LICENSING —
A STRATEGY FOR PROFITS

LICENSING — A STRATEGY FOR PROFITS

- Why consider licensing in the first place —

- Why some companies should not license —

- Is it more important to license out or to license in —

- How to negotiate the best deal — Royalty evaluation — Protection of property rights —

- Plus a practical discussion of "how not to", based on actual experiences.

By Edward P. White

Commissioned by
Licensing Executives Society (U.S.A. and Canada), Inc.

Published by
KEW Licensing Press

Library of Congress Cataloging in Publication Data —

Author: Edward P. White
Title: Licensing — A Strategy for Profits
Library of Congress Catalogue Card Number: 90-91582

ISBN 0-9626017-0-5

Published by:
KEW Licensing Press
907 Linden Road
Chapel Hill, North Carolina 27514-9162

CONTENTS

PREFACE...ix

Part One

Chapter I
WHAT IT'S ALL ABOUT 3

    Four different businesses with four different and
    successful licensing experiences. 3

    Questions and doubts...5

    Definition of licenses, franchises and technical joint-
    ventures...5

    Definition of a good license..8

    Protection with patents, trademarks, copyrights and trade
    secrets...8

    Importance of licensing "in" as well as "out." How some
    companies fill a special market niche.............................11

    Planning and the use of licensing and joint-ventures to
    reach objectives...12

Chapter II
DECIDING WHETHER, WHY & WHEN.............................15

    Licensor advantages..15

    Licensee advantages..15

    Advantages of shared technology...................................16

    Disadvantages for licensor and licensee.........................17

    Competition..18

    Expectations and cautions...19

    Opening up new markets...20

    A primary income source..20

A secondary income source...20

R&D technology and spin-off licensing for a secondary
income...21

Licensing know-how when the market is right.....................23

Protecting know-how and trade secrets..............................23

Licensing as an alternative to suit.......................................24

Compulsory licensing. 26

Protection of all types...26

Licensing computer software. 27

Licensing biotechnology. 28

Advantages of a coordinated program.................................29

Corporate planning objectives, strategies and tactics. 30

Chapter III
WHAT IS BEST FOR LICENSOR & LICENSEE 33

Standard licenses. 34

Licensing and joint-ventures with socialist and developing
countries. 35

Walk, do not run into negotiations. 36

Capability, a source of trouble. 36

Specifics of finding technology...37

Small licenses big. 38

N.I.H. A caution to both big and small. 38

Big licenses small. 39

Review..39

Chapter IV
LICENSING BOTH WAYS AT ONCE 43

General advantages. 43

USX Corporation. 44

Pfizer, Inc..44

F. Hoffman-LaRoche & Company..45

SAI Technology Company..46

SPS Technologies, Inc...47

DEC International, Inc. 48

Anaquest Division of BOC Group. 49

Stake Technology, Ltd. 50

Summary and the potential of cross licensing. 51

Chapter V
LEARNING FROM OTHERS

LEARNING FROM OTHERS...53

A tragedy of bad judgment. 53

More dumb mistakes. 54

The major problem for all. 55

Individual opinions. 56

Know your partner. 57

Two cases of disappointment. 58

Cautions on consultants. 63

More problems and how to avoid them. 64

Flexibility is the key. 65

Finances — a source of potential problems. 67

More solutions to finance problems. 68

Variations that help — Corporate Partnering. 69

Co-promotion another helpful variation. 72

Terms — friend and foe. 73

Negotiating the agreement. 74

Regulations — U.S. export controls. 74

Rising above the problems. 75

Part Two

Chapter I
ORGANIZATION FOR LICENSING

ORGANIZATION FOR LICENSING...................................79

The importance of top executives. 79

Licensing functions. 80

Organizing a licensing department. 81

Characteristics of the ideal licensing executive. 82

Executive development. 83

Responsibilities for the license department. 84

Reporting of the licensing function. 85

Organizations as they are...85

Service, contact and licensee morale..88

Consultants. 90

Using a consultant to the best advantage..90

The essential place of lawyers. 91

References for lawyers and consultants..93

Chapter II
ROYALTY AND OTHER COMPENSATION 99

Royalty systems. 99

Establishing values...101

Capitalized values..102

Know-how fee — a need for special emphasis................................103

Pricing decisions. 103

Setting the numbers..104

Increased royalty payments come with increased
importance of patents. 105

Duration of payments...107

Technical assistance fees. 107

Other costs and charges..108

Conclusion. 109

Chapter III
TYPES OF LICENSE AGREEMENTS AND SPECIAL
CONSIDERATIONS FOR FRANCHISES AND
JOINT-VENTURES...111

Patent licenses..111

Trade secret/know-how agreements. 112

Technical assistance agreements. 112

Copyright licenses..113

Trademark licenses. 113

Franchising. 113

Technical joint-venture. 114

Franchising — business opportunities and cautions (also
see Part One, Chapter I, p. 7). 115

Franchise cautions. 117

Joint-ventures — questions and key points. 118

Advantages of joint-ventures and some cautions.........................118

Joint-ventures vs. licensing without equity. 122

Chapter IV
WHY, WHY NOT & HOW TO FIND A PARTNER.......................127

Advantages for the licensor. 127

Advantages for the licensee. 129

Disadvantages for licensee and licensor. 130

Finding the right one. 132

Licensor background. 133

Licensee background. 135

Licensor-licensee mutual background. 136

Chapter V
INTELLECTUAL PROPERTY RIGHTS 137

PATENTS. 137
    Definition 137
    Patent Planning 139
    Patent Importance — A Summary...141

TRADE SECRETS AND KNOW-HOW. 143
    Definition Of Trade Secret 143
    Definition Of Know-How..143
    Protection Of Trade Secrets 144
    Trade Secrets vs. Non-Proprietary Know-How.......................145
    Trade Secrets vs. Patents..145
    Duration Of Agreements 147
    Combined Use...148

TRADEMARKS. 149
    Definition 149
    Planning And Registration..150
    Licensing Of Trademarks 152
    Trademark Value 153

COPYRIGHTS..154

MASK WORKS AND SEMICONDUCTOR CHIPS. 156

Chapter VI
COMPUTER SOFTWARE — A SPECIAL CASE 159
　Protection of intellectual property rights 159
　Licensing considerations. 160

Chapter VII
AGREEMENT TERMS ESSENTIAL AND NOT SO
ESSENTIAL 167
　License grant 168
　Definitions 168
　Exclusive or sole license 168
　Field of use 168
　Territorial rights 169
　Patent coverage 169
　Patent infringement notices and patent defense 169
　Patent identification 168
　Patent warranty 170
　Trademarks 170
　Trademark defense 170
　Quality requirements or diligence provisions 170
　Royalty, know-how payments, technical service fees 171
　Exchange control 171
　Accounting and reporting. 171
　Taxes 171
　Technical assistance 171
　Guarantees and warranties 171
　Improvements and grantback 172
　Visitation 172
　Most favored nation 172
　Arbitration/forum and dispute resolution 173
　Governing law 174
　Language 174
　Waiver 174

Modifications or changes..175

Force majeure 175

Approval 175

Notices 175

Sublicense rights 175

Assignability 175

Bankruptcy 176

Notice of breach...176

Termination...176

Schedules 176

Summary..176

Chapter VIII
SPECIAL NATIONAL RESTRICTIONS 179

General cautions...179

Communist countries. 180

Developing countries. 181

Chapter IX
NOTES FOR NEGOTIATING 183

Preparation..183

Entry readiness. 185

Negotiation. 186

Strategies and tactics..187

Performance...191

Part Three

Chapter I
LICENSING IS NOT JUST "HIGH TECH"...195

Royalty is paid in product..195

Metal stamping shop works with individual inventor. Both
succeed..196

Chapter II
CONCRETE BLOCKS THAT LOOK LIKE CUT STONE.............197

What is the Designer Blocks technology? 197

Who was the incubator? What is the relationship? 198

How did we find our licensees? 198

What are the key terms of our license agreement? 199

How do we support our licensees? 199

What have I learned and what would we do differently? 200

Chapter III
A BUSINESS BUILT UPON ACQUIRED TECHNOLOGY 201

Chapter IV
GROWING WITH THE TECHNOLOGY 203

Chapter V
SOLVING THE PROBLEM OF DAVID VS. GOLIATH 207

Novices to licensing. 208

Organizing for the work of licensing. 209

Plan for it and try it...210

Chapter VI
POOLING BRAINPOWER 213

Chapter VII
A CASE HISTORY: 'WORKMATE' 215

Chapter VIII
LICENSING INFLUENCE IN CORPORATE STRATEGY 219

Chapter IX
UNIQUE INVENTION CHANGES AN ORDINARY
PAPER BAG INTO WORLDWIDE USE AS A HEAVY
DUTY SACK 225

Chapter X
HOW A LICENSING PROGRAM BECAME THE BASIS
OF A COMPANY WHOSE 1986 REVENUES EXCEEDED
$29 MILLION 233

Commercializing the Dolby System.......................................233

Chapter XI
INVENTOR SUCCEEDS WITH A DEVELOPMENT
LICENSE..239

Chapter XII
THE STORY OF THE EASY OPEN CAN END 241

Chapter XIII
HOW AN AUSTRALIAN FIRM INTRODUCED ITS
ROLLING DOOR TO THE WORLDWIDE MARKET 245

Chapter XIV
STEEL WIRE MANUFACTURER FINDS REASONABLE
RETURN FROM INTERNATIONAL LICENSING
NETWORK...251

Specific features of agreements. 255

Conclusions. 257

Chapter XV
THE PROGRESSION OF A CORPORATE PARTNERING.........259

Relationship. 259

Part Four

IN CONCLUSION..267

Part Five

Appendix A
TEXT COMMENTS...271

Appendix B
SOME OF THE PROFESSIONAL ORGANIZATIONS
INVOLVED IN LICENSING CONSIDERATIONS...........................273

Appendix C
SEMINARS AND CONSULTATION GENERALLY
AVAILABLE...275

BIBLIOGRAPHY...277

Reference marks and notes:..277

PREFACE

The importance of small and mid-size business — and the reason why this book was written:

"In North America today, small companies with less than 20 employees are responsible for creating a disproportionately large share of all net new jobs," claims David L. Birch, President of Cognetics, Inc. a marketing-consulting firm in Cambridge, Massachusetts. The National Institute of Business Management in the October 9, 1989, issue of *Research Recommendations* observes that companies of 100 employees or less are responsible for 80% of all new jobs and that these firms are also more innovative than those of 500 or more employees. Whether speaking of the United States, Canada or other countries, these comments emphasize the importance of small and mid-size businesses throughout the commerical world.

The purpose of this book is to point out the variety of licensing activities now carried out by such firms, to outline the opportunities of licensing for those not already involved, and to show how and why it is successfully done.

Among questions to be addressed are:

> *"What must be my commitment in money, personnel and effort in order to start a licensing program?"*
>
> *"How can I find a license partner:*
>
> > *"To acquire a new technology or product line?"*
> > *"To use my technology and bring me extra profits?"*
>
> *How can I organize a successful licensing program — or, should I do it all?*

The author has received help and advice from many friends, in and out of LES, and from the proverbial "four corners of the world." Special thanks go to Jack S. Ott, editor and helper. Specific thanks also go to the following:

*E.G. Astolfi	*B.I. Friedlander	K.E. Payne
Tony Andraitis	R. Goldscheider	H.L. Pocklington
Wm. Bailey	E.P. Grattan	F.S. Reed
C.W. Baker	R.L. Grudziecki	P.C. Ridgeway
S.E. Baker	*G.J. Houle	K.B. Ridler
R.E. Bayes	*N.A. Jacobs	*Marcia Rorke
D.L. Birch	M.F. Jager	J.S. Saxe
H.O. Blair	D.R. Jaine	I. Schotz
T.R. Brown	F.C. Jesse, Jr.	C.A. Shields
*B.G. Brunsvold	H.L. Johnson	*D.B. Smith
W.S. Campbell	K.F. Jorda	R.W. Smith
J.H. Coleman	K.J. Kanouse	*V.A. Smith
F. Contractor	H.B. Keck	G.P. Souther
V. Dagpinar	J.E. Kelly	G.F. Stuart
R.G. Davis	R.R. Kooiman	J.B. Townsend
W.T. Davis	*G.E. Lester	T.F. Tuttle
R.W Dean, Jr.	R. Lippert	*D.S. Urey
R.M. DeBoos	C.E. Martine, Jr.	David F. White
A.L. Early	J.W. Moorehead	T.E. White
J.P. Evans	*R.G. Moser	
*L.W. Evans	A.L. Ney	

Although the publication of this book is sponsored by the Licensing Executives Society (U.S.A. and Canada), Inc. and The Franklin Pierce Law Center of Concord, NH, the opinions expressed herein are those of the author, and in no way do they reflect opinions or policies of the Licensing Executives Society International, Inc., Licensing Executives Society (U.S.A. and Canada), Inc., any other LES chapter or Franklin Pierce Law Center.

Edward P. White
March 1990
Chapel Hill, North Carolina

*LES Review Committee

PART ONE

Experience of others
A planning guide for best results

Chapter I

WHAT IT'S ALL ABOUT

The Robert Dean story and reasons why small and mid-size businesses generate profits through licensing, franchising and joint-ventures.

* * * * *

Four different businesses with four different and successful licensing experiences.

After a review of his activities and plans for licensing special concrete block designs throughout the United States and Canada and in other countries outside North America, Robert W. Dean, Jr., President of Designer Blocks, Inc., commented: "I am beginning to realize that I'm not in the concrete block business! I'm in the licensing business." Mr. Dean's firm holds patents on the design and manufacture of specialty blocks and has established a successful program with licensee block manufacturers, a program that brings new and profitable concrete block designs to the manufacturers, unique specialty effects to the architects, and a profitable business to Robert Dean, President of Designer Blocks. The licensing program of Designer Blocks is covered in more detail in Part Three, Chapter II.

Many firms expand and increase business by acquiring new technology under license. G. Parks Souther, President of Parkson Corporation, reports on his company's success as a licensee for new products:

> *Parkson has grown to be a very profitable company with sales over $25 million per year through the licensing of cost effective products to our marketplace. We could not have afforded the time and expense associated with developing our own products in the early 1970's. It is*

> *also interesting to note that those firms who dominated the market when we started but who did not introduce new products have pretty much faded from the scene.*"

That statement clearly highlights an advantage of a sound, well thought-out program for licensing in. Mr. Souther's review of Parkson activities is found in Part Three, Chapter III.

———

K.B. Ridler, industrial consultant in Thunder Bay, Ontario, described an experience he had as Managing Director of Vesco Manufacturing, Division of Vulcan Machinery Co. A large Scandinavian firm was violating a Vesco patent for log handling equipment. The solution was a license. "When we finally got things settled, our relationship was ideal. The Scandinavian company had a new and useful machine to sell to its market, and I had extra profits coming from outside my own market." Subsequently, a similar license was negotiated for the same technology with Harricana Metal, Inc. of Amos, Quebec. Both of these licenses have represented useful extra income for Vesco.

———

Larry Schotz, President of L.S. Research, Cedarburg, Wisconsin, utilizes licensing in yet another way. His audio-electronics firm has made licensing a principal part of the company's strategy and business plan. Mr. Schotz says, "We develop our own ideas and inventions, and we do specialty research work for others, but we don't want to get into manufacturing. So, we license our patented inventions to others and keep a good profitable business going."

———

These and other experiences demonstrate how and why managers of many small and mid-size businesses have found additional profitability by incorporating licenses into their business program either licensing in to obtain a new product, a new design or a new process or licensing out to sell a technology to others for increased profits through royalty. A license can be an economical solution to a patent infringement as in the case of the Vulcan Machinery Company, or a deliberate strategy to tap a wider market, or get more profit from an in-house process. Whatever the reason for licensing, many small and mid-size businesses are using this route to expanded profitability.

Questions and doubts.

Many business people have expressed doubts about licensing, joint-ventures and franchising such as the "Twenty Questions" in Table I (page 6). For some, licensing can be a touchstone to new profits. For others, licensing should be avoided. These questions high-light the considerations of a thoughtful business person in determining the suitability of a license or licensing program.

Along with the uncertainty expressed in "Twenty Questions," there are still many who regard licensing as an activity that should be followed only by major corporations. They think that licensing is best practiced only by firms that have in-house attorneys and separate departments to specialize in license negotiation. Nothing could be further from the truth.

Definition of licenses, franchises and technical joint-ventures.

Technology, know-how, patents, and other intellectual property, are commodities that can be bought, sold, leased or shared. Licenses, franchises and joint-ventures are the mechanisms for buying, selling and leasing technology, know-how, trade secrets and all types of intellectual property.

A *license* is the granting of permission or rights to make, use and/or sell a certain product, design, or process or to perform certain other actions, the granting being done by a party who has the right to do so. A license agreement usually includes a variety of grants in which a licensor sells or leases to a licensee the use of certain industrial property rights and/or technical expertise. These "rights" may include patents, trademarks, copyrights, trade secrets, know-how and technical assistance. "License In" is a term used with respect to the acquisition of these rights through a license, whereas "License Out" is the term applied to the sale or provision of those rights. Essentially, the difference between a "domestic" license and an "international" license is the need for the international agreement to be compatible with the laws, regulations, customs, languages and performance standards of different countries. These variations make it essential to understand all elements of the agreement.[1]

TABLE I
Twenty questions, doubts and fears
as expressed by the small and mid-size business community.

1. What is licensing and how can it be used?
2. Must I spend a great deal of time on developing a licensing program when I am already putting in 60 or more hours per week on the job?
3. What are the complications and corporate commitments necessary to get a licensing effort going?
4. How much will it cost to start a license program and what does the cost cover? For lawyers? For consultants?
5. What is a "fair" or "reasonable" royalty?
6. What profitability can I expect and how soon for either licensing in or out?
7. What is the potential for getting more profit from old technology by licensing into less developed countries?
8. How should I look for a license partner:
   - To acquire a technology under license?
   - To license someone under my technology?
9. How do I organize for licensing? What should be delegated to others? To employees? To consultants?
10. How can I know that someone else's product or technology is what I need or want before I have made a commitment to spend money for it?
11. Will other companies or countries steal my technology? How do I protect myself from a license partner running away with my technology?
12. Do I need to be familiar with a myriad of foreign laws and regulations so as to license outside my country?
13. How should I handle negotiations?
    - What to look out for.
    - What to do if negotiations break down.
14. What kind of confidentiality or nonuse agreements should be used?
15. How long do negotiations take?
16. How do I protect myself if there is a license breakdown — confidentiality problem — unreimbursed costs?
17. Can license breakdown problems be avoided?
18. Are Japan and South Korea countries that should be avoided because of restrictive trade practices? What about other Asian countries?
19. Are the Soviet Union, China and other Communist countries to be avoided, or not? Why?
20. Is bribery common in other countries?
    - How should it be handled?
    - What are U.S. laws on the subject?

A *franchise* is sometimes compared to a trademark license, and there can be many similarities with respect to quality control and product identification. Fundamentally, however, franchising is the licensing of a business method or format with certain controls and identification requirements. Because of these similarities, franchising is mentioned and described in this study, albeit with a minor role, since our primary concerns are with respect to technology-related cases.[2]

At the same time, the franchise system of doing business is perhaps the fastest growing business system in the U.S. today, with respect to expanding sales and service companies. Licenses are generally not controlled or regulated as such. However, controlling regulations for franchising have been established by the U.S. Federal Trade Commission and a check list is available from the FTC to determine whether an agreement should be defined as a franchise. In addition to the FTC regulations, many states require registration of franchise agreements, disclosure of certain business details involved and regulation of certain aspects of the ongoing relationship. Failure to observe these regulations can result in significant fines and, in some cases, criminal prosecution. The definition of a regulated franchise may cover the licensing of a trademark, simultaneous with the furnishing of marketing or other assistance, the control of business or manufacturing methods and the payment of up front fees and continuing royalty. Competent legal assistance should be engaged to make sure that a simple trademark license is not construed as a more complicated and regulated franchise agreement.

A *joint-venture*, far more so than a franchise, is likely to involve technology, technology transfer and technology licensing. A joint-venture can be defined as a combination of two or more business interests that join forces in pursuit of a common business objective sharing profits and risks. Perhaps, the most important advantage of a joint-venture is that it can take many different legal forms. A participant can enter into a venture that it otherwise would not have the resources to pursue. Variations of the joint-venture are sometimes spoken of as "Corporate Partnering" and "Strategic Alliances." For the purpose of this book, joint-ventures involve technology and specific products — not those concerned solely with certain financial or marketing arrangements.[3]

Except when there are distinguishing features included in the latter two business agreements, the term "license" or "licensing" may refer to all such contracts.

Definition of a good license.

Robert E. Bayes, retired Manager of Process Licensing, Shell Development Corp., Houston, Texas, remembers taking his first negotiated agreement to his boss. The first question asked was, "Would you sign this agreement for the other side as well as for Shell? If so, it's a fair agreement and I'll sign it." This statement exemplified the Shell philosophy, fairness for all licensees and licensors.

The same basic philosophy was expressed differently by Dr. William T. Davis, Director of Licensing for Pfizer, Inc.:

> *It is vitally important for both parties in any license arrangement to have complete confidence in each other. In the case of large corporations dealing with small companies, this factor becomes even more important. Many small firms are afraid that the large firm will unduly exercise its size to create unfair advantages."*

It is the writer's opinion that most large and influential corporations do business fairly and equitably. If you are not sure about the reputation of a potential license partner, the best advice is to inquire about the other party through your bank, your lawyer, your business friends, and your professional society connections. It is the "test of time" that a good and fair license must be good and fair for all parties. Methods of finding a good partner are covered in Part Two, Chapter IV.

Protection with patents, trademarks, copyrights and trade secrets.

Many years ago, the author had an Army drill sergeant whose favorite comment was, "Ah cain't make you do anything but Ah kin shore as hell make you wish you had!" That statement fairly well describes the principle of why it is important to obtain optimum protection for intellectual property (patents, trademarks and copyrights). It also covers the question of what to do with unpatentable, proprietary know-how. You maintain a trade secret status. Libraries are filled with books, treatises and discussions on the detailed regulations and laws for patents, trademarks, copyrights and trade secrets, and it is not the purpose of this report to add to that collection of literature. These are questions that should be discussed with a lawyer who is competent in intellectual property protection. However, it is also important to remember:

- **Patents** provide highly desirable protection. They offer the patent owner the right to exclude others from making, using and selling the invention covered. Foreign counterparts may also be desirable. Widespread filing of foreign counterpart patents can get very expensive. Patents are probably the strongest protection for inventions and offer a sound basis for licensing, but have a limited life.

- **Trademarks** are visual symbols which identify the source and quality of products and services, and enable purchasers to distinguish between the products and services of different parties. Trademarks are valuable assets which may be protected perpetually if they are used correctly and policed diligently, and may serve as the proprietary basis for long-term licenses.

- **Copyrights** protect against copying original expressions of authorship such as literature, artworks, and computer program source code. Copyrights, unlike trade secrets, may protect these latter expressions from copying by others after public disclosure.

- **Mask works and semiconductor chip protection** as established by the U.S. Semiconductor Chip Protection Act of 1984. Exclusive rights belong to the owner of the mask work. For a general description of this relatively new form of intellectual property, see Part Two, Chapter V.

- **Trade secrets** can be established for virtually any type of information held in confidence and, if properly protected, can be the proprietary basis for very long-term licenses. However, they are always subject to independent discovery.

All of these parts of the "protection picture" for licenses are of considerable importance. They must not be overlooked. Table II (page 10) summarizes the characteristics of legal forms of protection in the United States. In many respects, these characteristics will be similar in other countries. Part Two, Chapter V has a more detailed review of these essential considerations, and the text of this study will refer often to the nature and use of intellectual property rights in licensing. Of particular interest to the reader will be some of the examples in Part One, Chapter V "Learning From Others" and Part Three "Stories of Licensing..." Both licensee and licensor must be careful that a license offers optimum protection for the technology that it covers. A competent patent, trademark and copyright lawyer should be a part of this aspect of any firm's planning.

TABLE II

General characteristics of legal forms of protection in the United States.*

CONSIDERATIONS	COPYRIGHT	TRADE SECRET	PATENT	TRADEMARK	MASK WORKS*
NATIONAL UNIFORMITY	YES	NO	YES	YES	YES
PROTECTED PROPERTY	EXPRESSION OF IDEA	SECRET INFORMATION	INVENTION	GOODWILL	SEMICONDUCTORS
SCOPE OF PROTECTION	EXCLUSIVE RIGHT TO REPRODUCE, PREPARE DERIVATIVE WORKS, PUBLICLY DISTRIBUTE, DISPLAY AND PERFORM	RIGHT TO MAKE, USE AND SELL SECRET AND TO PROTECT AGAINST IMPROPER USE OR DISCLOSURE	RIGHT TO EXCLUDE OTHERS FROM MAKING, USING, SELLING	PROSCRIBES AGAINST MISREPRESENTATION OF SOURCE	EXCLUSIVE RIGHT TO REPRODUCE CHIP
EFFECTIVE DATE OF PROTECTION	CREATION OF WORK	FROM DATE OF CONCEPTION OR RECEIPT OF SECRET INFORMATION	ISSUE OF PATENT	USE AND/OR FILING DATE OF U.S. APPLICATION ISSUING AS PRINCIPAL REGISTRATION ON OR AFTER 11/16/89	FIRST COMMERCIAL EXPLOITATION
COST OF OBTAINING PROTECTION	LOW	LOW	MODERATE	LOW	LOW
TERM OF PROTECTION	LIFE OF AUTHOR PLUS 50 YEARS, OR 70 YEARS	POSSIBILITY OF PERPETUAL PROTECTION, OR TERMINATION AT ANY TIME BY IMPROPER DISCLOSURE OR INDIVIDUAL DEVELOPMENT BY OTHERS	17 YEARS	PERPETUAL IF USED CORRECTLY AND DILIGENTLY POLICED	10 YEARS
COST OF MAINTAINING PROTECTION	NIL	MODERATE	MODERATE	MODERATE	NIL
COST OF ENFORCING RIGHTS AGAINST VIOLATORS	MODERATE	HIGH	HIGH	MODERATE	MODERATE

*See Mask Works and Semiconductor Chips — Part Two, Chapter V.

Importance of licensing "in" as well as "out." How some companies fill a special market niche.

The pharmaceutical industry is noted for its activity in licensing. Major companies, such as Pfizer, Hoffman-LaRoche and others license both in and out. Smaller pharmaceutical and health-care firms operate in the same way. Anaquest Division of BOC Group, Madison, Wisconsin, functions as a separate company with its own profitability as sole justification. As do many small drug firms, Anaquest will exploit products originated by larger firms when those products are unsuited to the originator's market or production scheme. Examples are a cardiovascular drug (anti-arrhythmic), used by cardiologists, anesthesiologists and emergency room physicians, and antiemetics, which are used by oncologists and anesthesiologists. Anaquest seeks to license such relatively small-volume highly specialized drugs from larger firms that find profitability in larger volume production.

Far from the health care industry are the licensees of Designer Blocks, Inc. (page 1). Rob Shouldice, President and owner of Shouldice Cement Products Limited, Shallow Lake, Ontario, Canada, claims that his license with Designer Blocks, Inc. is one of the major reason for the success his company enjoys. Other licensees of Designer Blocks from Quebec to Florida and California show the same advantages for their new products and licensee services.

People often think first of the licensor position when the subject of licensing arises, regarding it as "A new way to make some extra money based on our in-house technology." At the same time, with every successful licensor there must be a successful licensee. As is the case for Parkson Corporation, mentioned earlier, many businesses find it easier and less expensive to license in new technology or products than it is to develop them in house. Further discussion of this vital subject — licensing in — is covered in Part One, Chapter III, under the heading of "Specifics of finding technology"; in Part Two, Chapter IV; and in Part Three, Chapters III and IV. Bibliography references 3, 74 and 87 cover additional information on the subject.

Planning and the use of licensing and joint-ventures to reach objectives.

One of the very best examples of licensing in corporate strategy is the story of Consumers Packaging, Inc., of Etobicoke, Ontario, Canada as told by William S. Campbell. (See also Part Three, Chapter VIII.)

Consumers Packaging, Inc. started as Consumers Glass Company in 1917, a small firm with one plant. Its first license was taken by Consumers Glass in the early 1960s with Brockway, Inc., in New York State. Since then, through a series of licenses, in and out, joint-ventures and acquisitions, Consumers Glass has become a major factor in the packaging industry with broad capabilities in plastics as well as glass.

In 1986, Consumers Glass changed its name to Consumers Packaging, Inc., which describes its business more accurately. Today, Consumers Packaging is a significant factor in the world packaging industry, with operations in Canada, United States and the United Kingdom, totalling twelve manufacturing plants and employing more than 4,000 people. This corporate expansion and growth would not have been accomplished without a coordinated, well-thought-out licensing program incorporated into the strategic plan for the company. Mr. Campbell summarizes his paper with this conclusion:

> *If you have established a solidly-based licensing program that is active with full management support, you can have a major impact on the strategic direction of your entire company. As an aside, you most assuredly will be in a position to license out.*

In a completely different field and in a totally different way, the Ransberg Company established a position of dominance in the field of metal finishing through a patented spray painting method that has saved millions of dollars for industrially spray painted products. Supported by a strong patent position, a careful, high-quality service program and a well-organized series of field-of-use licenses, Ransberg built a business that brought in more than $250 million over the life of its basic patent. Today, Ransberg maintains its leadership through its well-organized technical service program, even though the basic patent expired in 1976.

In still another industry, Hatteras Yachts of High Point, North Carolina, is a very successful firm. The world's largest production builder of molded fiberglass yachts, Hatteras' annual sales are in the range of $150 million, and their employees total about 1,500. Production runs from 38 foot to 120 foot motor yachts. Herbert L. Pocklington, President of Hatteras International, points out that the corporate plan is to maintain a world market position by selling direct whenever possible and licensing production when necessary. Most interesting is the fact that the Hatteras program places no reliance on patents, is completely founded on know-how and trade secrets, is established through detailed market study work and is successfully maintained by thorough and regular contacts. The corporate plan is established in advance and followed with careful, hands-on management. This excellent example of corporate planning for licenses is highlighted here to show that careful corporate planning can include a productive licensing program even without patent protection.

These and other firms have used the licensing of technology and business methods, patents and trade secrets to their advantage. Proper planning and good strategy indicate that licensing both in and out should be considered for a part in the total corporate scenario. It is the purpose of this book to point out how this strategy can be implemented.[4]

FOOTNOTES:

[1] See Part Two, Chapter III.

[2] See Part Two, Chapter III and Bibliography 48, 49, 55 and 84.

[3] See Part Two, Chapter III and Bibliography 40.

[4] See Bibliography 3, 80, 82.

Chapter II

DECIDING WHETHER, WHY & WHEN

Brothers Research, Inc., Burlington, North Carolina, U.S.A. has 12 employees, a high quality product and does not want to license.

Beline Manufacturing Company, Ltd., Kindersley, Saskatchewan, Canada has 30 employees and a well-conceived license and joint-venture arrangement.

Both companies have made the right corporate strategy decision.

* * * * *

There are advantages and disadvantages for both the licensor and the licensee:

Licensor advantages.

- Increased income with little or no capital investment.
- New uses of technology.
- Can manufacture and sell with minimum capital/no staff.
- Avoid certain legal problems.
- Expand opportunities.
- Equity potential.
- R&D improvements from licensees.
- Market improvement.

Licensee advantages.

- Expanded rights (including new products and R&D)
- Expanded assistance (technical and commercial).
- Expanded marketing and sales.

- Expanded profits.
- Can avoid conflict or infringement suit if existing product is found to infringe someone else's patent.

Advantages of shared technology.

The UOP licensing story carries such clear examples of the advantage of licensing to both licensee and licensor that it deserves to be told. Tom Arnold partner in the law firm of Arnold, White and Durkee, Houston Texas, wrote the following account in the *1984 Licensing Law Handbook*:[1]

> *UOP has a very successful licensing program built upon the licensee's interest in future R&D. Some fifty or sixty licensees, I don't know how many, are too small and technically unsophisticated to do catalytic cracking R&D effectively. How do they compete with the eight major refiners in an area of continuously developing technology? UOP keeps one or more pilot plants continuously operating to try out new catalysts, new reactor temperatures, residence times, etc. And UOP collects grant-back[2] information from its licensees. Then UOP conducts annual seminars to give its licensees the latest updated technology. These licensees are licensees not just of past-developed technology but also of future-developed technology.*
>
> *UOP keeps catalytic cracking pilot plants running studies at all times and licenses its refinements in catalytic cracking know-how.*
>
> *Most of the world's refiners could not afford such an R&D effort and also could not stay competitive with the big eight or big ten oil refiners without access to such as UOP's ongoing research and development.*
>
> *Further, since UOP gets grant-backs[3] from its various licensees and the privilege to pass the technology from its licensees on to its other licensees, the many UOP licensees have access to still additional sources of technology that enable the small refiners to keep technologically competitive with the big refiners.*

While every licensing program may not develop worldwide technical feedback, it is reasonable to expect that a good licensor-licensee relationship will return advantageous but unforeseen developments. When two or more organizations work together, natural synergy produces complementary results.

REFAC Technology Development Corporation, is a firm that handles licensing in and out for many different clients. Phillip Sperber, Vice President of REFAC, outlines an example of non-monetary profit from licensing:[4]

> *The technical feedback values of license relationships, however unpredictable, often achieve unexpected magnitude. In fact, with proper administrative contact and cooperation, substantial feedback benefits are almost assured. For example, in the case of a worldwide licensing program for a patented industrial fastener, REFAC's Japanese licensee conducted expensive photoelastic stress studies that provided a technical rationale for opening up new opportunities for product application. The English licensee developed power tools that improved the economics of product installation. The French licensee established new product specifications that were incorporated into American product designs. They also engineered automatic quality-control devices that are now used by REFAC's U.S. client and by its licensees in other countries. The German licensee created a compound fastener that has become a standard part of the product line. The Indian licensee designed manufacturing equipment for short-run production that made it economically feasible for REFAC to set up licensed manufacture in smaller and developing countries.*

Disadvantages for licensor and licensee.

As for disadvantages, the following list gives problems cited as reasons not to license. Each can be a legitimate, well-founded objection, but most of the time can be avoided, if the parties involved think ahead and make adequate provisions to avoid the problems:[5]

- Limited opportunities beyond the license scope —

    For licensee unless future improvements are included.
    For licensor limited opportunity for management direction.

- Increased demands on management time of licensor —

    For licensee may result in insufficient service.
    For licensor may raise costs of service.

- Unforeseen technical problems for both licensor and licensee —

    Caused by insufficient production testing or market experience.

- Lack of control —

    Problem for licensor regarding licensee performance.
    Problem for licensee regarding service and help from licensor.

- Logistics difficulties —

    Possible for both licensee and licensor depending on geographical separation.

- Undesirable competition —

    Can create serious problems for the licensor

Competition.

As noted above, undesirable competition is a real concern. If there is no patent protection, a business must be extremely careful of disclosing critical, proprietary trade secrets. If a secret formula becomes known to unauthorized persons, deliberately or by accident, the "cat is out of the bag," and either the cost of legal action may be extremely high or there may be no recourse at all. Such is the case of Brothers Research of Burlington, North Carolina.

Dr. William Bailey, President, and Jerry Bailey, Vice President, owners of Brothers Research, are both accomplished and knowledgeable chemists. They have developed a car polish of exceptional performance that commands a premium price in a highly competitive market. Brothers

Research is concerned about its competition learning the secret formula. Everything possible is done to prevent its formula from being known by others. This policy means no licensing not even on the basis of a highly restrictive trade secret license. Present indications are that the decision is the right one. The company is taking all possible steps to protect and maintain its formula and methods as closely held trade secrets that can be defended in any court.

Expectations and cautions.

Expectations of licensees and licensors are established 90% of the time on the advantages and disadvantages cited in this Chapter and enumerated in Part Two, Chapter IV. However, a variety of factors influence the significance of these advantages and disadvantages:

- Competition is a factor that should never be overlooked. What retailer in his right mind would set up shop without knowing what other stores had for merchandise, and at what price? Availability and perceived cost for other or equivalent technology is sometimes overlooked to the later regret of would-be licensors or licensees.

- Industry practices should be investigated before entering into a licensing program. Accepted norms of royalty, or other practices can profoundly influence the terms acceptable for a license.

- Government regulations can sometimes represent a stumbling block. When a U.S. firm is extending a technology license outside the U.S., an export license, either general or specific, is required. Don't take your "goodies" abroad without checking. U.S. Department of Commerce, International Trade Administration, Washington, DC is the place to start. (Also, see Part One, Chapter V.) Regulations of other countries must also be considered.[6]

- Geographic and cultural differences education, training required, work ethic, basic communication habits, climate, language differences, and business practices can significantly influence the conduct and success of an international license. A very readable review of the effects of cultural differences on international business is found in *Going International* by Copeland and Griggs.[7]

Opening up new markets.

The Beline Manufacturing Company of Kindersley, Saskatchewan, offers a good example of how licensing can be used to open up a market otherwise tough to crack because of high shipping costs, high labor costs, high import duties and the difficulty of maintaining skilled sales and service without local manufacturing facilities.

Beline solved these problems by setting up a joint-venture in Mexico (51% Mexican, 49% Canadian) with a technology license to cover all aspects of the product line. The products of Beline Manufacturing are sophisticated applicators of granular chemicals and fertilizer with electronic and mechanical controls. By establishing a licensed joint-venture, Beline has put its quality product line in Mexico, with access to central and northern South American markets. It also has maintained control of patents and proprietary know-how by having a strong ownership position in the joint-venture. Suffice to say that problems of market access, profitable manufacture and skilled customer service have been met and solved through a technology license and joint-venture.

A primary income source.

In Chapter I the firms of L.S. Research, Inc. and Designer Blocks, Inc. were mentioned. Both are non-manufacturers that have certain patented and proprietary knowledge that is licensed to others for production applications. Technical and marketing support and good patent positions create favorable licensing situations. They are excellent examples of licensing programs that are principal profit sources.

A secondary income source.

More usual, however, are cases in which a firm develops a product and later turns to licensing for extra profits from markets not otherwise reachable. Television Technology Corporation of Louisville, Colorado, is a small firm that has developed low and medium power television transmitters that are suited for mountainous areas or in other circumstances where short-range transmission is advantageous. In 1983 Television Technology became aware of a need for the same type of equipment in China and made a trip over there to determine the potential.

How to satisfy the new market which they found? Direct equipment sale was not feasible. However, a phased licensing program proved to be an ideal solution, starting with a license for "kit" manufacturing or the assembly of imported parts and graduating on a controlled basis to a full manufacturing license. The ability to negotiate a license particularly suited to an individual situation produced increased sales of product plus royalty income from a license and the possibility for future product cooperation. As of 1990 the relationship continues, although at a much reduced activity. Indications are, however, that the project will be revitalized in the not too distant future.

R&D technology and spin-off licensing for a secondary income.

How can a company realize profits from an invention or innovation that it has developed, but which is outside the firm's normal business or production capabilities. There are two possibilities: start a new commercial endeavor or product line (which may cost too much money), or help someone else take on the new development. The latter course of action comes under the heading of "licensing spin-off technology" which can be both rewarding and frustrating. Tom Long, President of Tektronix Development Company (TDC), a high-tech instrument maker in Beaverton, Oregon, has described his company's practice of sponsoring small new businesses through an organized program of spin-off licensing as being very successful.[8] Under circumstances where technical capability is assured, such as in the TDC program, spin-off licensing can be successful.

Advanced Extraction Technologies, Inc. (AET) is an outstanding example of a spin-off license company with full technical capabilities in the sophisticated field of hydrocarbon processing. Formed in 1986 with a spin-off license from El Paso Hydrocarbons Company, a subsidiary of Burlington Northern, AET is the sole proprietor of the Mehra Process, a unique and widely patented technology for upgrading and processing hydrocarbon gas. With several patents granted and more filed in the United States and 21 foreign countries, AET offers to producers of natural gas, hydrogen and ethylene separation as related to the petroleum industry a new, cost-effective means of dramatically improving the production of existing process equipment with only moderate cost changes. AET offers the Mehra process at a very low royalty rate, believing it will be universally valuable to the petroleum refining industry. To date, the success of AET has been hampered by the depressed price of energy and the lack of a first commercial unit. However, AET management expects that this situation will improve as the petroleum industry begins to appreciate the potential for significant improvement of production and production efficiency. With technology excellence and a highly qualified staff, AET hopes to succeed in the petroleum industry as Dolby has done in the audio recording industry.[9] The Mehra Process should find wide application throughout the industry, in the industrialized countries and the developing countries, because of the excellence of the technology and the highly qualified staff of AET to support its licensees.

On the other hand, technical capability is a basic problem for successful spin-off licensing. Either the licensee should be able to carry on the work without technical help or the licensor should be in a position to offer whatever technical help is necessary. A licensee expects the licensor to furnish a viable product with the bugs worked out, both for production and use. The careful licensee will insure that there is adequate technical support and that the product or process will work "as advertised." Adequate licensor support is a primary concern. Technical validity must be established and maintained. But, how can proper support be assured for spin-off technology? How can a conscientious licensor convey a useful, valuable license when he has not and will not use the technology himself? How can a potential licensee be protected from unforeseen difficulties with an untried product? The answer for both licensee and licensor is to handle the question like a porcupine, very carefully.

These cautions are not prohibitions. Many companies have found an outside firm to take on their invention, because that outsider was particularly qualified to do so. Anaquest of Madison, Wisconsin, mentioned in Chapter I, has been successful in combining its internal R&D, with pharmaceuticals that were developed by others. Anaquest has developed its own organization so as to maintain good contacts with likely producers of spin-off pharmaceuticals as well as having a staff of analysts to judge manufacturing and sales suitability for potential new products.

Some companies however have had such unhappy experiences with licensing technology not in their normal product line that they will not consider granting spin-off licenses. "It's just not worth the time and trouble," says the Vice President of a technical device manufacturer. At the same time, however, the licensing of some spin-off technology may be well-suited to handling by a consultant firm. Qualified agency firms can offer contacts in a variety of industries, many on an international basis, and are in a good position to promote a licensable product or process as being a "raw development" without production or marketing background support.

Licensing know-how when the market is right.

Phillip Sperber points out that REFAC was able to structure a desirable license for a client based only on engineering and production know-how:

> *An American appliance manufacturer saw no possibility of licensing its electric stoves in Europe because of the lack of patent protection and established competitive products. REFAC identified established European appliance companies without an electric range line of their own, but with adequate plant capacity and appropriate marketing capability. A license was structured with one of these companies to whom the advantages of a well-engineered competitive product, ready-for-market, were particularly attractive.*[10]

Here is an example of know-how licensing when the competitive market situation was favorable.

Protecting know-how and trade secrets.

In contrast to the REFAC account, the following sad story is an example of the need to anticipate aggressive market conditions and to protect know-how with a well drafted agreement or else not to release useful technical information.

A leading U.S. manufacturer of industrial equipment, the Jones Company (not the correct name) was involved in a project with the U.S. Agency for International Development (A.I.D.) which sent an installation plus design and operating know-how to a South American Country to help that country improve problems related to food production. There were many assurances to the Jones Company that future sales and/or a profitable manufacturing joint-venture would be forthcoming from this helpful gesture. Nothing happened as far as Jones Company was concerned until about 18 months later when it was found that the equipment plans and sample installation of A.I.D. had made it possible for a manufacturer in the South American country to copy Jones Company's equipment, right down to the color of the paint! Jones Company had only know-how for design, engineering and manufacture, plus some trade secrets, but no patents on this equipment. As a result, Jones Company lost significant equipment sales in that market area. The Jones Company policy is now, "Do not license anyone, anywhere." While this policy might be changed someday, the price of any future license will be high, or the agreement will be "ironclad," or both. No one can reasonably object to this policy position. Releasing unprotected know-how is often risky.

Brothers Research has already been discussed, along with its situation and its valid, protective reasons for not licensing car polish composition. However, what would be the best strategy if a competitor were able to copy the Brothers Research formula? What if a major, well financed company threatened to take over this high quality market niche? Would it be smart for Brothers Research to sell its formula or to license the use thereof under certain terms based on trade secret status? Very possibly that approach would be a reasonable decision. Such a situation, if it ever happened, would be called "meeting a competitive challenge."

For all the cautions that are appropriate for licensing know-how and trade secrets, such licenses are still profitable and useful for many firms.[11]

Licensing as an alternative to suit.

Vesco Manufacturing, Division of Vulcan Machinery Company of Thunder Bay, Ontario, had patent coverage on its log handling machinery. When it was discovered that the patents were being infringed, the lawyers of Vesco were asked to make contact with the infringers and convince them either to stop production and pay damages or to take a license. After six months of no response, Mr. K.B. Ridler, Managing Director of Vesco, picked up the phone, called the President of the European company and asked him whether he wanted to fight a patent suit or negotiate a license. Both men agreed that a license was by far the best solution, and it might leave room for future cooperation. The European manufacturer said, "I'll meet you in Toronto." They met in Toronto, worked out a license in two days in a hotel and turned the matter over to their lawyers for final contract drafting. The contract was signed and Vesco collected very satisfying royalties for many years. The

European manufacturer was happy, too, because he had improved machinery to sell and good relations with a potential source of continuing technical improvements. This action is "licensing under duress." It might also be called "licensing as an alternative to suing."

If a patent position is strong enough, if it is not possible to avoid the patent, then the patent holder may have a strong commercial position worth defending in court. Maybe, but only maybe, the case would be worth the court suit. The case of *Polaroid vs. Kodak* for "instant camera" patent violation is now history, and Kodak has lost a lot of money. Stated very simply, Kodak thought they could make and sell an instant picture camera that would not violate the Polaroid patents. Polaroid disagreed and as soon as Kodak hit the market with its "instant camera," Polaroid sued for patent infringement. Kodak lost the suit. Polaroid damage demands have been quoted at $5.7 billion and more. Obviously, Polaroid feels that suit was worthwhile.

On the other hand, consider the story of Sony and its Betamax video cassette recorder and player. In 1975 Sony had the only system available on the market, Betamax. It had some patent protection and did not license these rights to others. Frustrated by a large commercial market that seemed to be unreachable, JVC (Victor Company of Japan) developed the VHS system outside the Sony patents and made it available under license to all comers. Today VHS clearly dominates the video system market, even though some say that Betamax is technically superior. Isn't it possible that Sony would have been better off to have licensed Betamax to the industry in the first place? Certainly the success of Dolby in the field of audio noise suppression would indicate the advantage of an industry-wide licensing program.[12]

Another case tells a similar story in a different market, the steel industry. A major U.S. company, pre-World War II, developed and patented an improved technology for continuous galvanizing of steel sheet. While it licensed several firms overseas and received a good royalty income from those licenses, its management believed its patent position to be sufficiently firm in the United States to eliminate competition, and would not license domestically. Unfortunately the competition, in order to have a share of the market, developed a different process, not covered by the original patent, and the original inventor company found itself with domestic competition and no royalties coming in.

A "dog in the manger" attitude is often an unwise position in the competitive, innovative, commercial world. Or, putting it another way: If you are going to "stonewall" the competition, you had better have a solid stone wall.

Compulsory licensing.

Some countries have compulsory licensing regulations. Under such conditions, a patent owner can be forced to license his patent if it is not being used by the owner or by a licensee. It may, therefore, be advisable for the patent owner to locate a licensee and negotiate a suitable license in that country rather than be forced to accept terms dictated by others. Such a situation is also "licensing under duress."

Protection of all types.

Sometimes a joint-venture can be combined with a technology license to give the licensor additional protection. Beline Manufacturing Company, as already mentioned, was concerned about proper supervision with a Mexican licensee for the necessary manufacturing and service of its agricultural chemical applicators and controls. The Beline management solved this problem with a joint-venture that contractually assured the maintenance of proper policies and supervision in spite of their minority (49%) ownership position. In this case, the patent coverage on Beline products had certain limits in addition to Beline's requirement for special technical supervision and custom service. The joint-venture contract was combined with the technology license to provide the necessary protection.

Proprietary technology, whether mechanical, chemical, electronic, organic or computer related, should be protected against unauthorized use by others. Part Two, Chapters V and VI review possible protection methods. A reading of that information is not, however, a substitute for a lawyer competent in the field of intellectual property rights. Rather, it is intended to help the reader to be better prepared in dealings with his lawyer.

Licensing computer software.

Two fast growing areas of technology are computer software and biotechnology. Software capabilities run from mechanical and/or time-dimensional activities to engineering design of structures, production control, accounting and financial analysis, even control of certain sophisticated biotechnology functions.

Part Two, Chapter VI, "Computer Software — A Special Case" outlines general protection means available for software and the basic considerations for software licensing. The most commonly used protection is a combination of trade secret and copyright. Patent coverage is sometimes possible and is desirable in addition to copyright when circumstances permit. Advice of a competent lawyer is essential in this consideration. While not yet recognized in all countries, proprietary ownership and initial exclusive rights by copyright is accepted in most circumstances. Certainly, U.S. copyright ownership, as well as a granted patent, gives a clear right to protect against illegal entry of software into the U.S. market. The Agency Committee of LES International has also announced the first draft of licensing guides on software and integrated circuits (March, 1990, issue of *les Nouvelles*, p. 7 blue pages). When completed, this work will also be very useful in determining optimum licensing terms.

It is on the basis of copyright that SIS Microelectronics, Inc., established a licensing program on its microcircuit design software for extension to various microchip designers. It is interesting to note that the SIS chip design software is itself based on a license received from a chip manufacturer.

With respect to general sales of copyrighted and/or patented software, the sales documents themselves should be drafted to negate any implied license under the copyright and/or patent to reproduce or copy. The sale price of such software should be sufficient to cover the manufacturing cost, distribution and dealer's cost and normal retail profit.

Whether the selected protection of software is trade secret, copyright, patent, or a combination of all three, the software developer is well advised to have appropriate legal counsel to establish defensible proprietary rights that can be exercised against unlicensed users. Then, any sale or use of such developed software should be made available for use by others only on a license basis.

Licensing biotechnology.

Biotechnology may have more direct effect on the health and nourishment of mankind than any other science. Its applications range from antibiotics and special diagnostic agents to waste disposal and agricultural product improvement such as plant development and livestock improvement. The most significant consideration for this field, therefore, is protection of innovation and invention along with the ability to profit from the resulting developments.

Biotechnology is protectable by utility patents, plant variety patents and trade secrets. Each of these methods has advantages and disadvantages. John H. Woodley, partner in the law firm of Sim and McBurney, Toronto, Ontario, reports on this subject in some detail in his paper "Capitalizing on Wealth in Biotechnology."[13] The rapidly developing world-wide situation for biotechnology intellectual property rights has been summarized in Dr. Albrecht Kreiger's paper "Status of World Intellectual Property Protection."[14]

Since biotechnology involves the use of living organisms, and since a given technology may be represented by such organisms (or parts thereof) as opposed to written data, formulae or designs, there are special considerations involved in licensing biotechnology. In his paper "Transferring Biotechnology," Waddell A. Biggart, partner Sughrue, Mion et al, Washington, D.C., points out:

> *Since living organisms reproduce, licensing of technology involving living organisms and/or parts thereof involves many different considerations than are involved in licensing of more traditional technology. The living organism is literally the entire biotechnology "factory." A technology transfer can thus include a transfer of intellectual property rights where the development transfer involves patent, trade secret and/or know-how rights. The technology transfer can also involve a transfer of personal property rights where the development transfer involves biological materials such as organisms, cell lines or parts thereof, e.g. plasmids, gene constructs, expression or promotion vectors, etc. As a result, control by the licensor of the licensor's technology after licensing may be more difficult after transfer and, importantly, after a license termination where biological materials, i.e. the biotechnology factory, have been transferred. Thus, a*

> *licensor must consider the value of his intellectual*
> *property rights in relation to his personal property rights*
> *to assess the value of the biotechnology he is planning to*
> *license and his risks in doing so.*

Anyone interested in the field of biotechnology as either licensee or licensor is urged to study the papers of Messers Woodley and Biggart, which cover the subjects of protection and licensing in some detail.[15] Mr. Woodley's paper includes several specific examples of licensing arrangements, while Mr. Biggart's paper reviews the terms of agreements that must be considered for licensing by a U.S. firm. Both papers emphasize that the licensing of biotechnology is similar to other licensing, but that property rights for living organisms need to be given special consideration. Clearly, the foregoing emphasizes the need to work closely with a knowledgeable attorney and possibly a competent consultant with respect to licensing plans in biotechnology. Further background material is found in Bibliography No. 97. The Agency Committee of LES International has also announced the first draft of a licensing guide on biotechnology (March, 1990, issue of *les Nouvelles*, p. 7 blue pages). When completed, this work will also be very useful.

Advantages of a coordinated program.

The story of Chester Carlson illustrates the advantages of licensing for an individual inventor, as well as a research and development company and, ultimately, a mid-size firm that has now become a major corporation through good business planning and a strategy that included licensing and joint-venturing.

THE CHESTER CARLSON STORY
One man's idea becomes a major industrial breakthrough
with the help of licensing and a joint-venture.

> *In 1938 Chester Carlson was granted a U.S. patent on*
> *his invention of a dry process for making copies. He con-*
> *tinued to pursue the idea until his money and any funds*
> *available from friends ran out, without having achieved*
> *a commercial result. In 1944 he achieved a license*
> *agreement with Battelle Memorial Institute in Colum-*
> *bus, Ohio, to the effect that Battelle would perform fur-*
> *ther development work on the process and bring it to the*
> *point that it could be sold or licensed for full commer-*

cial use. Mr. Carlson would share in any income from such a deal. Battelle's investment over a two-year period has been reported as $3,000. In 1946 the Battelle work was successful, and it licensed the invention to the Haloid Corporation, an enterprising company under the direction of Mr. Joseph Wilson, President, who then spent considerably more money to achieve a fully commercial unit.

As Haloid perfected the new copier, Mr. Wilson decided that his company name did not properly represent its activity. He changed it to Xerox Corporation, named after the new process which Chester Carlson called Xerography. In 1961 Xerox introduced its first office copier, the model 914, covered by more than 200 patents. A new industry was started, with profits for all, including Chester Carlson the inventor.

For international coverage, Xerox licensed the British firm, J. Arthur Rank, which had substantial marketing capabilities on the world market but no technology for making copiers. Rank-Xerox was the joint-venture outcome. It is now recognized as a leader in the field of copy machines and related office equipment outside the United States.

Once again, licensing and joint-venturing proved to be an effective, significant part of business planning.

Corporate planning objectives, strategies and tactics.

A company's plans for licensing should go hand-in-hand with the overall corporate strategic and tactical planning. If the latter does not exist or is not clearly identified, then it will be difficult to have a licensing plan and organization that is other than haphazard.

In a thought-provoking article in the March-April 1981 issue of *Harvard Business Review*, David Ford and Chris Ryan state:

Corporate management of technology requires careful planning of the relationships among a company's technologies, its markets, and its development activities. . . .

Current management wisdom says that a company invests its skills and resources in developing products or services that are of value to its customers. However, we argue that, to maximize the rate of return on its technology investment, a company must plan for the fullest market exploitation of all its technologies. These technologies may, but need not necessarily, be incorporated into that company's own products or services. . . .

Thus, a company's marketing strategy may and probably should provide for the sale of technologies for a lump sum or a royalty. . . .

The foregoing, are considerations that business managers should look at as they plan for the future. Not everyone will find that licensing is the best move in corporate strategy. However, some may decide that it can be a principal source of profits. Most will agree that the possibilities of licensing deserve serious attention as a part of business planning. In certain cases, a good strategy may be to prepare for licensing but not actually to do so until the time is right. Meanwhile prepare for the proper protection of proprietary technology. Part One, Chapter V has a few examples of what happens when valuable intellectual property is not handled properly.

FOOTNOTES:
[1]See Bibliography 6.
[2]See Part Two, Chapter VII, "Agreement Terms — Improvement and Grant-back."
[3]Ibid.
[4]See Bibliography 51.
[5]See Part Two, Chapter VIII.
[6]See Part Two, Chapter IX.
[7]See Bibliography 50.
[8]See Bibliography 56.
[9]See Part Three, Chapter X.
[10]See Bibliography 51.
[11]See Bibliography 63 and 64.
[12]See Part Three, Chapter X.
[13]See Bibliography 68.
[14]See Bibliography 90.
[15]See Bibliography 67 and 68.

Chapter III

WHAT IS BEST FOR LICENSOR & LICENSEE

Designer Blocks, as noted in Chapter I, has developed a good business in "licensing out" a special design of concrete block. Designer Blocks President, Robert Dean, looks for concrete block manufacturers with good territorial coverage and dependable manufacturing competence, firms that will make good licensees.

Anaquest of Madison, Wisconsin, was mentioned in Chapters I and II as a health care firm that is interested in obtaining technology by "licensing in." Anaquest looks for a product that fills a need and has been developed by a technically competent firm hopefully a product with established production methods and the necessary approval of the U.S. Food and Drug Administration.

* * * * *

Both licensee and licensor want to expand technology use, sales and profitability. The licensor turns to his licensee for expanded market coverage and for use of the licensor's technology. He must assure himself that a prospective licensee will give him the competence necessary to make the licensed product or use the technology effectively and, in the case of product licensing, will market the product effectively. The considerations for licensee selection should include all elements of effective manufacturing and marketing. Company size, market served, facilities, number of employees, present products, current profitability and general reputation are all factors that should be considered in selecting a licensee.

The licensee must determine much of the same information with respect to the licensor. The licensee also must determine to his own satisfaction both the suitability of the licensed product or process and the suitability of the licensor and the experience that the licensor has had in working with other licensees. Part Two, Chapter IV, gives preliminary information checklists made up from the experiences of many licensors and licensees. Bibliographic references 3, 57, 58, 59, 60 and 74 have additional significant comments.

In actual practice, of course, many license arrangements are put together without the complete licensor/licensee analysis indicated in the check lists. Sometimes certain information is simply not available when needed. A judgment call must then be made by the executive in charge of the program, and negotiations will either be stalled until the information is available or will proceed without the missing information. The real key to success is to distinguish between information that is necessary and that is merely useful but not critical.

Standard licenses.

Most of the firms responding to this study have indicated no use for standard licenses, and appropriately so. The use of a "form" or "standard" license is sometimes just a substitute for thinking. However, there can be a good reason for having a standard license arrangement, namely when there will be so many licensees that it would be impractical to have a separate, individually negotiated license for each. A standard license may also be used to assure that all licensees are given the same terms.

An example of appropriate "standard term" licensing is seen when the Ransberg Company[1] found it necessary to develop a series of standard terms for their licensing program which covered over 2000 companies in the U.S. and approximately the same number outside the U.S. The Ransberg program covered a unique system of electrostatic spray painting. License terms were based on production type, products and category of product. All companies with the same product types received the same terms. Without such a standard arrangement, Ransberg would have had a very difficult task of keeping track of royalties and licensee obligations. A similar situation existed for Dolby when that company started its licensing program to the audio recording industry for the elimination of unwanted static hiss. The practical solution was a standardized license.

In 1963, when Aluminum Company of America (Alcoa) initiated its licensing program for Easy Open Can Ends, two standard licenses were established one for U.S. can manufacturers and one for can makers outside the United States. Terms for these two standards were different because the patent coverage was different and because licensee production rates would be significantly different. While the U.S. licensees were relatively few in number, it was essential that the same terms be applied to all. For the international market, it was necessary not only to have absolutely the same terms in order to be fair to all but also to have a system that could accommodate what was ultimately 75 different licensees from all parts of the world! Here, again, the "standard" approach was the practical solution. Further discussion of this program is in Part Three, Chapter XII. While a "standard license" eliminates flexibility, it can change a potential management nightmare with multiple licensees into a workable business arrangement.

Licensing and joint-ventures with socialist and developing countries.

An interesting caution is emphasized by several executives. The remarks come both from managers of mid-size and large corporations and from individual agents or consultants. The caution is, "Be very careful about licensing or selling into the socialist countries and into the developing countries." The caution is not so much a question of reliability, but of time and effort that will be necessary in both negotiation and license servicing. In the case of socialist countries, the familiarization, selling and negotiation time can be so long and arduous that the result simply may not be worth the time spent. Granted, the ultimate "prize" may be big, but one should be prepared with the "Three P's" — patience, patience and patience, plus the finances to support the patience. Technical competence and required training should be studied with particular care. If the prospective licensor does not have an in-house expert on the country, it is well-advised to engage a consultant or designate an employee with time to study the situation.[2] As this book goes to press, it is difficult to say just how this situation may change in view of the current political upheavals in most communist countries. Present wisdom, however, still indicates a real need to continue with caution and the "Three P's."

These remarks on socialist countries also hold for the developing countries, but with more emphasis on technical competence and training questions and less on negotiation problems. Furthermore, many developing countries have restrictive laws on licensing which must be accommodated.[3]

Walk, do not run into negotiations.

A U.S. manufacturer was enthusiastic about a license and joint-venture possibility with a manufacturer of the Peoples Republic of China. The result of this arrangement was to have great success in filling a need in China and supplying a world market for certain products. After the first meeting, the U.S. company wanted to start right away, and the Chinese were eager to close the deal on the basis of what the U.S. firm representatives said were "general" or "approximate" costs for the contract with the U.S. company. Fortunately, the U.S. manufacturer engaged a consultant and took time to study the situation carefully after the initial meeting. Further review with the consultant showed that training and technology transfer costs would unquestionably be much greater than first anticipated. They returned for the serious negotiation stage with a proposal considerably more expensive for the Chinese than the original estimates. Negotiations promptly came to an end when the Chinese learned that the "new" price was substantially higher than the original figure. In spite of this outcome, the management of the U.S. company was ultimately pleased that they had "done their homework" before long negotiating time was spent or embarrassing legal commitments were made. While the deal did not take place, the U.S. firm had clearly saved a lot of money and avoided later complications. Incidentally, the consultant involved clearly earned his fee in cost saved for his client.

Capability, a source of trouble.

As previously mentioned, the capability of both licensee and/or licensor can be critical to the success of a license or joint-venture. If the licensee is not sufficiently capable to operate the license without a great deal of help, the licensor may be required to spend excessive time and money in training. Similarly, if the licensor is not prepared to help a licensee adequately, the licensee firm can find itself burdened with impossible performance obligations.

In discussing the licensing of R&D results or undeveloped technology, one technically oriented company has said that it will not license a technology unless it has already used that technology successfully. Reason: too many headaches in handling technical questions from a licensee when those questions have never been faced "at home."

Robert Smith, Vice-President of DEC International, Inc., a manufacturer of dairy and food related equipment in Madison, Wisconsin, insists that licenses not be extended to firms in locations that are geographically remote, unless they are exceptionally competent. Otherwise, the cost and time needed for providing technical assistance is not acceptable to DEC International, according to Mr. Smith.

Herbert L. Pocklington, President of Hatteras International, has terminated licenses when the licensees were not performing at a required level. Fortunately for Mr. Pocklington, he has the foresight to include provisions in his licenses that make such termination possible.

Both technical and marketing performance demands are critical for licensor and licensee and should be carefully reviewed in every contract by all participants. Prior experience in licensing is often a revealing factor and should be explored by every prospective licensee and licensor as they enter into preliminary discussions and ultimate negotiations. People do not like to talk about unhappy experiences. For that reason, specific experiences of incompetence are not generally available. These problems do happen, however, and performance capabilities should be thoroughly searched on both sides. Chapter VI includes more on the subject.

Specifics of finding technology.

The advantages of locating and acquiring technology from others and the need to do so in an organized, logical manner are of utmost importance. Suggestions on this subject are covered in Part Two, Chapter IV. Two actual experience stories of licensing in are covered in Part Three, Chapters III and IV. Parkson Corporation conducted a very precise and organized program for acquiring equipment technology in the process industry. E.M.I. Corporation, on the other hand, expanded through a less formal series of equipment and technology licenses in the plastics field. Both accounts are interesting and informative.

The importance of licensing in and the requirements for doing so successfully and profitably must be emphasized. Often the strategy of licensing is considered primarily from the viewpoint of the licensor, overlooking the fact that a sound, satisfying license arrangement must be useful and profitable to both licensee and licensor. The entire subject of technology search, acquisition and implementation has been studied in depth by the LES, USA/Canada Committee on Technology and is reported in all aspects in the article "Technology Acquisition Process,"

December 1989 issue of *les Nouvelles*.[4] This report covers the various vital aspects of:

- Identification of Need
- Scourcing of Technology
- Assessment of Technology
- Negotiation of The License
- Technology Transfer
- Financial Options
- Implementation
- Termination of The License

Bibliography references 3 and 74, along with 61 and 86 emphasize the clear and constant need for competence in both technical and business strategy considerations.

Small licenses big.

It is always a pleasure to point out experiences that prove in a positive way how well things go when technical competence is present on both sides. One typical such experience covers both the licensor's interests and the licensee's point of view. Stake Technology, Ltd. of Oakville, Ontario, Canada, developed unique specialized technology and equipment for converting forest and agricultural waste into useful chemicals, cattle feed and fibre products. Stake Technology has 20 employees, and its principal licensee is a French corporation with 4,000 employees. Technip, the French licensee, is technically capable, is doing an excellent job of handling the European market and is clearly delighted with the technology from Stake. Stake on the other hand, finds Technip to be a competent, dependable partner in business, and both firms are well satisfied.

N.I.H. A caution to both big and small.

N.I.H. stands for "Not Invented Here." Expressed or unexpressed, the N.I.H. attitude can well be the most dangerous thinking in any firm that is interested in forward progress through the acquisition of technology under license. To be overly critical of or opposed to an idea or a technology from the outside is both a natural human reaction and a dangerous barrier to progress. N.I.H. should be eliminated from any firm that is devoted to progress and development. The presence of

N.I.H. in any firm will be a deterrent to forward progress through intelligent, selective licensing.

Big licenses small.

A firm already mentioned, Anaquest of Madison, Wisconsin, carefully avoids N.I.H. and derives substantial technology under license from others. With considerable experience, Anaquest searches the field of new product possibilities after determining the most needed medical and pharmaceutical products suited to its manufacturing and marketing scheme. Thorough investigation of available technology for patent and other protection, for FDA approval stage and for other special market considerations, helps Anaquest to determine the most desirable licensing arrangements. Highly regarded by the major pharmaceutical firms, Anaquest is able to negotiate licenses that are successful for both Anaquest and its licensors, most of whom are large, multinational firms. Having a reputation for top quality production and a hard working sales organization, Anaquest is well regarded as a high-performance organization, a firm that can be counted on as a top-quality licensee partner. In the field of pharmaceuticals and medical products, Anaquest is a good exception for firms who refuse to license spin-off technology.

Review.

The following account is interesting as a summary of the considerations and principles discussed thus far in Chapters I-III — how licenses fit into good business strategy — why and how license situations change — what can be the favorable results of a properly handled license program. Alcoa's Closure Division could be thought of as a separate company, since its product line, manufacturing and sales force operate substantially outside the "mainstream" mill products of the parent company. This experience, then, can be considered as a 20-year licensing experience by a mid-size company. While the time span of this account is more than twenty years old, the circumstances represent situations still valid in international licensing.

CLOSURES FOR BOTTLES AND JARS
Twenty years licensing experience with changing circumstances.

Alcoa's worldwide licensing program for closures or caps for bottles covered some of the classic do's and don'ts of licensing from the late 1950s to the middle 1970s. In the late 1950s, a licensee was established in Mexico to manufacture many of the Alcoa "roll-on" closures (a unique design of bottle cap). The situation was ideal, an improved product for an expanding market and a market in which Alcoa could not effectively compete through the export of U.S.-made closure products. Soon after that license was established, a similar arrangement was completed in Colombia. In each case an equity position was established by capitalizing certain manufacturing equipment supplied. In another two or three years, a small closure manufacturer in Ecuador applied for a straight license with no equity and was accepted as such. In the same time period, closure manufacturing licensees were also established in Venezuela and Argentina. All these licenses carried royalty requirements and (with one exception) minimum payments. The arrangement was good. Licensees were happy with their new product line, and a network of closure licensees gave effective coverage in a market area that could not be covered effectively by export from the United States.

As time went on, however, situations changed. The Ecuadorian licensee really didn't want to expand its operation and aggressively pursue the market. What it really wanted was for Alcoa, as licensor, to prevent the Colombian manufacturer from entering the Ecuadorian market, an action that Alcoa would not take. The Ecuadorian license was terminated amicably. Then, market economics turned sour in Mexico and Colombia, and royalty payments were in trouble. Arrangements were made to reduce royalty requirements. Ultimately, it was realized that all of these licensees required more continuing technical help than could be supported by future royalty payments. Since good, friendly relationships had been maintained throughout this period, it was possible to terminate the licenses on individually negotiated schedules in such a way that all parties remained friends. The licensee manufacturers were able to continue operation, each at a limited rate to suit the individual market circumstances.

While these license activities were going on in Latin America, licenses were also established in Germany and Japan. The German licensee, a competent, though small, individually-owned firm, was looking for a strong partner with the possibility of expansion support. An initial limited product license period constituted a highly satisfactory "get acquainted period" which was ultimately followed by a 100% Alcoa equity and expansion. Wholly owned by Alcoa, the facility is a major supplier to the European closure market. The Japanese licensee ultimately established a partial equity of Alcoa in the firm with further expansion for the Japanese and general Asian market.

In each of these cases, royalty payments and good relations maintained a commercial participation for Alcoa in markets otherwise not possible. Through the maintenance of friendly associations, it was possible to find relief from situations that became commercially burdensome due to changing circumstances. Finally, the intimate knowledge possible between licensor and licensee opened the door to even closer and more profitable equity relations with certain selected partners.

FOOTNOTES:

[1]See Part One, Chapter I.

[2]See Part Two, Chapter VIII, also Bibliography 1.

[3]See Part Two, Chapter VIII, also Bibliography 1, 52, 53, 54.

[4]See Bibliography 86.

Chapter IV

LICENSING BOTH WAYS AT ONCE

For several years two unrelated corporations, one a major firm in the metals industry and the other a major firm in the chemical and fibres field, collected roughly $10 million dollars each per year in royalties on technology licenses. They also paid approximately the same amount in royalties and fees for technologies acquired under license.

* * * * *

General advantages.

The foregoing examples illustrate that there can be as many opportunities and advantages in buying technology (licensing in) as in selling it (licensing out).[1]

As the opportunities of licensing both in and out are appreciated, many firms extend their licensing work to include the acquisition of technology as well as the sale, or vice-versa. Often a special advantage is found from such dual activity. There is a closer touch with relevant industry and one hears more technical "gossip," information on who is doing what in a given field. Business in some industries, such as the pharmaceutical and chemical industries, seems to enter into the action of "both-at-once" more readily than others. Perhaps rapidly changing technology is the reason for this phenomenon. It also appears that many large corporations with well organized licensing programs are involved in both technology acquisition and sales.

Unfortunately, only a few of the small and mid-size businesses contacted by the author during this study had been involved in a two-way street of licensing or joint-ventures. To give the proper emphasis on simultaneous in and out licensing this chapter will discuss the activity of larger corporations as well as smaller firms that have profited from such a strategy.

USX Corporation.

In 1981 John R. Pegan, Senior General Attorney Intellectual Property for United States Steel Company (now USX Corporation) told the Licensing Executives Society:[2]

> *In my opinion it is a hallmark of good business and technical people to recognize that one can learn from others. This includes purchasing better technology when and as it can be obtained and applied more efficiently and economically than it can be developed independently. . . . U.S. Steel recognizes the need for building tomorrow's strengths and successes upon a solid technological base today. We are proceeding with a careful view toward a proper balance of internal development and judicious acquisition of technology for our own use, and a policy of transfer of our technology to others at a fair price.*

Pfizer, Inc.

As already noted, the pharmaceutical industry is substantially devoted to both licensing in and licensing out. An example of this practice is Pfizer, Inc. According to Dr. William T. Davis, Director of Licensing, Pfizer has historically accepted the fact that acquisition of technology from the outside is an important factor for growth. It is impractical, he points out, to support the goal of 15 percent annual growth with internal research alone. Of the four major new products described at the 1986 annual meeting of Pfizer, three were the result of licensing in. Overall, 50 percent or more of Pfizer's products are the result of licensing in for either product or process in spite of more than $400 million annual research expenditure.

A notable example of Pfizer's licensing in policy is known by the technical name of Tetrahydrozelene and the commercial name of Visene. Synthesized several years ago in the garage of an individual inventor, Tetrahydrozelene was licensed to Pfizer with the result of significant profits to the inventor and a long-term profitable product for Pfizer.

The patent coverage on Visene ran out years ago, but the product and its name identification continues as a valuable item on druggists' shelves.

Current licensing activities are related to current product and business strategies and thus are not available. However, one example of licensing out is Pfizer's arrangement with the firm of Molecular Genetics. Pfizer has developed a very useful adjuvant (material that makes vaccines more effective), and Molecular Genetics is in the business of making vaccines. Pfizer has extended to Molecular Genetics a nonexclusive field-of-use license to incorporate the Pfizer adjuvant into the Molecular Genetics vaccines. The final products are significantly improved. Molecular Genetics is happy, and Pfizer is able to obtain profit through the use of Pfizer technology in an application not otherwise in its normal product line.

F. Hoffman-LaRoche & Company.

Jon S. Saxe, Vice-President, Licensing and Corporate Development, Hoffman-LaRoche, Nutley, New Jersey,[3] expresses principles for licensing in and out that seem to coincide remarkably with those of other major pharmaceutical and health-care firms.

For licensing out:

- Financial income is important, but of equal importance is the creation of "owe-me's" with other creative health-care firms. In other words, the quid pro quo aspect is significant among firms that are likely to produce other useful technologies.

- A primary importance is the humanitarian aspect of licensing a drug or commodity in order to make it available for use when that use has a special need.

For licensing in:

- Consider the opportunity costs, the market need, the cost to bring the product to consumer readiness, and the ability to sell the product for the necessary profit but do not hesitate to take on an outside technology because of N.I.H.[4]

SAI Technology Company.

D.K. Layser, President of SAI Technology Company, San Diego, California, gives a useful account of his firm's experience in licensing in and out.[5] The following is a summary:

SAI Technology (SAIT) is a wholly owned subsidiary of Science Applications, Inc. (SAI). SAI is a mid-size, privately owned company that provides R&D studies and has a strong computer software capability. SAIT is the manufacturing arm of SAI.

In the late 1970s and early 80s SAIT manufactured and sold an electronic laboratory instrument, the ATP photometer, under a license from its inventors. The ATP in the name of the instrument referred to adenosine triphosphate and the instrument is used in general purpose laboratories to measure the amount of biological mass in a sample. Prior to undertaking any consideration of a method to obtain this technology SAIT did its homework on profit potential, market, ease of production in SAIT facilities, etc. SAIT's management also determined that it could probably develop its own ATP instrument that would not infringe the patents of the original ATP photometer. However, a decision was made to take a license after SAIT management considered:

- Terms of the license offered.
- Time required for development.
- Low business risk.
- Familiarity with the basic technology.
- Cash investment.
- Impact on earnings.

SAIT executed an exclusive license agreement with the inventors and for a period of four years successfully (and profitably) manufactured and marketed the ATP photometer. Mr. Layser, says: ". . . licensing proved to be a desirable way to meet the risk exposure, earnings, and cash flow objectives of an R&D growth company."

Based on internal design and development, SAIT also manufactured sophisticated high technology electronic or electromechanical product lines. One was a highly sophisticated plasma display terminal capable of operation while withstanding substantial mechanical vibration and shock (used largely on military equipment such as tanks). SAIT's management felt there was an opportunity to increase income from the display terminal technology by entering the market of the NATO countries of Western Europe. In considering this possibility, SAIT reviewed the options of direct sales through its own sales office in Western Europe, a joint-venture with a Western European firm, a wholly owned facility in Western Europe or a license with a competent firm in Western Europe. A decision was made to license a West German military electronics company to manufacture and sell plasma-display terminals using SAIT technology.

Considerations for the final license were:

- Qualifications of the licensee.
- Terms of the license.
- Cash flow.
- Earnings.
- Engineering resources of SAIT.
- Senior management involvement.
- Risk.

In summary, Mr. Layser comments:

> *I am not sure that the business factors that I considered in these two cases apply to all other licensing situations, but I suspect that several of these factors are shared with most R&D growth companies. Cash flow, earnings impact, optimization of engineering resources and senior management time are, I believe, important considerations to other companies which are similar to SAIT.*
>
> *In any event, I personally, am sold on licensing as an effective way to leverage my assets or to limit my business risks in many situations. I will continue to use licensing whatever and whenever it has a good fit with the objectives of SAI Technology Company.*

SPS Technologies, Inc.

The licensing program of SPS Technologies of Jenkintown, Pennsylvania has been noteworthy in respect to licensing both in and out. An account published in 1979 by A.L. Ney, attorney with law firm, Ratner and Prestia, reviews the SPS reasons for licensing in and out:[6]

SPS Technologies is a manufacturer of precision fasteners, fastener installation systems and precision metal parts. It sells to manufacturers of airframes, aircraft engines, motor vehicles and capital equipment — and companies than handle and store parts. SPS licenses out, to establish multiple sources of SPS fastener products. While it would prefer to be a sole supplier, customer demands and commercial pressures dictate that licenses be granted to competitors. In addition, SPS licenses its technology to subsidiaries and joint-ventures, thus enhancing their equity positions. Beyond those two basic purposes, SPS also licenses certain by-product technologies for the sole purpose of generating additional income.

SPS licenses in to fill certain needs in established product lines. it takes these licenses from competitors, noncompetitors and individual inventors. A second and equally important reason for SPS to license in is diversification. SPS believes that a practical and viable way to diversify is to identify a business area of interest and then buy the best available technology to enter that business. In the opinion of Mr. Ney, this approach is generally cheaper than buying a going business. While not as quick to show results as when buying a business, licensing or buying technology is considerably faster than developing the technology internally.

DEC International, Inc.

SAIT licensed out to reach foreign markets for its own in-house technology, and licensed in to obtain the know-how and rights to new product technology which would be profitable. DEC International, Inc. of Madison, Wisconsin, a leader in dairy-related equipment, licensed in for technology and patent coverage, refined the technology, made a specialized product line from it, and licensed it out to companies in Australia, South America and Europe! Combining internal technology with intelligent licensing in, DEC International manufactures products ranging from milking equipment, dairy farm automation and cheese making equipment to spray driers, heat recovery systems and special food processing equipment. Patents and trade secret know-how have been taken under license selectively by DEC for development into products and processes ranging from a remote liquor system and bottle control apparatus to estrus detection for cows, milk meters with automatic detachers for milking machines and automatic feeder systems with specialized computer software. DEC supplies dairies and related food processing firms throughout the world from their manufacturing facilities in Madison, Wisconsin and vicinity.

With respect to recent licensing activity, DEC started by making an agreement with Pillsbury on several patents related to filtering and drying. DEC's management believed that this patent coverage and technology could be very useful in building a line of equipment known today as the DEC Filtermat Spray Dryer. This development was so successful that DEC ultimately purchased the Pillsbury patent outright. The performance of the equipment created a sufficiently large market that DEC licensed the technology to A.P.V. Bell Bryant for New Zealand and Australia, to Sumitomo for Japan, to Electrogeno A/S in Denmark for coverage of Western Europe and to Meiter, S.A. in Argentina for the South American market.

Other licensing out activities of DEC have included tower drier technology into Brazil, and bulk tank cooler technology into England. In the latter case, there were no patents, simply trade secret know-how developed over a period of years. In order to maintain proper controls by DEC on the unpatented technology and to assure FABDEC, Ltd. (the licensee) of continued technical contacts, the final arrangement was a 50-50 joint-venture. Established in 1962, this relationship continues to this day.

Anaquest Division of BOC Group.

Robert Lippert, Director of Licensing and International Development for Anaquest, identifies a principal reason for licensing out, the need to license for "quids." Anaquest, like many pharmaceutical firms, depends to a large extent on the technology of others. Such technology can be licensed in and handled by Anaquest for certain of the specialized markets it serves. With licensing both in and out being such a universal matter for the drug and health-care companies, firms such as Anaquest must be careful to work cooperatively with other firms in the industry. Many times a license will be either taken or offered on the basis of serving mutual interests. "Quid pro quo" is frequently mentioned, and that reference explains why Mr. Lippert is careful to define his portfolio for licensing out in terms of its "quids," while direct royalty income potential may even be a secondary item. The licensing activities of Anaquest have also been discussed in Part One, Chapters I, II and III, also in Part Two, Chapter I.

Stake Technology, Ltd.

Licensing in and out simultaneously can also be used by a small firm to establish worldwide leadership in a new technology. With 20 employees, Stake Technology, Ltd. of Oakville, Ontario, is a perfect example of a small firm with scientific solutions to worldwide problems of waste disposal. Stake Technology is making optimum use of business techniques, such as licenses and technical collaboration, to achieve the most favorable overall strategy. In Chapter III, Stake Technology was mentioned for development of equipment and process technology to convert forest and agricultural waste into chemicals, cattle feed and fibre products. To date Stake Technology has licensees in Paris, France, (Technip); in Cincinnati, Ohio, (Vulcan); and Tokyo, Japan, (Nissho Iwai and Hitachi Zosen). These licensees apply the Stake Technology method of biomass conversion, with Technip being the primary manufacturer of equipment for applications outside of North America. In their program for leadership of the world market in biomass utilization, Stake Technology has also taken exclusive and nonexclusive licenses for related patents and know-how from Finnish Sugar Company of Helsinki, Finland; from Dr. B.V. Kota of the University of Quebec and from Forintek, an R&D organization funded by the Canadian Government and the forest industry of Canada. The result of this carefully planned strategy for licensing in and out is to place Stake Technology in a position of clear world leadership in the field of biomass and waste product conversion for forest and agricultural waste material.

The success of Stake Technology is graphically described in a Summer 1988 article in the *Penny Stock Journal* which described licensing activities and plans for Brazil, the Soviet Union and unnamed locations in Eastern Europe, Central and South America. With regard for licensing policy, *Penny Stock Journal* quoted Jeremy N. Kendall, Chairman and CEO of Stake Technology, as saying:

> *"Our (licensing) revenues will come from three basic sources cattle feed, paper manufacturing, and the conversion of plants into numerous products by breaking down the lignin. A fourth application, fiberboard production, is a bit farther off."*

With respect to license planning and business strategy, Mr. Kendall also says:

> *"We're licensing much of our technology, but we're keeping the United States and eastern Canada for ourselves."*

The May/June, 1989, issue of *Penny Stock Journal* reports:

> *Stake Technology, Ltd., has received three new contracts that during the first half of calendar 1989 should "translate into the first significant operating income in the company's 15-year history, but more importantly establishes our technology as the leading edge in paper pulping," Jeremy N. Kendall, Stake chairman, told security analysts recently.*

Summary and the potential of cross licensing.

Managers and CEO's sometimes think only of licensing out, getting more mileage, more profit, from their technology. They may fail to look for opportunities to acquire technology such as a new product or an improved process. However, as more companies realize the advantages of "both at once" there will be an increasing influence of these companies on the growth of product lines and the improvement of production processes.

Included in this activity will also be "cross licensing," or the mutual exchange of technology between two firms on a licensed basis. The cross licensing concept offers an opportunity for a company to exchange the use of its own technology for the advantages of another's development. Each firm thus has a new technology for process or product improvement. At the same time, a minimum of cash money changes hands because the technology evaluations tend to compensate each other. These variations indicate again the versatility of licensing as a business strategy. An example of such strategy is seen in a March 22, 1989, headline in *The Wall Street Journal*: "Genetics Institute and Genentech Agree to Cross-license Drug for Hemophiliacs." Other imaginative licensing strategies are reviewed in the following chapter under "Corporate Partnering" and "Co-Marketing."

FOOTNOTES:

[1]See also Part Two, Chapter IV, "Why, Why Not . . ."

[2]"Technology Transfer at U.S. Steel," paper presented at the 1981 LES (U.S.A. and Canada) annual meeting.

[3]See Appendix A-2.

[4]See Part One, Chapter III, "N.I.H. A Caution to big and small."

[5]See Bibliography 62.

[6]Taken from "Ingredients for Success" by Andrew L. Ney — publ. in the December, 1979, issue of *les Nouvelles.*

Chapter V

LEARNING FROM OTHERS

What *not* to do and some special tips on what *to* do.

* * * * *

The mistakes of others can provide valuable instruction. For example, there is the case of a firm which spent a significant amount of money in royalties on a patent license for several years after the patent had expired! Too many times costly mistakes are the result of errors of oversight.

It is not easy to persuade people to talk about their mistakes. Successes and triumphs we all like to publicize, but failures or near-failures are usually kept from public view. Nevertheless, the details of an authentic disappointment can be as instructive as the story with a happy ending. The following accounts are examples of actual incidents with names protected as necessary in certain cases.

A tragedy of bad judgment.

The worst instance of mishandled licensing uncovered in this study must be described without identification. It is a case of a highly competent inventor who had tragically poor business judgment.

In the late 1940s an inventor developed and patented a piece of equipment that proved to be popular with the manufacturing industry. Sales grew and the business expanded, but the inventor was more interested in R&D than in manufacturing. Ultimately the inventor's sales manager persuaded the inventor to turn the business over to him, the sales manager. However, the inventor kept the patent ownership and did not give the sales manager a license under the patent. He merely said, "You are a good friend so just go ahead with your own company."

A year or so later, another firm approached the inventor. It asked for and received a license to make and sell the device. Unfortunately, no one did anything about the original sales manager, who was still permitted to make and sell under the original "understanding." The second licensee firm did not pursue the market vigorously and ultimately sold out to a third firm. The third firm was, likewise, not successful in sales and, without any compelling minimum payments in the license, had no incentive to try harder. Meanwhile, the inventor was developing and extending further improvements to his licensees and becoming more frustrated because no one was producing good sales results.

Finally, the inventor made arrangements to go back into the manufacturing business himself, and he hired a "hot-shot" consultant to help. This new man proved to know very little about running either a license program or a small business. As time went on, the new consultant/manager also proved that he did not know how to handle the people already in the inventor's organization. The result was that half of the inventor's small staff left him.

Licensing, as a business strategy, was not at fault in this case. The fault lay in several poor decisions, including poor judgment in how to set up and operate a license program. Unfortunately, the inventor still thinks that it was licensing not business judgment that caused his problems.

More dumb mistakes.

The first paragraph of this chapter speaks about a situation where most business people would say, "Not me! Never!" Well, believe it or not, the following have been cited many times as licensing "blunders" that have cost money for different firms.

Licensee Mistakes:

- Royalties paid when licensed patents had expired.

- Payments made after royalty terms have been satisfied.

- Payments made under a trademark license when the trademark is not used.

- Patents covered in a license no longer cover products that are currently made, yet royalty is paid against the patent coverage.

- Royalties paid at the wrong rate, i.e. one higher or lower than provided.

Licensor Mistakes:

- Failure to take action if royalty payments cease when they should not, e.g. prior to expiration of the patent.

- Failure to monitor royalty payments, e.g. sudden reductions or failure to meet minimum royalties that could trigger a change from exclusive to nonexclusive or termination of the license.

- Failure to stay in technical contact with the licensee, with the result of licensee not interested in paying royalties, in maintaining quality, or keeping good records.

The major problem for all.

A 1983-84 survey by the Licensing Executives Society U.S.A./Canada shows that the biggest difficulty between licensors and licensees was communication. Perceptions of difficulties appeared to be almost evenly divided between "in" and "out." Licensors felt that their licensees did not properly handle the information given. Licensees felt that they were not given the proper help. In some instances, it is quite apparent that the party accused was, indeed, not living up to agreed performance. It is also evident that some of the problems could have been resolved if the two sides (or perhaps just one side) had done a better job of describing a question or filing a request or making a complaint while it was minor instead of waiting until it was a major problem requiring major efforts and drastic solutions.

Too many times one party to an agreement will do something wrong or improper, not bad enough to breach the agreement, but still wrong and improper, and the other party will not say anything. When a minor mistake or improper action is not politely, diplomatically, straightened out, another similar incident will surely occur. A series of minor problems becomes a major unhappiness and the license is in trouble.

Problems of significance reported in the survey include royalty payments (late, missed, or deposited to wrong bank account number), exchange rate and timing, failure to use airmail, failure to use correct address, telex number or bank account deposit number, notices, and failure to respond in a timely manner to requests from the other party, misunderstanding of terms and conditions (license or related agreements), licensor's organization (inadequate support), licensee's organization (incapable, confused, "turf" problems), performance guarantees, defense of infringement suits, and royalty term.

The LES study came to two conclusions:

- Most problems arise from misunderstandings, lack of thoroughness, carelessness, or failure to administer the agreement at all, i.e. no one in authority is responsible for administration.

- Seldom do license problems originate with an unavoidable circumstance.

Of the two, the second is the most significant. Problems can be avoided by careful, knowledgeable action based on awareness and timely communication.

Individual opinions.

In a 1986 LES Panel Presentation,[1] titled "Learning from Mistakes of Others," four experts, each with many years' professional experience gave several extremely appropriate comments:

P.F. Casella, President of Intra Gene, Inc., and retired Director of Patents and Licensing for Hooker Chemical and Plastics Corporation, offers cautions on negotiations:

- Don't be a "show-off" when in negotiation.

- Don't grant sub-licensing rights to competitors.

- Don't charge too much.

- Don't take the wrong person on your negotiation team.

(Also see Part Two, Chapter IX, "Notes for Negotiating.")

J.P. Ciarimboli, President, PCT Technical Services, Inc. recognizes potential problems and the need for constant alertness.

- Full and complete commitment is required in any major project.

- In planning a licensing program, realistic, achievable goals are essential.

- Regardless of how good a technology may be, outside circumstances may render it only partially useful, too expensive, replaceable by a different technology, or unnecessary due to outside circumstances. Whenever possible, plan accordingly.

D.A. Guthrie, Vice President, Gulf South Research Institute says that problems result from factors in the planning process which have been carelessly carried out:

- Fuzzy thinking and fuzzy ideas.

- Personnel problems.

- Misjudging the market and the competition.

- Insufficient technology.

- Inadequate marketing.

Ivan Axelrod, C.P.A., Laventhol & Horwath lists the following problems that occur in performance under the agreement:

- Difficult relationships (communications) between licensor and licensee.

- Poor understanding of the contract.

- Improper or inadequate accounting and reporting.

Know your partner.

A major U.S. firm which must be given the fictitious name of Toppem, Inc., nearly had a disastrous confrontation with a foreign technical joint-venture partner because of a misunderstanding in accounting. The accountants of Toppem were, to say the least, dismayed when they discovered how the foreign partner handled profits. After deducting the appropriate costs and determining profits, the partner had for years made "contributions" to a local church. Typically these "contributions" were 75% of total profits. The church would then return 95% of the "contribution" to the partner (some "under the table" and some to compensate for certain "services"). The partner was delighted to have this "found money" on which no government tax was then paid, and the church was happy with the 5% that it would not otherwise have received. Neither the partner nor the local churchman saw anything wrong in this arrangement!

For reasons of company policy and legal regulation, Toppem, Inc. could not be associated corporately with a firm that performed that way. There were some difficult negotiation conferences with the joint-venture partner before Toppem succeeded in persuading the partner that the joint-venture could not continue unless this practice were stopped. The moral of this story is "Learn how your joint-venture partner conducts business before signing the agreement."

Two cases of disappointment.

Mr. Harris L. Johnson, President of Shipp-Johnson, Inc., Greensboro, N.C. and retired Director of Licensing for Burlington Industries, Inc., tells about two important experiences.[2] These two cases cover what can happen when a license is not drafted to cover all potential developments and what can happen when the marketplace changes the value of a new technology.

CASE I:

> *Licensing experience today, as a viable alternative to international business, is far more sophisticated than it was 25-30 years ago. This first case deals with a major textile machinery innovation developed as a result of a U.S. textile man touring one of the less prosperous countries of the world shortly after World War II. This innovation was licensed exclusively, worldwide, to a small U.S. firm. The fact that the license was worldwide meant that the licensee could manufacture and sell the machine on a protected basis anywhere that the licensor's patent rights existed. That seems simple enough. Let's look at the advantages:*

- *Licensor or patent owner had only one licensee to deal with. Royalties came from one source and technology flowed to one point.*

- *Licensee had a terrific market since the licensor had patents in all the major countries.*

But the original parties to the agreement failed to deal with at least two very important aspects of an international exclusive license.

The licensor had failed to insist on a clause requiring the licensee to attempt to sub-license equipment manufacturers producing equipment that fell within the claims of the patents.

The licensee had failed to insist upon a clause requiring the licensor to take legal action against firms that produced competing equipment coming within the claims of the patents.

As a result, a program that was reasonably profitable to both licensee and licensor on an international as well as domestic front, only partially generated the return it should have. The reason was simple. International manufacturers soon discovered the value of the product and out-produced the small, but now growing, U.S. licensee. At first, the licensee was not too concerned with the international market because of the high growth rate achieved in the U.S.

Soon, however, the international manufacturers began to poke into the U.S. marketplace. It was at this point that my own involvement began. The next few years were frustrating because (a) the licensee would not sub-license its competitors, and (b) the licensor would not litigate and risk its patents without having the flexibility to resolve the litigation through sub-licenses. Countless meetings failed to reconcile these problems. The result was less sales for the licensee and less royalty income for the licensor.

Let's look back at this case. Recognizing a viable business alternative in licensing the product or process, great care must be taken to examine a licensing alternative from a policy/practical standpoint as carefully as if an investment were being made in plant and equipment. Selection of the proper licensee is the key element. Just as location is everything in real estate, selection of the proper licensee is the secret in licensing. The agreement should be negotiated by individuals experienced in the nuances of licensing technology. Great attention must be paid to local laws and customs. Firm decisions must be made and incorporated into the agreement for expected technological, market and legal developments. The case we have just examined really only suffered from inattention on how to deal with success.

The licensee, succeeding beyond its wildest expectations, was unwilling to share that success with competitors even though it was impossible to capitalize on the success of the technology by offshore manufacturing and broader marketing by the licensee.

Risking the patents without complete freedom to settle was the last thing the licensor wanted to do because a win did not gain a market broader than the licensee was then serving. A loss meant that even the licensee would stop making its royalty payments.

This case was a major success yielding less than it should have because of poor licensee selection and poor attention to the ramifications of the silent intent of the agreement.

CASE II:

Let's examine a licensing effort that was designed for success and featured a product that was the answer to a manufacturer's dream.

An innovation developed by a major international think-tank was acquired by a textile manufacturer under an exclusive license with responsibilities for worldwide sub-licensing after additional R&D work was ac-

complished. When that work was completed in about 18 months, the licensing team took their dog-and-pony show to the largest U.S. firm on its list of potential sub-licensees in order to learn if the licensee's market research and that done by the think-tank was correct on the potential value of the innovation to the industry.

To the utter dismay of the exclusive licensee, the large domestic firm rejected the innovation in a rather hazy, unfocused manner. The exclusive licensee was not able to penetrate and understand (this reasoning) until several years later when the large domestic firm closed the division that would have been manufacturing the innovation. In the meantime, anxious because a million or so dollars had been invested in R&D, the exclusive licensee went to a large number of potential domestic and international sub-licensees. The result of this saturation activity was also somewhat disturbing; happily so, however, since everyone approached wanted the product.

The exclusive licensee went through a series of decision-making exercises to locate the proper sub-licensees. Early reference has been made to some of the reasons why licensing is a viable option to generate sales in otherwise difficult-to-reach offshore markets. Let's examine the specifics needed in this instance.

The sub-licensee would have to invest several million dollars in further R&D, training, sales aids, advertising, customer trials, and management costs. Therefore, it had to be a large company. The whole world was the market so the sub-licensee had to be able to cover the globe with its marketing and technical support. The investment and marketing scope meant that an exclusive sub-license would be the only way to find the "right partner."

After the potential sub-licensee was selected, negotiating the license agreement was the easiest part of the entire project since the sub-licensee selected was sophisticated and recognized that an equitable document was the joint goal of both parties. This is not to say that many hours, many meetings, much travel and many drafts were not *necessary. They were, but always they were undertaken in a spirit of cooperation. The agreement was executed by a U.S. division and the European home office of the exclusive sub-licensee.*

The exclusive textile manufacturer licensee selected an exclusive international sub-licensee with sales of several billion dollars and with selling and support services around the world, including the communist countries. Obviously, patents did not exist in every country. But since the manufacturing facilities of the sub-licensee were located in countries covered by patents, a mutually-convenient and legally-acceptable method of royalty payment covering the non-patented countries was agreed upon. For the record, this was possible because products processed in non-patented countries were invariably sent back into patented countries, thereby becoming subject to the patents.

So accept, if you will, that unlike our first case which floundered along because not enough attention was paid to the requirements of each party, this program was well conceived, well documented, and undertaken with enthusiasm by all concerned. The selected sub-licensee was signed. This sub-licensee, with manufacturing plants in the U.S. and Europe, brilliantly refined the innovation and, as those in licensing like to say, the product became technically commercial. Sales were made in all major countries. And, despite some early "teething" problems, the product was used successfully and met the objectives of the innovators and the customers. It was a strong effort, involving an international think-tank firm, a very large exclusive licensor, and a multi-billion dollar sub-licensee, properly structured, properly researched, properly patented, properly introduced to the market and properly supported by all.

Money was made by the innovative international think-tank firm and money was made by the exclusive licensor, but only by combining royalty income with savings generated through use of the innovation in its own manufacturing facilities. Money has not been made by the sub-licensee! Why? Very simple, the worldwide

*economic situation forced customers to change produc-
tion schedules from large volumes which the innovation
was designed to accommodate to small volumes, which
have no requirement or need for the innovation.*

*A failure? Probably not. Overly structured? Probably
not. It was and remains all that it was developed to be.
Perhaps its time will still come. Licensing was the only
viable way to get the product to market with this particular set of conditions.*

*The moral is that great care and attention does not as-
sure a successful licensing program any more than it assures success in any business transaction. The ultimate
customer makes the final decision.*

Cautions on consultants.

Recommendations for choosing a consultant are outlined in Part Two,
Chapter I. Final comments follow in respect to selection of the right
one. Prepayment requests for work to be done should always be sub-
jected to close scrutiny to determine why the prepayment is necessary.
Even if a prepayment request sounds reasonable, it is recommended
that at least one more consultant be asked to quote and advise on the
project. Many high-principled consultants perform a certain amount of
work before submitting an invoice. Also, when the invoice is submitted,
the work done should be described for the client's understanding and
approval, with the costs as quoted.

A good consultant can be a tremendous help particularly when the
small to mid-size business person has not had previous experience in
licensing. However, all consultants are not as successful as it may appear to the uninitiated.[3] The March 22, 1984 *Pittsburgh Post-Gazette* of
Pittsburgh, Pennsylvania, carried a feature article about Invention
Marketing, Inc., at 701 Smithfield Street, Pittsburgh. In part, the article
said:

*Now believed to be the largest firm of its kind in the na-
tion, IMI advertises in magazines, newspapers, radio
and TV throughout the United States and in some
foreign countries.*

For a fee that can run between $2,500 and $5,500, it promises to try to find manufacturing contracts for the ideas of "garage inventors" who think they have a touch of Thomas Edison in them.

Yet, IMI's President, 47-year-old Martin Berger of Squirrel Hill says, when asked, that IMI markets very few products and only a "very small number" of its clients have ever made more money than they paid to the firm.

IMI warns customers in writing that chances for success in the invention field are very slim. Still, widespread customer dissatisfaction has caused the company to be the target of formal consumer complaints and legal inquiries in several states.

Right now, for instance, IMI is being investigated by the Pennsylvania attorney general's office.[4]

Regarding bogus consultants, Calvin D. McCracken, inventor, businessman and author, says:[5]

There are a number of organizations preying on inventors who would try to convince you that it doesn't take a lot of money. (To develop a commercial product from an invention.) Sign up with them, they say, for a fee, and they will develop your product, prepare drawings, file a patent application and make every effort to find you a licensee. . . . It is estimated that there are some 250 idea brokers doing about $100 million a year in business and servicing some 100,000 hopeful inventors. Although they are not all frauds, many of them are, so be very careful.

More problems and how to avoid them.

Regardless of the country in which licensing is being done, most potential problems are the same. Experienced licensing professional, Crispin Marsh of F.B. Rice & Company, Balmain, Australia, lists the following reasons for license failures:[6]

- Failure in the evaluation of the technology.

- Failures in the selection of partners.

- Failures in the conduct of the negotiations.

- Failures in the agreement itself.

- Failures in the implementation and servicing of the license.

Mr. Marsh offers the following pointers:

- A successful licensing relationship is a long-term one.

- Analyze the technology in great detail before going into it. Talk to people in the industry. Read the journals in the field. Investigate and probe.

- Apply the same analysis to your proposed partner. Can he provide what you lack? Is there a synergism between the parties?

- Negotiate fairly. Don't screw your proposed partner for short-term gain. Don't destroy the trust. Do ensure that what has been verbally agreed gets put on paper accurately.

- Seek an agreement that has positive incentives to achieve the desired results.

- Take care with the implementation and ensure your licensee continues to value your license throughout its life.

- Last, but not least, structure the license so that if it does fail the parties may disengage cleanly.

Flexibility is the key.

LES Australia/New Zealand devoted[7] its 1987 Annual Conference in Melbourne to an analysis of an Australian firm which was newly formed and was also dealing in a very new medical technology. The business concept of the firm involved both domestic (Australian) and international licensing. The firm is IVF Australia, Pty., Ltd. a firm organized to conduct in-vitro fertilization procedures based on research conclusions developed at Monash University. Various aspects of the IVF Australia program were reviewed from proprietary rights to international licensing, technology transfer and necessary business arrangements. Mr. B. Moses, Managing Director of IVF Australia, summed up his analysis of "Business Opportunities" for the conference with the following significant observations:

> *If there is a moral to this (licensing) aspect of the IVFA story, it is that agreements pertaining to the establishment of new businesses, whether they be investment agreements or licenses should:*
>
> - *do everything to reflect the "actual views and expectations" flowing from the meeting of the minds at the time the original agreements are negotiated, but they should also;*
>
> - *recognize that circumstances not only can, but will change, and therefore such agreements should contemplate the possibility, indeed the probability, that it will be in the best interest of the parties to the agreement and the company itself to allow for periodic reexamination of the terms of the license.*
>
> *Certainly at the initial IVF Australia negotiations with investors, neither investors nor the founding management of the company anticipated some of the start-up requirements for funds and human resources. Likewise, the agreement between IVFA and Monash (Monash University, technology source), revolutionary at the time, clearly did not anticipate all events which have subsequently developed.*
>
> *As a closing comment I would offer this: there are simply too many unknowns surrounding the start-up of most new businesses to allow for the creation of perfect agreements and therefore one must be extremely careful not to rely too heavily on the strength, logic and lasting nature of terms and conditions embodied in these initial agreements.*
>
> *Far more important is the ongoing working relationship between the parties to the agreement.*

Finances — a source of potential problems.

It is almost axiomatic to say that finances are a concern for many small and mid-size businesses. Often a properly conceived licensing arrangement can contribute to the solution of such difficulties.

D.K. Layser, President of SAI Technology Company, San Diego, California, refers to the cash-short position of SAIT as a new and developing company (Part One, Chapter IV). SAIT found that licensing was a good business strategy both "in" and "out" that permitted it to take certain development moves with a minimum of risk to cash flow or capital funds.

As another example, T.E. Larsen, Chairman, Detector Electronics Company, points out that his company existed because of a license and was helped by other licenses. In the final analysis, however, its success depended on solving financial problems.[8] In 1972, Mr. Larsen was International Marketing Manager for the Apparatus Control Division of Honeywell Corporation. Detector Electronics was formed in 1973 through a licensing agreement with Honeywell for the production of a highly sophisticated apparatus for detection of fires, with a prime market in oil drilling and refining operations. Honeywell was going to phase out the production of this line, and Mr. Larsen was interested in continuing its production and worldwide sale. Honeywell was cooperative in business matters, but it did not function as a bank. Therein lay Mr. Larsen's problem. He obtained the necessary financing through the Northwest Growth Fund who also forced him to hire an accountant, take a Northwest man on his Board and, ultimately, assisted Detector Electronics in going public, a corporate move that permitted a needed refinancing.

All the products of Detector Electronics are manufactured in the United States, yet 90% of them are sold outside the United States. During the early years of business, a major share of its sales were with the Soviet Union. In 1982, business was shut off with Russia, and at the same time the world oil glut forced a cutback in orders from other customers. It was at this time that Detector Electronics "went public" with the assistance of Northwest Growth Fund. The sale of stock generated enough funds to pay off high-interest bank loans as well as supply funds for further activity. In addition, Detector Electronics expanded its product line through licensed acquisition of a touch-sensitive CRT screen from Control Data Corporation and a safety system for aircraft from Systron-Donner Corporation. Increased sales also resulted from working with Honeywell, Foxboro and other firms that quoted on oil well and refinery control systems. The result has been successful selling to a world market that is still 90% outside the United States, and is largely located in less-developed countries.

As the business has developed, Mr. Larsen points out, several vital considerations have become clear:

- Licensing can form a basis for a sound company business. Licensing can also be used to diversify and bring in new products to supplement the existing product line.

- Without a sound, dependable technical base, a license cannot be successful.

- In order to serve a world market, it is necessary to have a good domestic base of operations for technical service and a dependable means of obtaining payments due.

- All of the above may be achieved, but a business will not succeed unless it has its financing and its cash-flow requirements under control.

More solutions to finance problems.

For lack of money a business was lost. The message in this restatement of an old saying highlights one of the most serious problems facing many small and mid-size businesses and entrepreneurs. Consultants and consultant firms sometimes are qualified to assist in this problem area. A few firms function not only as licensing consultants, but also as financial and management advisors. Albert L. Early, Vice President, Marketing, H.L.P.M., Inc., of Louisville, Kentucky, says there are three essentials for the commercial success of a technical venture:[9]

- *Technology:* essential for soundness and viability.

- *Management:* with abilities in entrepreneurial deal making, financial operation and manufacturing sense.

- *Money:* "Patient Capital" investors who are willing to wait for a while to receive returns on their investment.

Mr. Early points out that many small and mid-size firms, and virtually all individual inventors find the latter two factors are especially difficult to handle. Point one, technology, is probably well under control. After all, technology is the vital part of any technical venture. Point two, management capability, may also be at least partly under control, if the company is already in operation with a manufacturing organization, a good idea how to use the technology and an effective marketing organization. However, financing is most likely to be a major problem. In-house expertise may not be available to manage cash flow, proper handling of manufacturing and sales expenses, short-term loans, long-term debt financing, and taxes. Yet they are ultimately as important to the firm's success as the original invention. Financial consulting firms, especially those with a licensing knowledge, or licensing consultants with financial services, can be particularly helpful. Also to be considered is "patent enforcement insurance," which will reduce the financial risk of patent litigation, protecting against the expense of lawsuits on patent enforcement, indemnification and invalidity.

In addition to venture capital firms as sources of additional funding, there are state grants or loans for new business projects. Among them are the Ben Franklin Partnership of Pennsylvania, Massachusetts Technology Development Corporation and the Thomas Edison Program of Ohio. In addition, Innovation Development Institute, Swampscott, Massachusetts, monitors federal and state grants. Consultation or reference to such organizations, especially the last mentioned, could well uncover useful sources of much-needed financial support.

Variations that help — Corporate Partnering.

Corporate Partnering represents another imaginative way to solve some types of financial problems.[10] It is a concept that might be described as being midway between a straight license and a joint-venture. Corporate Partnering has been defined as any contract in which two or more companies agree to work together to pursue a commercial opportunity.

Small Business Motivation for corporate partnering can range from financial to technical help, as for instance:

- Funding for new technology and new products.

- Access to management resources.

- Acquiring new customers.

- Accessing market and distribution networks.

- Gaining credibility with investors, lenders and customers.

- Access to special production techniques.

Concerns and hazards may include:

- Loss of independence for management, marketing and financing.

- Changes in personnel or management thinking on the part of the corporate partner.

- Inability of corporate bureaucracy to adjust to unexpected developments.

- Misunderstandings from lack of communication.

Big Business Motivation for corporate partnering includes:

- New and special technology and products.

- Access to entrepreneurial energy and developments.

- Better utilization of facilities.

- Opportunity to identify, investigate and promote future acquisition of the smaller partner.

- Increased profit.

Concerns and hazards for the large corporation can be:

- Funds expended do not produce intended results, because project needs were misjudged.

- Reduced control over project.

- Difficulties in protecting know-how from personnel in the partner company who may not be bound by secrecy unless specifically so covered.

The following examples were cited by Frank Jesse in his 1987 LES Workshop on Corporate Partnering:

Medical Graphics of Minneapolis developed screening systems for cardiopulmonary diagnosis with Medical Invest Svenska A.B. of Sweden. Svenska purchased 150,000 shares of Medical Graphics at $8 per share with warrants to purchase another 150,000 shares. Medical Graphics has exclusive manufacturing and marketing rights. Between the two firms there is some shared R&D as well as shared technology.

Minntech (formerly Renal Systems) of Minneapolis has unique technologies in electronics, hollow fibres and certain liquid solutions. In combination with C.R. Bard Company, a major hospital supply company, they have developed new membrane oxygenation technology and a Catheter reuse system. In this corporate partner arrangement, Minntech does research and manufacturing, and Bard has exclusive marketing rights.

Lifcore Biomedical Company, a biomaterials company, developed an FDA-approved haluronic acid that has potential applications in many medical areas. Lifecore uses corporate partnering with Coopervision. Coopervision has funded research by Lifcore for applications in ophthalmic surgery. Lifcore agrees to sell the product exclusively to Coopervision, and Coopervision has taken an equity position in Lifcore.

Lifecore also has a corporate partnering arrangement with Biomet, an orthopedics company. Both companies share the costs of developing a fluid for orthopedic uses. Product is made by Lifcore and marketed exclusively by Biomet. Profits are shared equally.

Lifecore also partners with Orthomatris for the development of bone shaft material, a project in which Lifcore owns and controls the technology and does the manufacturing.

The following is a special partnering arrangement which must be described without company names to maintain confidentiality of the participants:

Big Company wanted to have some elaborate software to allow for paperless shipping and record keeping of parts among its plants. Small Software Developer could create the software, but wanted the right to license the developed program to others. The final license agreement terms were an excellent example of flexible corporate partnering:

- The license was based on a final product to be developed thoroughly described and defined.

- Up-front payment ($50,000) by Big Company to Small Software Developer.

- Big Company gets royalty-free license to use the program developed.

- Small Software Developer pays a per-unit royalty to Big Company for each program unit licensed to others until the up-front royalty is repaid.

- Small Software Developer after paying back the up-front royalty retains total profits on further sale of software.

Co-promotion another helpful variation.

Co-promotion is described by Jon S. Saxe, Vice President of Hoffman-La Roche, Nutley, New Jersey.[11] Co-promotion is a unique and relatively new method of expanding and strengthening the market for a product, which involves both the licensing of technology and the licensing of a sales and marketing program. Mr. Saxe points out that the rewards are substantial for having a coordinated sales and marketing program with another company. At the same time, the potential problems of arranging and controlling such activities are enormous, and these considerations are in addition to the normal difficulties of a technology transfer license. In spite of the problems, the advantages of the concept are:

- Enables firms to concentrate simultaneously on the sale of a single product instead of having similar products under different names which may cause confusion in the marketplace.

- Combines the established strong market recognition of one firm with a new product development of a second firm.

- Enables one firm to establish a better recognition in a market segment by combining its sales effort with a second firm.

While the advantages are clear, the difficulties of this innovative approach are related to the need to establish complete confidence and understanding between the partners. Partners must work with the closest possible harmony and understanding on both technical and marketing matters.

It may well be that the pharmaceutical industry is showing other industries a new and workable business strategy. Table III lists the co-promotion agreements in effect as of October 1988, according to Mr. Saxe.

TABLE III Co-promotion agreements In 1988.			
Drug Name	**Co-Promoter**	**Original Inventor**	**Drug Application**
Zantac	Glaxo	Roche	anti-ulcer
Ceftin	Glaxo	Roche	anti-infective
Baypress	Miles	Roche	cardiovascular
Versed	Roche	DuPont	sedative/anesthetic
Cipralan	Roche	Glaxo	anti-arrhythmic
Inhibace	Roche	Glaxo	ACE inhibitor
Inhibace HCTZ	Roche	Glaxo	ACE inhibitor/diuretic
Cholotec	Squibb	Roche	in vivo radiodiagnostic
Isotrex	Stiefel	Roche	topical dermatological
Neupogen	Amgen	Roche	cancer, infectious disease

Terms — friend and foe.

The subject of license terms always arises as negotiation time approaches. A lack of mutual understanding of terms can be a source of serious trouble between either license partners or license negotiations.

It is important to identify terms that are necessary and those that are mere window dressing. Definitions, restrictions, obligations, license grant, royalties, termination are common terms that are essential to a well drafted license. Other terms should also be included as appropriate. The most commonly used license terms are defined in non-legal words in Part Two, Chapter VII.

Negotiating the agreement.

As with royalties and payments, the subject of negotiation continues to receive much attention.[12] The establishment of the most favorable terms including royalties will, to a large extent, depend on the abilities of the license negotiator. Therefore the process of negotiation should be considered carefully along with the terms of any license, joint-venture or franchise. Part Two, Chapter IX summarizes the comments regarding negotiation of many of the licensees and licensors contacted in this study, as well as several licensing professionals known to the author.

Regulations — U.S. export controls.

In wrapping up a discussion of problems and how to learn from others, one consideration must never be overlooked in licenses between U.S. individuals or companies and foreign persons or companies, U.S. Government Export Administration Regulations. These regulations apply to goods, services, technology and/or technical information. They exist as regulations to protect the safety and well-being of the United States of America and its citizens. Violation of these regulations carries significant fines to the company and the individuals involved and prison terms for individuals. These regulations are subject to change from time to time; so it is incumbent on a U.S. licensor to stay up-to-date with these changes as they occur.

Obtaining export approval (an Export License) is a procedure fairly well laid out in the Export Administration Regulations. Most of the time an export license is no problem. However, depending on the equipment/technology and/or the country involved, license approval may not be obtainable. For example, certain computer hardware and software may not be approved. Technology related to national defense concerns may not be approved. U.S. Department of Commerce, Bureau of Export Administration (BXA) is the place to start checking out the need for an Export License.[13] In addition, BXA has a telephone "hot line"

for questions and consultation: (202) 377-4811. After consulting with
the BXA, consider the regulations of the U.S. Treasury Department
and the U.S. State Department. Regulations which are coordinated with
other countries (COCOM regulations) are handled through the BXA
and the State Department. While this subject may not be critical for
most cases, it must never be overlooked or ignored. Certainly, it makes
no sense to invest time and money in preparation for a deal that will not
be approved.

Rising above the problems.

Sometimes a recitation of difficulties leaves the feeling that, whatever
the game, it is not worth pursuing. Of course there are business people
who think that licensing, joint-ventures and franchising are the wrong
approach. Examples of non-licensing choices were examined in Part
One, Chapter II. However, some companies have had bad experiences
because the license adventure was poorly handled, not because the procedure was the wrong strategy. Some business people have heard a
couple of "horror stories" and were scared away. In Part Three, we
bring a little more realistic light on licensing, corporate partnering and
strategic alliances which are bringing a greater measure of success to
many small and mid-size businesses.

FOOTNOTES:

[1]Part of the program for the 1986 LES (U.S.A. and Canada) Annual Meeting, held in Los Angeles, California, October 1986.

[2]"Experiences with Three Licenses," *les Nouvelles*, March 1984, Bibliography number 1, page 3F 205.

[3]See Bibliography 82, "Dream Weavers."

[4]The Pennsylvania Attorney General ultimately filed a suit against IMI, which was settled by a payment by IMI of $62,500. IMI has since operated through affiliated companies, two of which are named Invention Submission, Inc. and Intromark, Inc. (See also Bibliography 82, "Dream Weavers.")

[5]See Bibliography 17.

[6]See Bibliography 65.

[7]Australia-New Zealand chapter of Licensing Executives Society International. Also see Appendix A-1.

[8]Paper given at Midwest Regional Meeting of LES (U.S.A. and Canada), June 20, 1987.

[9]Paper given at Midwest Regional Meeting of LES (U.S.A. and Canada), June 20, 1987.

[10]The theme of the 1987 LES Midwest Regional Meeting was "Intellectual Property Transfer between Small Business and Big Business — Everybody Wins." With this as a central topic both workshops and plenary session papers were interesting and to the point. Of particular interest was the workshop on "Corporate Partnering" led by Frank Jesse, International Counsel, partner in the firm of Gray, Plant, Moody and Bennett in Minneapolis, Minnesota.

[11]"Innovative Licensing Techniques and Marketing in the Pharmaceutical Industry" by Jon S. Saxe, Vice President and Chairman of the Corporate Licensing Committee, Hoffman-La Roche, Inc., Nutley, New Jersey, given on October 27 at the 1988 Annual Meeting of LES U.S.A./Canada, Inc.

[12]See Bibliography 34, 35, 36, 37 and 38.

[13]See Bibliography 75.

PART TWO

How to do it in your own company

Overworked
Chief Executive

Eager
Licensing
Executive

"No, I can't be bothered
seeing any crazy researcher.
We've got a battle to fight."

Author Unknown

Chapter I

ORGANIZATION FOR LICENSING

Organizing for a license or a license program has several aspects even for those who are in a small or mid-size business. First, the concept must have top executive support. While it may or may not be desirable to use a licensing consultant, it will certainly be necessary to have a competent lawyer. This chapter will discuss those points and more.

* * * * *

In 1983, after several months of no response through his firm's lawyers, K.B. Ridler, Managing Director of Vesco Manufacturing, Division of Vulcan Machinery, Thunder Bay, Ontario, phoned direct to the President of a Scandinavian equipment manufacturer to discuss the latter's infringement of a Vesco patent, the Scandanavian's response was immediate: "I'll meet you in Toronto in two days."

Would the Scandinavian have reacted that cooperatively to anyone of a lesser title at Vesco?

Probably not.

* * * * *

The importance of top executives.

Granting that the answer supplied to the question above is pure supposition, nothing is more important to a successful licensing program than the full support of "the boss." The Chief need not do all the negotiating or the planning but he should always be aware of and give full support to the ongoing program. This principle has been evident with every successful licensing effort noted in our study.

> *"Unless you are committed to licensing as a basic strategy of your business, don't try it."*
> > *Willim F. Silva*
> > *President, Catalysts and Process Systems*
> > *Union Carbide Corporation*[1]

> *"The most essential requirement of any comprehensive licensing program is the total commitment of the senior management with support in strategic terms from the Board of Directors."*
> > *William S. Campell*
> > *Executive Vice-President*
> > *Consumers Packaging, Inc.*[2]

> *"However, all of this activity would come to naught without a corporate commitment to licensing."*
> > *Edgar H. Philbrick*
> > *Vice President, Planning and Development*
> > *Merck and Company, Inc.*[3]

The litany goes on. Fortunately for most small and mid-size businesses the man at the top is likely to be directly involved with all decisions of a policy or strategic nature. In any case, and regardless of the size of the company, the potentials for licensing in and out should be clearly understood by the CEO and his staff even though day-to-day operation may be handled by others.

Licensing functions.

Before noting activities and approaches of various companies, it is important to point out a few principles of operation. The licensing function can perform in three different ways:

- *Profit Center* — A "self-starter" or commercially aggressive operation that seeks either to optimize the potential income from corporate technology or to acquire new products or processes or combines both "in" and "out" licensing programs for the optimum corporate strategic advantage.

- *Support Group* — Generally works with various divisions of the company and is largely governed by the initiative of others, whether licensing in or out. Such a group coordinates different elements (technical, legal, accounting), but does not normally initiate a licensing activity.

- *Administrative* — Principally concerned with accounting, record keeping, and handling of miscellaneous administrative and service details, all with respect to existing licenses. An administrative group has essentially nothing to do with setting up for or initiating new licensing programs.

Anyone with experience in company organization will quickly recognize that there can be a wide variation in the above three categories, depending on the corporate technology and the people involved. Each type of organization can be of real significance to a company. The Profit Center is the most visible and may contribute most when there is good potential for licensing technology or for bringing in new commercial opportunities. The Administrative function can make a great contribution in a relatively small company where one or two executives must carry the entire load of corporate progress, and they need someone to make sure all the details are properly handled. The Support Group function, then, is most apt to be an evolvement of an Administrative function that has demonstrated the ability to take on more responsibility. For the small or mid-size business, the preferred organization is likely to be the Support Group with basic initiation and decisions by the CEO or an Executive Vice President.

Organizing a licensing department.

An organization for an ideal licensing department might be set up as follows:

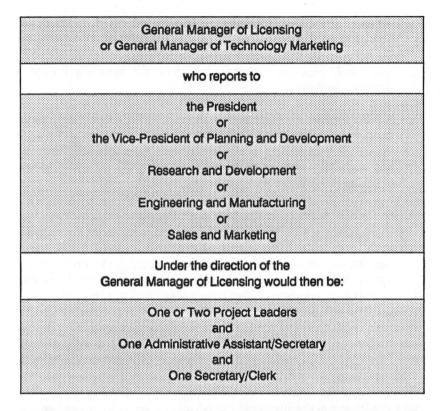

General Manager of Licensing or General Manager of Technology Marketing
who reports to
the President or the Vice-President of Planning and Development or Research and Development or Engineering and Manufacturing or Sales and Marketing
Under the direction of the General Manager of Licensing would then be:
One or Two Project Leaders and One Administrative Assistant/Secretary and One Secretary/Clerk

In this arrangement, the services of technical, legal, patent, etc. would come from other corporate departments or from outside counsel.

A reduced-version of a licensing department would be one man and one secretary, with support work coming from other parts of the company.

In any case the General Manager of Licensing should have strong executive support, and he or she must be a good salesperson within the company. Otherwise it will be difficult to accomplish the objectives of either licensing out the company's "precious know-how" or licensing in technology not invented by the company's own people.

Characteristics of the ideal licensing executive.

According to most licensing professionals, the desirable qualities for a licensing manager include all imaginable business characteristics rolled into one, including the ability to walk on water!

Desired traits or abilities of the ideal licensing executive should include:

- Entrepreneurial and business management skills.

- Sales and marketing abilities.

- Technical (scientific and engineering) abilities and/or perception on a broad spectrum.

- Patent and general legal familiarity.

- Financial and corporate structure appreciation.

- Good knowledge of total corporation product line and capabilities.

- Thorough background in corporate policy and philosophy.

- Ability to work with others and to get other people to help.

- Maturity.

- Ability to adapt to and do business with foreign cultures, customs, languages.

- Physical stamina, willingness to work long hours when necessary.

- Setting aside the last four characteristics, the most important "strong points" of a good licensing person should be in the area of sales/technical/corporate familiarity with legal/financial and pure entrepreneurial being secondary.

Executive development.

In respect to overall corporate planning for personnel, Human Resource Planning, a licensing operation can be an outstanding place for a young, or middle management, executive to receive special training. This activity will expose and strengthen:

- Negotiation abilities.

- Business opportunity perception.

- Sales, financing, business law, technical perception and entrepreneurial instincts.

- Overall acquaintance with corporate affairs.

- General management characteristics.

Properly treated in corporate planning, a licensing activity could function as a good training ground or exposure for ambitious, capable managers.

Responsibilities for the license department.

While very few companies may be organized to the extent indicated here, many operate with the following responsibility areas covered in one way or another:

- Have a voice in all technology transfer activities, whether by purchase or sale of assets, joint-venture or simple license.

- Maintain a corporate technology audit (inventory and assessment).

- Consult with R&D as well as Operating and Sales regarding value to the company of retaining certain technology packages on a proprietary basis.

- Consult with R&D, Operating and Sales on what new technologies would be desirable.

- Recommend to Executive Management for final decision whether a given technology should be made available for license and under what circumstances. Obtain from Executive Management approval on new technologies to be sought.

- Appraise domestic and foreign markets for technology and obtain executive approval for appropriate approaches to these markets.

- Locate prospective licensees or licensors and obtain executive approval to negotiate a suitable agreement.

- Negotiate the contract with responsibility for direction of the corporate negotiating team.

- Supervise the servicing of the license.

Reporting of the licensing function.

Many small to mid-size firms will have only a limited licensing program, whether the program is for licensing out or licensing in. When only two or three licenses are granted or taken in a period of five years or so, the President may find that his best organization is to have an ad hoc committee separately formed for each project and reporting directly to the President. Each committee membership would consist of those directly involved with the license. For a more substantial license program the different needs of the company should be considered on a standing-committee basis, covering the interests of:

- Sales and Marketing.
- R&D.
- Engineering and Manufacturing.
- Financial.
- International.
- Legal.

The best answer to the question of reporting is usually to have the licensing responsibility report to that Executive Officer whose activity will be most involved or whose activity and objectives are most similar to the responsibilities being handled under license.

Organizations as they are.

During 1980-81 Dr. Farok J. Contractor, of the Graduate School of Management, Rutgers University, New Brunswick, New Jersey, conducted a study of several major U.S. corporations with respect to their organization to handle international licensing. The reactions that Dr. Contractor received varied widely. A corporate planner in the Chicago headquarters of a large industrial equipment manufacturer indicated that licensing played only a minor part in the company's international operations. The consumer electronics division of a large conglomerate indicated that licensing was the dominant, if not the company's only, viable international strategy. Organizations to support these operations varied in accordance with the importance ascribed to licensing. Even for the most active in licensing, the organizations did not always follow clear-cut lines. Authority and action tended to follow the lines that worked best while disturbing the basic corporate organization the least.

As mentioned in Chapter I, licensing is a major part of the business of L.S. Research in Cedarburg, Wisconsin. The firm locates its licensees as a result of its research work in electronics and sound reproduction. Contract negotiating is accomplished by Larry Schotz, President. The final agreements are drafted either by the local general law firm for L.S. Research or by the firm in New York City that handles its patent work. Contract service and administration is carried out under Mr. Schotz's direction.

DEC International, Inc., of Madison, Wisconsin, is alert to the development of new apparatus and is perceptive to ongoing needs in the dairy and related food industries. New ideas are generated by internal R&D as well as the technical and marketing staff of the various DEC Divisions. Robert W. Smith, Vice President and General Counsel, handles all licensing activities. In this instance, the General Counsel carries commercial responsibilities with his position as Vice President. Whether licensing in or out, Mr. Smith coordinates all work, with the technical and commercial background from the various Division Managers. Original initiation of a licensing project may be from a Division, from Mr. Smith or from another DEC International executive. Legal details, contract negotiations, and contract execution are performed by Mr. Smith or are under his direction.

Rosemount, Inc., of Eden Prairie, Minnesota, started business in 1956. Within a few years Rosemount granted its first license, and since then the practice of licensing both in and out has been a part of the company's business plans and strategies. Briefly, the company is a leader in the field of sophisticated measurement, analytical and control devices for the chemical, food and other process industries. Sales are to a worldwide market. Licensing out is done selectively to reach markets that cannot be effectively served by Rosemount through its domestic and international sales organization. In some cases products that have become obsolescent or unsuited to the company's manufacturing and sales program may also be licensed selectively. Licensing in is done on the basis of new technology that may come to the attention of Rosemount through a variety of circumstances. Recommendations for licensing either in or out will come from different parts of the company, such as marketing, planning and product division management. A specific license project is pursued by the initiating group, the contract drafting being done by the corporate law group. Final negotiation is carried out by the initiating group and the corporate law group working together. Final approval is obtained from top management.

Anaquest of Madison, Wisconsin, maintains its own R&D, but a large number of its products come from new ideas and inventions of other firms. Some firms are not able to bring their R&D products to commercial reality in all potential applications because of the special requirements of certain limited, or niche, markets. Anaquest, in its own market range, can often take such products on a license basis and achieve considerable success as pointed out in Part One, Chapters I, II, III and IV.

The sophistication of Anaquest's organization emphasizes the importance of the licensing function to the company's total business. The Vice President for Commercial Development has reporting to him the following:

- Director of Licensing and International Development
- Director of Business Development
- Director of Strategic Planning

Reporting to the Director of Licensing and International Development are:

- Manager of European Licensing
- Manager of North American Licensing

The Orient and the Pacific areas are handled directly by the Director of Licensing and International Development.

From this organization line-up it is plain to see that Anaquest's business planning and development depends in large measure on the licensing function. The product line expansion is carefully handled in accordance with the long-term goals and special strengths of the company as determined by the Director of Strategic Planning. With these goals, Licensing and International Development works directly with the Director of Business Development to achieve the corporate objectives through licensing both in and out. As pointed out in Part One, Chapters III and IV, Anaquest uses this organization to maintain an enviable reputation for sophistication and quality of products and performance. Their use of licensing could form a good model for many firms.

Service, contact and licensee morale.

While most people think of the glamour of marketing and negotiating a license and collecting royalty, many forget that it is equally important to operate the process or to make the product that has been licensed. Probably more licenses have fallen apart because of service problems than for any other reason. In this context, "service" covers everything from organizing support in the licensor company, to technology transmission, to continued technical service contacts, to royalty payments and business contacts between licensor and licensee.

Compensation and profitability of a license can also be measured in ideas and technical interchange as well as money. When such opportunities exist, it is highly desirable that the licensee contributions are appreciated by the licensor firm, especially at management levels.

Technology transmission and its proper handling is a key to success for every license involving know-how of any sort. If it is possible to have the entire licensed technology summarized in a confidential report, this technique should be used and that report given to the licensee with appropriate ceremony. The more complete the report, the better. Typed directions, specifications, drawings and other relevant material should be included, and copies or sufficiently complete duplicate records should be kept by the licensor showing exactly what is given. If it is not possible to have a complete report and summary of technology, all verbal instructions should be outlined for record purposes. Simple routines of this nature may seem unnecessary, and the licensee may appear to have obtained all the needed information. However, that licensee is likely to have more questions, or may not understand fully what he did receive. When this happens, it is important to have a complete record of what has been covered.

Continuing service is usually necessary as well, depending on the nature of the technology. Proper service may require establishing a licensee technical service operation. An alert license service department will maintain contact with licensees in such a way as to keep them up to date with technical information, as well as other pertinent subject matter such as market surveys, advertising and new developments. It is this contact that fosters best a thorough interplay of information and feedback of relevant information from the licensee. Doing a proper job in licensee service requires time and thought. A good job is rewarded with a healthy, happy and profitable licensee who not only pays royalties but also contributes new and useful ideas on the licensed subject.

In addition to straight technical service, new developments may be important to a licensee. How quickly new ideas can be made available should be properly defined in every license, and a definite schedule maintained for review of the service of new developments.

Servicing licensees is also one of the best ways to maintain contact. Designer Blocks, for instance, has a 2-page, 4-color newsletter service with items of interest for architects and builders. This letter shows various applications of Designer Block licensed products, as made by various licensees, and features the architect, contractor and owner of the building described. Markets covered are schools, churches, recreational and industrial buildings. The letter is sent out by Designer Blocks to lists of customer prospects which have been submitted by the various Designer Block licensees, and it carries the imprint logo, address and phone number of the specific licensee, plus a postage paid postcard to Designer Blocks, Inc. for those who may want further general information. Even though this extra service has a nominal charge to the licensee, it is both appreciated and widely used.

At least one major U.S. corporation has an organized competition between its licensees and joint-venture partners in various countries throughout the world, covering a number of consumer oriented products. Awards for "Licensee-Partner of the Year" are made on the basis of annual market share and percent annual increase, product innovation, profitability of product and expansion into other product lines licensed from the U.S. licensor. While the judging for this award gets a bit tricky when balancing results from more developed to less developed countries, nevertheless, the concept appears to be very popular. Awards are made with suitable ceremony at annual international company meetings.

A number of firms report sponsoring annual or biannual technical review meetings in which all licensees gather for a two- or three-day session at the licensor's headquarters. These occasions usually turn out to be especially useful because the licensee representatives get together and swap ideas and experiences. The licensor management also gets some useful "feedback." This informal exchange of ideas and discussion of mutual problems sometimes proves to be as valuable as the formal presentation program. A fascinating story of how one company profited from a program of regular licensee conferences is told in "Pooling Brain Power," which is reprinted in Part Three, Chapter VI.

Various schemes are used to "stay in touch." The most successful are arranged to suit a particular situation. When licensors and licensees are separated by large distances and there is not a lot of correspondence or other contact, simple touches such as birthday cards, anniversary cards and Christmas cards help to maintain a valuable personal relationship.

Consultants.

At this point, the potential contribution of an outside licensing consultant should be mentioned. In both organization development and on specialty assignments, a good consultant can make a significant contribution, even to a large Profit Center type organization, can be of considerable help in developing and coordinating a Support Group mode and can be invaluable to the smaller firm that must depend upon the executive staff for basic policy questions and negotiations, while turning day-to-day details over to an administrative manager.

Using a consultant to the best advantage.

A licensing consultant may also be called a consultant in technical management, and can be useful to corporations of all sizes. An experienced consultant hired for a specific job with a major transnational firm may be more cost-effective than educating junior staff or pulling experienced people off present activities, especially if the job in question is regarded as a one-time project. In the case of smaller firms, the consultant can either perform single jobs or conduct a continuing program. Examples of such work are:

- Organize a licensing function.

- Assist in the organization of a licensing department.

- Perform licensing functions and assist the client on a retainer basis.

- Conduct a technical inventory and identify licensable technology.

- Assist and advise on industrial property rights management to protect technology through judicious use of patents, trademarks, copyrights and trade secrets.

- Advise on potential technology market areas.

- Advise on special aspects of foreign markets combining with political risk analysis to analyze political issues, their economic significance and trends.

- Identify needs for new technology or new products.

- Locate and assist in negotiation for new technology.

Normally, the licensing/technology management consultant will have a background in business, sales and marketing, technical and legal. While he probably knows less than the inventors or innovators regarding a specific technology, the consultant will bring an objectivity of judgment in respect to licensing potential, an understanding of related factors and the ability to describe the technology in terms readily appreciated by the executive management of his client and/or his client's customers. In respect to the purchase of technology, the consultant can also contribute a balanced third party judgment and a counterbalance to the N.I.H. (Not Invented Here) syndrome, if it exists.

Technology audit services often turn up opportunities within an organization that have been overlooked because the possibility of outside uses was not appreciated. Technology survey and audit services can also be useful consultant contributions. Previewing on a third-party basis the potential application of new technologies, products or process innovations is an example of such a service. This type of assistance applies to domestic and foreign markets and considers both licensing out and licensing in.

The consultant can also appraise and assist in strengthening industrial property rights, the filing of domestic and foreign patents and the protection of trade secrets. A licensing consultant must be prepared to guide and assist in all aspects of licensing and the planning of license programs. Thus, the consultant can become a valuable contributor to both the long-range strategy and the shorter-range tactics of corporate planning by bringing an informed expertise along with the ability to make candid judgments and to state them without fear of "criticizing the boss."

The essential place of lawyers.

A license is a legal contract, and anyone who would sign or be a party to a legal contract without competent legal advice deserves what he will probably get — trouble. The licensing of technology and other intellectual property rights is a part of doing business and, as such, should be guided and controlled by a businessman. At the same time, the license contract is a legal document and must be handled with all the considerations appropriate to a document that legally requires certain performance on the part of those who are governed by that contract. Are these statements double talk? No. Do they indicate the need for licensing in a careful, knowledgeable fashion? Yes.

A lawyer must protect his client, the businessman, from foreseeable legal problems. A lawyer should be knowledgeable as to what the businessman wants to do, the protection that exists and how strong that protection is for the technology or property rights that are to be licensed. Further, the lawyer should know what laws will control, the tax and antitrust consequences, the future obligations of the licensee and/or the licensor and the different laws of the different states, provinces or countries involved. For reasons such as these, a competent, understanding lawyer should be acquainted with a proposed license agreement as early as possible and as thoroughly as possible.

At the same time, the businessman must make the final judgment while balancing one risk against another. He must be one who looks for opportunities, who sees ways in which a given "deal" might be worked out. His role is the optimist's role while the lawyer, then, can be the careful, loyal pessimist, and it is the businessman's acumen that determines final success.

Some business people have stayed away from the possibility of licensing either in or out simply because they had heard that there would be frightening legal fees or serious legal obligations or trouble caused by "dealing with the lawyers." Such an attitude is unnecessary. The lawyer's place is simply to help the businessman do what he wants to do legally and without legal trouble. If legal problems are avoided, the lawyer is indeed the businessman's best friend. If the lawyer keeps his client out of trouble, even when it means turning down a proposed license that sounds "too good to be true," the client is well served.

To conclude the discussion of the essential place that lawyers have in licensing, a few words should be spent on the question of "How and where can I find a good lawyer to work with me on my licensing ideas?" Unfortunately, there is no pat answer. However, a number of observations can be given. Some are personal to the author; some have come from other licensing professionals:

- Finding the "right" lawyer is similar to finding the "right" doctor. Final choice is a combination of competence in the field under question and personal actions or reactions of the principals involved. Ask questions about what the lawyer has done and what the results have been.

- Is the lawyer willing to admit that he needs help in some matters; does the lawyer know where to get that help; and will he do so?

- Is the lawyer a fighter? Will he aggressively pursue all potential advantages within the law? Will he be innovative in establishing his client's best advantage and will he fight and work hard for that advantage?

- What experience has the lawyer had in the field of licensing? What are his professional society activities, such as the Licensing Executives Society?

- Is the license or joint-venture being considered for one or more foreign countries and is the lawyer knowledgeable on the laws and regulations of those countries? Does he know where to go to get good, competent foreign counsel?

- What is the lawyer's background knowledge of patents, trademarks, copyrights, trade secrets, know-how? A thorough and professionally qualified knowledge of this field is necessary.

- What experience and knowledge has the lawyer developed in the technology and business area of the firm in question.

References for lawyers and consultants.

The A.I.P.L.A.[4] has available a list of patent lawyers who will give a 30-minute, no-charge consultation regarding potential patentability and possible licensability of a given invention or innovation. LES U.S.A./Canada[5] can furnish a list of consultants who are willing to give an hour, no-charge consultation to an inventor, innovator or small/midsize business person interested in considering the licensing of their invention or technology. Possibly business friends, bankers, and other professional acquaintances can recommend lawyers or consultants. Additional references may be found through local city, county, state or provincial Bar Associations. Sometimes lawyers are listed by their special areas of law, such as "licensing," "technology transfer," "patents" or "intellectual property." It is particularly important to obtain the services of a lawyer experienced in these fields. A general lawyer may not be adequately informed in these matters. Regrettably, however, there is no way to know whether you have made the right choice except to make your decision and work with the individual, perhaps on a first-trial basis.

THE BROCKWAY GLASS STORY

Brockway Glass Company of Brockway, Pennsylvania, has for many years maintained a reputation of being one of the most efficient low cost producers of glass containers in the U.S.

The organization of Brockway Glass for selling technology to noncompetitors outside the United States is such a perfect story that it is being used here as a final example of what can be done when a complete licensing organization is planned. The story is taken from "Transferring Glass Technology" by J.P. Poole, Vice President, retired, International Division, Brockway Glass:[6]

> *The purpose of this paper is to describe the development and operation of a new division created within the Brockway Glass Company. The responsibility for the development of our International Division became mine in 1973. The objective of the division was to sell advanced glass container production technology to noncompetitors outside the United States. This plan seemed to be desirable for a number of reasons. It could produce revenue which would help support its continuing and expensive R&D program; it would give Brockway an opportunity to see what was developing in other parts of the world which could then give new direction to its own R&D.*
>
> *Stanford Research Institute was hired as a consultant to give us needed direction in the establishment of this new division, including its policies, structure, agreement form, and many other such details. The next step was to make a market survey of all of the foreign glass companies producing containers in the western world. One hundred thirty-seven glass companies in 61 countries represented 85% of the population of the areas studied. Of these 137, 71 companies were already committed. Of*

those left, the small companies which appeared unable to generate enough sales to pay for the cost of operating a contract were deleted.

We started with 41 potential clients located in 25 countries. It was decided that the division should have three separate developmental phases. Phase I would be an attempt to sell complete technical assistance agreements to major glass companies in the developed world. Phase II would consist of partial sales, such as pieces of equipment and special techniques which could lead the respective licensee to develop confidence in our ability to handle a full technology exchange. Phase III would consider a development of new businesses, which could include specialized equipment developed for specialized purposes, R&D for a particular client, turnkey plants, operating contacts, joint-ventures, and, perhaps, completely new businesses.

Once a list of glass companies in the various countries that were potential clients had been established, the next step was to visit them. We presented technical papers at various foreign and national meetings which attracted glass technologists.

An international seminar was held in Brockway, P.A., to which management and technical representatives from 17 glass companies in 14 countries were represented. The international seminar was very successful and is held every three years. Its purpose is to acquaint all licensees that we already have with the developments that they can anticipate being transferred to them in the. very near future while the potential licensees get an appreciation of the expertise that is available to them on a contract basis.

It eventually became possible to become familiar enough with the individual company's operations to make suggestions to them to the effect that if they could do in certain areas as well as Brockway was doing, they could save themselves a lot of money, increase their productivity, and increase their profits. This led, in many cases, to an opportunity to make a detailed technical audit utilizing a team of staff specialists from Brockway who would study and evaluate the potential client's plant in great detail.

From this, a detailed report was prepared which compared various significant parts of the production operation of Brockway to those of the company being investigated. If the audit showed that the improvement that could be expected was not sufficient to pay for the effort of technology transfer, no agreement was even sought. Agreements had to be cost-justified.

Fees are primarily based on the savings that could accrue over at least a five-year period combined with a complete knowledge of the cost of managing the contract to make the technology transfer. The fee schedule varies, depending upon the amount of help that is needed and the amount of effort that will be put into the contract, so that each agreement is distinctly different from any of the others.

The contracts usually include two audits or eight man-weeks of service performed in their plants at our cost each year. The purpose is primarily to permit us to monitor the progress under the contract, so that training adjustments can be made and efforts redirected, if necessary. In general, all the training is carried out in Brockway at no additional charge to the client. Additional time beyond that which is specified in the contract, that involves training away from the normal workplace of the staff trainer, is charged to the client.

Each contract is assigned a Contract Manager from Brockway and a Contract Coordinator from the client's company. All communication passes between these two people and is copied and redirected by them to the intended recipient. This is essential if the technology transfer is to be completely coordinated by both sides.

Routine communications are established, between the two coordinators, daily by telex, phone, and as well by monthly project and progress reports. The clients' plants and company are treated exactly the same as any Brock-

way plant. We assume the same responsibility for success with the technology transfer to the client as we do to our own plants.

The contract manager works in such a way that contract renewals are likely because of the continual development, improved technology, and expanded services which include marketing, long-range planning, facility planning, principles of cost-accounting, etc., to the client. In addition to full agreements with glass container producers, we have executed engineering contracts for complete plants, parts of plants, taught composition control techniques, and done trouble-shooting for fiberglass and flat-glass operations, and for glass containers.

After 10 years, we are still in Phase I, but working well into Phase II and are beginning to implement Phase III of our original plan. As of this date, all of our clients have renewed their contracts, our first having extended for over a period of 20 years. Our international operation permits us to see what is going on in the world, to predict for our friends abroad what will probably happen to them, and it helped pay for our own significant R&D effort which helped us to maintain our high level of technology.

FOOTNOTES:
[1]See Bibliography 66.
[2]See Bibliography 72.
[3]See Bibliography 73.
[4]See Appendix A-3.
[5]See Appendix A-1.
[6]"Transferring Glass Technology," *les Nouvelles*, December 1982.

Chapter II

ROYALTY AND OTHER COMPENSATION

For most licensors and licensees the terms for royalty payments and other charges are critical. Evaluation of technology and determination of a fair royalty have been the subjects of many meeting papers, professional articles and court suits. They will continue to receive much attention. Unfortunately, specific royalty details are seldom available for specific license agreements. Therefore it is not possible to cover here royalty terms in reference to particular firms. However there are a number of considerations and determination methods which will be summarized in this chapter.

Royalty systems.

Royalties can be paid in a variety of ways, from lump sum figures to running royalties to combinations of payment methods. For instance, one firm whose principle income is from licensing charges an initial fee, plus a running royalty with a minimum. The following terms are generally accepted as describing the normal royalty systems:

Lump Sum is a single amount established to cover the value of the technology, and, sometimes, also the cost of technology transmission. It can be accomplished as a single payment "up front" (on signature of the license), or with several payments. A typical breakdown might be:

- 25% to 50% on signature.

- 25% to 50% at different stages of the project.

- Remaining balance on project completion, with perhaps 5% or 10% withheld until guaranteed production is reached.

This latter system is used in many arrangements for large projects.

Initial fee is often used along with other payment forms such as annual royalties. It is a common situation to have an initial fee set up to handle an evaluation of the basic know-how and/or the cost of technology transfer. When both are combined, it may be possible to balance out certain costs or evaluation figures of one versus the other.

Another type of first payment is advance royalty. This system simply assures the licensor of a certain initial minimum income while assuring the licensee of the opportunity to "work off" the advance by use of the license.

Running royalty is a practical method of establishing a royalty that is fair to both licensee and licensor with payment on the basis of either production or sale of a licensed product (or on the product of a licensed process). This system permits the licensee to pay on the basis of license use and adds a certain incentive for the licensor to assist the licensee as much as possible for the end result of maximized royalty.

The percent-of-sales system is particularly useful as a means of compensating for inflation, since the royalty amount automatically goes up when the sales price goes up.

Annual fixed fee payment is useful when a suitable running royalty base is difficult to determine. Such fees are generally set for use of a process, method or machinery for which no definite use measurement is reasonable.

Royalty Base is a means of measurement or a base of computation. If a process is involved, the volume, or weight of product, or total unit production of the process may be the best measurement. If a product is the licensed subject matter, percent of sales price is probably most appropriate. In some cases, the input of a raw material can be appropriate measurement.

Royalty rate, whether percent of sales or a payment per unit of production, is just as important as the royalty base. Taken together, these elements determine the answer of whether a license is profitable for either side.

Several studies have been made of royalty percentages (normally taken as a percent of final sales price). Seldom does the percentage go over 5%, even less often will it be lower than 1%. Well-protected devices in high demand may take 10% or more.

Guaranteed annual royalties can assure certain licensee performance and can assure the licensee of extra reward for extra good performance. These arrangements are guaranteed annual minimums and guaranteed annual maximums. The first assures the licensor of a certain base return, while the second offers increased income to the licensee once a certain performance is achieved.

The importance of easy accounting should not be forgotten. Regardless of the system chosen, a well-founded royalty base and royalty rate must permit the licensee to account for and report the royalty with relative ease. A difficult system will tempt the licensee to use sloppy accounting practices. Nothing can break down a good license relationship faster than arguments over money. Consequently, it is most important to establish a sound, useful royalty base and an appropriate royalty rate.

Establishing values.

Consideration of the value of a license for either licensee or licensor should cover the following:

- Probable cost to self-develop technology or "invent around" the patent offered.
- Cost to maintain technology.
- Probable cost of related improvements.
- Potential profitability to the licensee.
- What substitutes are available?
- Would it be worthwhile to challenge the patent?
- Is the licensed product or process badly needed?
- Is the market for license use growing?
- How fast will increased profits be realized?
- Will the license be exclusive, sole or nonexclusive?
- What is territory and duration of the license?

In addition, the value of a license will be influenced by various inter-related considerations, as shown on the following page.

What is the Licensed Subject?	Proprietary Protection Available
Process or Product or Both Raw Material Intermediate Product Component of Final Product Final Product	Patent Application(s?) Patent(s?) (Utility, Design, Plant) Trademark Copyright Trade Secret FDA Information/Registration
Industrial Product Consumer Product Specialty Product	Use General or Restricted End Product Process
Simple Technology Complex Technology Know-how Turn-key Plant	Foreign Protection Basic Invention Improvement
Established Market New Market Size of Market	Broad License Field of Use License Territorial License
High Profit Margin Average Profit Margin Low Profit	Exclusive Nonexclusive Established Market Competitive Equivalents Difficult or Easy to Police Litigated Patent Short-term Protection

Capitalized values.

When highly valuable know-how and/or patents are involved, the licensee may not be able to pay the full price of the evaluation or the licensor may not want a valuable property to "escape." In these cases, it may be possible to capitalize the know-how and/or patents to establish an equity by the licensor with the licensee or to establish a joint-venture, in which the licensor's contribution is largely the capitalized know-how. There are advantages to this treatment from the licensor standpoint:

- Licensor gets more control over the use of the license.

- It may be possible to raise the stated know-how value.

In this arrangement the licensee often has an advantage of being able to obtain more technology more easily because of the equity relationship. Any arrangement of this sort should be handled only with competent legal and tax advice.

Know-how fee — a need for special emphasis.

Often, licenses that involve a substantial body of technology should involve an initial "know-how fee", particularly when know-how is more important than patents. In these cases, a proper evaluation is especially important, considering all of the evaluation factors just mentioned.

Pricing decisions.

"How much can be charged?" "How much should be paid?" These are the two dominant questions for licensor and licensee. Unless a reasonable answer is found, the license will be in serious danger.

"Reasonable Royalty" is a term often used in discussing the pricing of a license. Of course, what seems reasonable to one may not appear reasonable to another. The fact is, however, that both parties to a license must agree on one payment system that is acceptable to both, and this system is referred to as a "reasonable royalty."

Aside from the various economic factors already mentioned, there are a few additional observations that are pertinent to price determination and the setting of a "reasonable royalty":

- A licensor is not compelled to extend a license (except in cases of compulsory license as may be required by the laws of some countries outside the U.S.).

- It is possible in many circumstances for a licensor to license one or more firms on a selective basis. (This practice can have U.S. antitrust implications and should be regarded with care.)

- It is possible to license the same subject matter to different licensees for different prices or royalties. (Again, caution should be taken for U.S. antitrust violation.)

Setting the numbers.

A "Rule-of -thumb" sometimes used for the pricing of licenses is 25-35% of estimated profit" or "10% of capitalized cost" or a combination of the two. Such systems are likely to be workable. At worst they offer a starting point. However, it is very much preferred to have some logic better than the fact that others do it this way.

Good business judgement will often bring out a good solution to the question of "how much?" However, it is important to be sure that the judgment is good.

Sometimes corporate executives who are not familiar with licensing insist on setting the price on the basis of their "business judgment," and this method may lead to disaster. In one case, for instance, the executives of a firm that will be called "Acme Metals" established a royalty payment for a recently perfected technology based on its high cost of development, without regard for the probable reaction of potential licensees. The technology was a new and much needed environmental protection process, and it received substantial favorable notice when first announced. Unfortunately, when faced with a very high compensation demand, several potential licensees decided to develop their own parallel technology, outside the patents of Acme. Two of these independent developers then proceeded to license their own processes. Thus Acme Metals lost most of the license market by putting the original price too high. The original high cost of process development was a "sunk cost." The process had been developed for internal use by Acme. By putting a high price on their process, Acme played into the hands of their competition, which turned out to be very inventive in their own right.

Generally, a product or process, patented or not, is developed with the idea of direct sale of the product or internal use of the process. Therefore, the cost to develop should be regarded as a sunk cost of secondary importance with respect to establishment of an appropriate royalty. Only when a technology is developed specifically for licensing to others should the cost of development be significant for the establishment of royalty. Further, to be "fair" or "reasonable," a royalty must permit the licensee to obtain a fair or reasonable return from the use of the license. This last consideration must be overriding.

In the author's judgement, one of the best articles to be published on the subject of license royalties is "Negotiating Compensation in International Licensing Agreements" by Franklin R. Root and Farok J. Contractor.[1] They present a detailed and interesting discussion of factors such as "economic rent" and "opportunity cost." They point out that the licensor's minimum acceptable royalty is the amount of the transfer cost, while the licensee's maximum acceptable royalty is the lowest of four values:

- Licensee's incremental profits from use of the license.
- Cost of technology from an alternate supplier.
- Cost to self-develop.
- Cost of infringement or obtaining technology "over the transom."

The negotiating range is thus established in the minds of both licensee and licensor, according to how well each has assessed its own situation and the position of the other party. In this discussion it is interesting to note the attention paid to "opportunity cost" for the licensor which is the amount of potential profit from the licensed property (from sales or other means) that has been given up by licensing the property to someone else.

Sometimes the necessary details are simply not present for proper use of sophisticated cost accounting methods. Accurate figures may not be available to determine the "opportunity cost" of Messers Root and Contractor. Decision theory analysis may be difficult to apply when decision alternatives are unknown. Present value and discounted cash flow is useful in many decisions such as the advantage of lump sum payments vs long-term annual royalties, but these options are often not available. Nevertheless, the successful licensing businessman should be acquainted with such systems. Sound judgment has no substitute, but that judgment can be made more sound by intelligent use of all available tools.

Increased royalty payments come with increased importance of patents.

R.P. Whipple, President of Whipple International Development Company, calls attention to two significant events that occurred in 1983.[2]

These events add special emphasis to the potential of licensing and increase the likelihood of royalty income for both certainty of action and payment amounts.

First, the Circuit Court of Appeals for the Federal Circuit (CAFC) was established in that year to hear the appeals of patent infringement cases on a national basis, as opposed to having such cases heard by one or more other Circuit Courts which might not be well versed in matters of technology and the patenting of technical/scientific inventions. Furthermore, the CAFC seems to favor a position of validity for patents granted.

The second event of 1983 was the decision by the U.S. Supreme Court that interest should appropriately be paid on back royalty awarded as a result of patent infringement. The case was General Motors vs. Devex, and its results have been seen in subsequent infringement case awards.

CAFC decisions have not only brought together much needed technical and legal criteria with respect to patent infringement but also raised the level of damage or royalty compensation paid to successful patent owners suing for infringement. The General Motors vs. Devex decision has further raised the compensation awarded on infringement cases settled in favor of the patent owner.

The message here is, "Have you checked over your intellectual property rights lately? Have you taken inventory of your business and its total values in technology, design, production and marketing?" The federal courts have established certain market and financial factors as being useful in determining "reasonable royalties." They have also strengthened the position of a patent holder in obtaining "prejudgment interest" on a "reasonable royalty" award.

The July 3, 1988 issue of the New York Times described this situation in an article headlined, "The New High-Tech Battleground." One of the lead paragraphs summarized the situation:

> *American industry in general, and high-technology companies in particular, are increasingly resorting to patent and copyright litigation as a source of new revenue and as a competitive weapon. Companies are viewing such intellectual property rights as key corporate assets to be exploited to the fullest in an increasingly competitive environment.*

With this background, a U.S. patent owner today is in a good position to establish a sound license program with improved support from the U.S. court system. Likewise, the patent licensee can look forward to an equally firm position of rights under a license, supported by the patent. All of these factors indicate the logic of considering a licensing program in the business plan of any company dealing with technology and patent rights.

Duration of payments.

Duration of a license influences many obligations of licensee to licensor and vice versa, not the least of which is the payment of royalties. If a license is based on a patent, it may make sense to operate for the life of the patent. If the license is on know-how only, the duration will be based on the importance of present know-how, future know-how and its status as a trade secret. Many general know-how licenses are written for at least five years, but seldom more than 10 years. Well-protected, valuable, trade secret licenses may last for 20 years or more. In the case of general technology in which the licensor has a "one shot" special expertise, a know-how license may be shorter than five years and covered by only one or two payments. In some cases it may be appropriate to discontinue royalty payments but to continue the license with respect to licensor-licensee information exchange, secrecy obligations, and other commitments. Such arrangements tend to emphasize the value of a license over and above the simple payment of money.

Technical assistance fees.

Similar to the know-how fee is an established rate for technical assistance. It is good business that the licensor should estimate in advance the extent of technical assistance that is anticipated. It may be that a certain amount of this assistance should be required as opposed to being merely offered. The pricing of the required assistance can be established on a set-fee minimum while help on request is established on a per-diem rate for travel and living expenses for the licensor's personnel, plus a fee for the personnel time.

Many times it is possible to include in the license, on a separate annual fee basis, a certain number of man-hours for on-site consultation, licensor laboratory service, question answering, technical seminar, quality improvement recommendations and follow-up. On other occasions, the foregoing can be offered as a special extra service, which would include a thorough annual review of improvements and new developments. Pricing of such a service would, of course, depend on many factors. Under certain circumstances, a limited amount of service could be free. If a trademark license is involved, or if the quality or performance of the licensed product is critical for its use, the licensor may want to require time for a licensor quality-control inspection of the licensee's operation. The cost of that effort could be covered through royalties, set annual fee, or other nonnegotiable arrangement.

If these arrangements are not clear to all concerned, the license can experience severe difficulties. The understanding of technical-assistance charges should also extend into the operations and technical departments of both licensee and licensor organizations. These units of the companies involved will be most concerned with the matter, and a lack of understanding and agreement at the operating level can cause severe frictions.

Other costs and charges.

In addition to royalties, know-how payments and technical service fees, other costs must also be compensated or at least provided for in every license. While these elements may not be subject to discussion and opinion in terms of amount, they nonetheless should be included by specific provision. Examples are:

- Payment of patent taxes (in licensee's country in the case of an international license).

  In countries where patent taxes exist, it is proper to consider whether licensee or licensor should pay. There are arguments for both sides.

- Costs of new patents (in licensee's country in the case of an international license).

  The cost of new filing by the licensor, and prosecution charges may be handled by either licensee or licensor. Final decision should include the question of ownership rights going with payment as well as payment for use by licensee.

- Costs of patent litigation and distribution of any proceeds from suit.

  Generally allocated to licensor for first decision on whether suit should be filed, with later decision for licensee if licensor does not file suit. Party filing suit should bear costs and take proceeds.

- Patent Indemnification.

  Should be regarded with great caution. Any indemnification, if given at all, should be limited to the amount of royalties received by licensor or a portion thereof.

- Cost of technology or patent licenses obtained from third parties.

  Should normally be shared on an equitable basis.

- Governmental taxes and fees.

  Should usually be paid by licensee, except for income taxes on royalties as levied by licensee's country. The latter can be paid by licensee out of royalty due when tax treaties permit a tax credit to the licensor.

Conclusion.

Money Problems should not exist, but they may if proper care is not exercised. If the agreement is properly made in the first place, and if both parties are punctual in following their obligations, there should be no serious difficulties. However, payments are not always made on time. Licensor/licensee confidence can be seriously damaged by negligence such as late payments. Royalty accounting, reporting and payment should always be completed on time. If not, the licensor should immediately, firmly and diplomatically inquire as to the reason for delinquency. The right of the licensor to inspect the licensee's records for royalty determination can be an essential strength in a licensor's inquiry into delinquent payments.

If there is a valid reason for inadequate royalty payment, that reason should be recognized, and formalized by written waiver or other suitable adjustment when royalty minimums are involved. No absence of payment should be permitted to continue beyond the prescribed period without proper notice being given. Occasionally, it is discovered that the circumstances surrounding a license have changed from the time of original negotiation. In such cases it may be appropriate to renegotiate certain payment obligations.

In addition to royalty payments, the licensee should promptly pay other obligations such as technical assistance charges and patent costs. Further, the licensor must be sure to submit promptly all statements of payment due. A lax system of payment-due invoicing cannot impress a licensee with a need for prompt payment. To be well run and permanently satisfactory, a license program must be handled in the same manner as any other business, with complete attention to prompt notification and prompt payment of all obligations.

The basic philosophy of all successful businesses is to treat customers and suppliers fairly and to expect fair treatment in return. The same is true for license, franchise or joint-venture arrangements. A one-sided deal is bound to create trouble.

FOOTNOTES:
[1]See Bibliography 14.
[2]See Bibliography 81.

Chapter III

TYPES OF LICENSE AGREEMENTS AND SPECIAL CONSIDERATIONS FOR FRANCHISES AND JOINT-VENTURES

One of the advantages of licensing for both strategy and tactics of business is the fact that a license agreement can be constructed in many different ways to suit the needs of the parties involved. In addition to the various terms and conditions which can be adjusted, the very form and nature of a license agreement can change to suit the technical, commercial and legal conditions. The different types of agreements are outlined in the following pages. In addition, two specific types of agreements are given particular attention — Franchising and Joint-Ventures. Both of these business methods belong in the consideration of licenses in a general sense. At the same time, they also deserve special attention for the conditions and restrictions which may be involved. The critical aspects of these considerations are reviewed here in order to give the reader a more complete appreciation of the business decisions involved.

Patent licenses.

- For specific apparatus, product or design coverage.

  Examples would include a specific apparatus whose essential element is patented or a refinement or even a "convenience feature" that makes an existing standard product more saleable. A "field-of-use" license can be appropriate to a specific patent coverage in a limited field of application.

- For a specific process or method of manufacture.

  Such as a metal-finishing process that is the only way to achieve a certain decorative or functional surface quality or the method of economically forming a manufactured element or a chemical process for deriving a certain synthetic material.

- For the combination of both of the above.

Usually to achieve a complete, marketable product.

Trade secret/know-how agreements.

- Cover specific secret or otherwise difficult to obtain (expensive) information on formulas, processes, industrial techniques. This type of coverage can range from a secretly held chemical formula to a special manufacturing technique that has been developed over many years.

- Often are used in connection with patent licenses to complete the subject coverage.

- In technical areas can be equal in importance to patent agreements and greater in value than trademark licenses.

- Have certain defensible protection in respect to industrial property in many countries, but in most cases are not as secure as patent licenses, and in other cases have no status at all for industrial property rights.

- In certain trade secret cases the license can have a significantly longer life than a patent license.

Technical assistance agreements.

- Involve continuing supply to the licensee of scientific assistance, en gineering services, training and management guidance.

- Usually are embodied in licenses that involve know-how.

- Often involved with patent and patent/know-how agreements, sometimes as separate agreements to assure proper remuneration.

Copyright licenses.

- Cover certain registered artistic creation.

- Widely accepted for computer software licensing.

- Must be carefully controlled to guarantee the continued proprietary position.

- Can be entered into with or without concurrent patent and know-how coverage.

Trademark licenses.

- Cover unregistered and registered proprietary identification.

- The owner of the trademark must monitor and control the nature and quality of the goods or services sold under the trademark by licensees in order to maintain the value of the trademark and to prevent a loss of trademark rights due to uncontrolled licensing.

- Can be entered into with or without concurrent patent and know-how coverage.

- Often recommended to be handled in documents separate from those covering patents or know-how.

- Can have a duration considerably beyond the term of a patent license.

- Control the use of the trademark.

- May establish a sales or marketing territory.

Franchising.

- Controls the use of:

  Business name or trademark; may also include other intellectual property rights.

Business methods including manufacturing and selling.

- May establish an exclusive sales or market territory.

- Furnishes on-going support to the franchisee principally in training, marketing, merchandising and selling, and also in quality control and business methods.

- The franchisor must monitor and control the nature and quality of the goods or services sold under the business name and trademark by franchisees in order to maintain the value of the business name and trademark and to prevent a loss of rights due to uncontrolled licensing.

Technical joint-venture.

- Involves equity participation of two or more legal entities.

- Usually established with one or more of the license features listed above.

- Not limited in duration except as may be specifically stated in the formation agreement or as may be regulated by the government of one of the participants (generally the socialist countries).

* * * * *

Franchising — business opportunities and cautions (also see Part One, Chapter I, p. 7).

Franchising has been described as the licensing of a business system. *Franchising In The Economy 1985-1987* is a report of the U.S. Department of Commerce, International Trade Administration (Bib. 48). The "Study Results" of this report start with: "Franchising sales of goods and services in more than 498,000 outlets are expected to reach more than $591 billion in 1987, about 6% higher than a year earlier and about 77% over the level of sales at the start of the 1980s." The U.S. Federal Trade Commission's Rule of October 21, 1979, has established certain regulations in respect to franchisor-franchisee relations, and these may be obtained from the U.S. Federal Trade Commission, Bureau of Consumer Protection, Washington, D.C. *The (Annual) Franchise Manual* (Bib. 49), has a summary of these "regs" as well as a discussion of "package" and "products" franchises. This same manual carries a review of legal requirements, sample contracts, business information and franchiser listings in the U.S., Canada and "Overseas Listings." The International Franchise Association at 1350 New York Avenue, N.W., Suite 900, Washington, D.C., 20005-4709 has a large list of franchise related publications. Anyone interested in franchising would be well advised to contact the I.F.A., the U.S.F.T.C. and the Bibliography references 45, 46, 47, 48, 49, 55, 80, 89 and 91.

The following excellent discussion of franchising is taken from *Evaluating A Franchise* published by the Australian Government Publishing Service, authored by the Australian Department of Industry, Technology and Commerce:

> *What is a franchise?*
>
> *A 'franchise' is a business arrangement in which knowledge, expertise and often a trademark or trade name are licensed to an operator. The franchise business is run along lines agreed to between the parties. 'License', 'exclusive distributor' and 'dealership' are some of the other terms applied to such arrangements.*
>
> *The 'franchisor' is the seller of the franchise and the 'franchisee', the buyer.*
>
> *A franchise can involve:*

- *A product, where the franchisee acts as a wholesaler or retailer (as in the motor vehicle retailing and petrol reselling);*

- *A system, where the franchisor permits the franchisee to use a unique method of doing business (as in fast-food outlets, laundries and motels);*

- *A manufacturing arrangement, where the franchisor provides an essential ingredient or know-how (as in the soft-drink industry).*

What are the advantages?

For the franchisee, franchising can offer the opportunity of sharing in some of the benefits of larger business (such as an established reputation and image, skilled management and a large-scale advertising program) while offering much of the independence of a sole proprietor.

For the franchisor, franchising is a way of expanding service outlets and distributing products with a limited amount of ready capital. It is a way of obtaining conscientious and dedicated personnel who work hard to safeguard their investment.

While some franchise arrangements work well for the mutual benefit of franchisor and franchisee, problems can arise, particularly when the aims of the parties are opposed.

What are the problems?

These include:

- *The terms of the franchise agreement may place franchisees in a position where they cannot achieve the return on investment they expected.*

- *Export markets may be restricted.*

- *Assistance promised by the franchisor to the franchisee does not always materialize.*

- *Threat of termination by the franchisor may be used as a lever against franchisees, putting them at a disadvantage in negotiations and forcing them to accept company decisions which they see as disadvantageous.*

- *Lack of independence in operating the business leads some franchisees to complain that they are no better off then employees, yet without the benefits and security that employees enjoy.*

- *Some franchisees are temperamentally unsuited to work under the terms of a franchise arrangement.*

- *Some franchisees have been falsely persuaded they can make quick profits with little work.*

Franchise cautions.

With all the glowing reports on franchising, there are unscrupulous or incompetent franchisers and franchisees. The article "Fear of Franchising" in the June 1987 issue of *INC.* magazine covers the details of such an unhappy situation. The same careful, commonsense judgment outlined for other licensing applies to the franchising business as to all other business. In addition, there are regulations which must be observed in the U.S. and in one province of Canada (Alberta). U.S. regulations consist of the F.T.C. Disclosure Requirements and Prohibitions as well as separate regulations of 15 states in the U.S. Violation of regulations in at least one state (New York) may involve criminal court proceedings. These factors emphasize the need to differentiate between the substance of a license which is not regulated and a franchise which is regulated. The author is not aware of any regulations on franchising other than those mentioned above.

* * * * *

Joint-ventures — questions and key points.

Joint-ventures are an often-used strategy for combining the strengths of separate firms, whether the objective is market presence in a foreign country or market expansion in the same country as the originating partners. For example, in May, 1989, Exide Electronics, based in Raleigh, N.C. and GS Japan Storage Battery Co., Ltd. of Japan announced the formation of a joint-venture to manufacture, sell and distribute advanced uninterruptible power systems in Japan. On the other hand, the April 10, 1989, issue of *Business Week* carried an article which described a joint-venture between Procter and Gamble, Cincinnati, OH, and Syntex Corp. of Palo Alto, CA, to market a non-prescription version of Naprosyn, Syntex' antiarthritis drug as well as a 50-50 joint-venture between Johnson and Johnson and Merck to market certain over-the-counter drugs derived from Merck's prescription drugs.

Advantages of joint-ventures and some cautions.

Flexibility determines the popularity of the joint-venture concept. Just as the virtue of licensing is its flexibility in rights, obligations, payments, etc., so the versatility of a joint-venture is in its flexibility of establishing ownership, operating responsibilities and degree of independence. Often a technology license will be an integral part of a joint-venture. (See pages 122-124 for a comparison of a joint-venture and a straight license. Also see page 69 for notes on Corporate Partnering.)

Depending on local limitations, a joint-venture can combine cash, equipment and capitalized know-how with land, labor, utilities, infrastructure and market accessibility from the other side to bring profits to both. Sometimes one contributes the technology while another brings the sales force and a third supplies manufacturing facilities. Perhaps one joint-venture partner has the most economical raw material source, while one or more other partners supply manufacturing and sales. Ownership percentage is usually negotiable at least within certain limits and the licensing of critical technology by one of the partners can often bring that partner the assurance of extra income from a licensee with whom there is a solid equity relationship.

Along with these positive factors, there are a few negatives. For instance, some authorities claim that a joint-venture should not be undertaken when either partner has a gross sales figure of under $1 million or where the ultimate joint-venture would anticipate an ultimate gross sale less than $1 million. Certainly, the expense involved in planning, manning, training and participating in a joint-venture indicates that the project should be sufficiently profitable to support the effort. Whether the $1 million figure is valid for every case is a matter of opinion. Some cautions are covered in the following discussions. Other more detailed concerns should be covered with qualified experts or consultants in the fields indicated.

Planning for a Joint-Venture must include discussion of the following questions:

- What are the reasons of each partner for forming the joint-venture, i.e. the objectives of the joint-venture.

- Will one or more parties continue to operate independently in other product lines?

- Will one or more parties be limited in future actions by reason of the joint-venture?

- Will the joint-venture operate on its own (arms-length) or will its actions be subordinate to one or more of the parties?

- In the case of a dispute between the founding parties in respect to purpose, objectives and actions of the joint-venture, how is that difference of opinion to be settled? Does one party have a controlling vote?

And if an international joint-venture is the subject, also consider:

- What are host government requirements for export?

- Will the host government grant the required duty protection to permit economical operation?

Joint-Venture Management Objectives and Methods are considerations that can be the source of greatest friction between parties:

- Who will manage and direct the operation?

- How will the directors and managers be chosen?

- What are the authority limits of the CEO?

- How is the management staff chosen what are the job requirements for each position?

- Does the management (and CEO) understand and agree with the Corporate Planning Objectives?

- What are the total personnel requirements and has the entire operation been broken down by job description?

- What are the training requirements for the various levels of all employees?

- For international joint-ventures, what will be the expatriate staff requirements?

- As the joint-venture develops, are there provisions for changing the Management Objectives and Methods and whose responsibility are they?

- If an international joint-venture, what are the host country living requirements for expatriates such as cultural differences, freedom of action and movement, religious restrictions (as in Moslem countries)?

Policies for Joint-Venture Sales or Marketing should be established in respect to local and export markets.

- How sales are handled — joint-venture sales personnel — agencies representatives.

- Requirements for product quality, product liability and product servicing.

- What are the inter-company sales policies and needs between the joint-venture and the partners.

Financial Policy and Financial Considerations can be a subject of concern for both partners.

Dividend Policy or Profit Sharing should be settled in advance.

Accounting Practices may vary between partners and may be influenced by local government and/or partner company's home government.

Local Government Regulations can represent problems or advantages in the case of an international joint-venture. These questions vary significantly with international joint-venture formation, and particularly with respect to developing countries and communist countries. In order to cover these matters adequately, it is necessary to study the local regulations in detail, as well as to research various other information sources, such as:

- The Licensing Executives Society's publication *les Nouvelles*

- U.S. Department of Commerce

- Business International Corporation

- UNIDO

- Various national trade councils

Special problems in international joint-ventures may surprise the unwary partner in regard to a number of details. For example:

- When a family group is a significant local partner, what is the policy on hiring and firing family members?

- Do all family members have voting rights, management rights, veto rights?

- How can differentiation be made between bribes and "facilitating payments"?

- Are "facilitating payments" illegal, standard practice, accepted with limits?

- Policy on gifts, entertainment, special perquisites for "family" owners.

- What is tax avoidance and how is it defined and/or practiced?

- How do local practices influence or impinge upon the "home country" legal responsibility of partners (i.e., U.S. Foreign Corrupt Practices Act, U.S. Anti-Boycott Regulations and Export Control Regulations or simply U.S. tax laws)?

- Governments may change the rules.

- Religious and/or cultural backgrounds of certain countries can and have created problems for expatriate employees.

Joint-ventures vs. licensing without equity.

The fields of licenses and joint-ventures overlap and yet they are different. A joint-venture often (but not always) includes a license. A license may be an integral part of a joint-venture formation, or it may be an entirely separate contract, with or without a joint-venture. The following comparison of similarities and differences helps to explain the relationship of the two concepts and to assist those considering such arrangements.

A Comparison of Similarities and Differences Between Licenses without Equity and Those Joint-Ventures Which are Established for Production and Sale of Products
Taken from
"Licensing vs. Joint-Ventures: Differences and Similarities"
by
J. Peter Killing and David J. French
1982 Licensing Law Handbook, Chapter 4 (Bib. 4)

Objective of Parties	
LICENSE AGREEMENT	JOINT-VENTURE
Licensor seeks monetary (royalty) returns without significant involvement in the management of the technology recipient's operation.	Technology supplying partner seeks participation in joint-venture operation: to establish a market presence; to obtain local market experience and to share in potential profits.
Licensee seeks new technology at minimum cost and obligations.	Local or recipient partner seeks to establish a successful continuing venture.
Licensor's royalties will be maximized by maximizing licensee's sales; as opposed to licensee who seeks to maximize his profits.	As owners of equity, both parties have the same objective of maximizing profits.
Contributions of Parties	
LICENSE AGREEMENT	JOINT-VENTURE
Licensor grants permission under patents and supplies an initiating amount of show-how and know-how; may also grant trademark rights and continuing access to new technology for term of agreement.	Technology partner supplies technology, management services and capital; and ongoing support under all three headings indefinitely.

Licensee pays royalties, accepts limitations on use of licensed technology and may grant back rights in improvements.	Local partner supplies local market distribution facilities and knowledge, existing production facilities and continuing participation. May voluntarily limit actions to avoid competition.

Character of Parties

LICENSE AGREEMENT	JOINT-VENTURE
Licensee has basic ability to carry on alone once initiated.	Both parties have substantial but incomplete skills or resources that are complementary.
Licensor lacks resources or inclination to invest in the local market.	Licensor is prepared to invest more substantially in the local market.
Parties are potentially more likely to compete rather than cooperate in conflicting territories.	Parties are less likely to become competitors, due to mutual control over internal management of the technology exploiting entity.

Common Factors

Both involve the transfer of technical knowledge from a technology supplier (foreign) to a technology user (local).

Both involve the existence of special proprietary rights or market advantages based on patents, trade secrets and know-how that pass from the foreign supplier to the local user.

Both involve some degree of limitation or constraint on the marketing freedom of the entity exploiting the transferred technology.

Both are a substitute for direct foreign investment by the technology supplier and serve as an alternative to creation of a 100% controlled subsidiary.

Both overcome political barriers prohibiting 100% foreign control in jurisdictions which limit foreign ownership.

Both are likely to include arrangements limiting in part the market freedom of the technology receiving entity.

Both provide some scope for the technology supplier to provide exports to local foreign production in the form of precommitted tied purchases.

Both require a serious commitment of employee time to planning, preparation for and coordination of the technology transfer process.

Differentiating Factors	
LICENSE AGREEMENT	JOINT-VENTURE
Less involvement between parties.	Continuing cooperation and commitment between parties.
Limited in time.	Unlimited in time. (Note, not necessarily so, for most communist countries, and some developing countries, Ed.)
Fixed royalty payment terms; possibly including guaranteed payments.	Equity participation of licensor allows for deferred payment.
No capital investment by the licensor in the licensee.	Technology supplier provides capital or equivalent in resources.
Licensee is free to exercise own management discretion.	Parties must cooperate and obtain a consensus on management decisions; depends on type of venture.

126

Chapter IV

WHY, WHY NOT & HOW TO FIND A PARTNER

Chapters I and II of Part One discuss some of the reasons that several small and mid-size businesses have included a form of licensing in their business strategy — or, for good reason, have decided that a license program is not appropriate for them at the present time. There are advantages and disadvantages in licensing, and no single company can demonstrate all such considerations in one case history. The following outline of pros and cons, along with necessary information on prospective partners, will summarize the considerations that should always be taken in regard to any license or license program of strategic corporate importance. (See also Bibliography 3, 11, 42 and 43.)

Advantages for the licensor.

Some of the most significant advantages to the licensor are:

- *Income*

    Increased income through royalties, potential sale of related materials, fees for services rendered and other related business transactions.

    Income through sale or license of unused or old technology.

- *New Uses of Technology*

    Application of a technology into a different field of use or geographic area without large capital outlay.

    To employ "by-product" or "fall-out" technology.

- *No Capital/No Staff*

    Capital investment may not be necessary. Licensing is usually an inexpensive way of operating within a foreign country or distant market.

There is usually no need for the licensor to maintain a permanent staff of administrative and technical and sales personnel in a foreign country or even in a more distant domestic market.

- *Avoids Legal Problems*

  The jurisdiction of a foreign government does not have any direct effect on the licensor in respect to labor and social legislation, etc.

  Where patent and trademark laws require either a loss of patent rights or compulsory licensing, for continued nonuse of those rights, licensing affords protection under the local patent and trademark position.

  Can be a practical settlement to an otherwise unpleasant patent infringement suit or a trade secret controversy.

  Avoid antitrust or trade regulation problems.

- *Expands Opportunities*

  Licensing expands the opportunities of foreign operations, and can complement or supplement exports and/or direct manufacture — also expands opportunities with distant domestic markets.

  Licensing may be the only avenue open to a market when export sale is blocked and equity associations are not immediately possible.

  Cross licensing may open significant technical or commercial opportunities.

- *Equity Improvement*

  If a company has an interest or an equity in a foreign (or domestic) operation, a licensing agreement can have an extra protection or binding influence, especially if a minority interest is involved. Royalties from such a license can be another way to obtain profits from a subsidiary.

Large and profitable equity operations often have their beginning with a mutually advantageous license agreement.

- *R&D Improvements*

Reverse flow of a license's new improvements and developments is often advantageous to the licensor. Licensee may even have known capabilities and R&D facilities for developing technology further.

Increase returns on R&D.

Support future R&D.

- *Market Improvement*

Maintain goodwill contacts and technical rapport with others.

Reach fields of use not covered by technology or patent owner.

Better market coverage through other licensed manufacturers.

Possible sale of special related products or raw materials.

Can be the answer to acceptance vs. nonacceptance in certain high-production industries that cannot accept single supply sources of material or parts.

- *Preparation for Other Markets*

May be a means of testing or proving product suitability when testing cannot be done in licensor's home territory.

Advantages for the licensee.

If the licensee does not derive sufficient advantage from an agreement, he will not be interested in keeping it, and all the legal talent in the world cannot salvage or protect against an unhappy partner. Licensees should look for the following provisions:

- *Additional Rights*

Rights to use patents, trademarks, designs, know-how, etc.

Rights to future innovation of the licensor firm.

Rights to sell the products of the licensor firm (especially in the case of a foreign license).

- *Assistance*

Technical services and assistance.

Cheaper and faster development of product or process in comparison to self-developed technology.

Management assistance and manpower development.

General marketing help such as sales promotion, advertising, public relations, etc.

- *Expanded Marketing Potential*

Possible expanded export market using the licensed product.

Rapid market entry with new product.

Use of a good trademark or reputation of the licensor.

- *Expanded Profits*

Potential prestige factor, which may help with marketing contacts, financing and other factors important to an expanding business.

Potential for cross licensing with improved technology and improved products.

Disadvantages for licensee and licensor.

There are also disadvantages of licensing to both the licensor and the licensee. Unless these disadvantages are properly understood and dealt with, a license contract may turn into a source of problems instead of profits. Most of the recognized disadvantages can be summed as follows:

- **Limited Opportunities**

  Licensor may be limited in profit possibilities, perhaps at a fixed royalty, without the opportunity to continue or expand participation beyond original terms.

  Licensing does not offer the same opportunities for growth and expansion as an investment in a direct manufacturing operation.

  Licensor usually has no direct voice or participation in the control or management of the licensee.

  Licensor may have control problems in a trademark license.

  May limit ability of licensee to work with competitors of licensor. May limit ability of licensor to work with competitors of licensee.

- **Extra Costs**

  Demands for education, training, technical assistance, supply of technical data, and supervision on quality control and production standards may make the program so costly that it is impractical for the licensor. In such a case either the licensor does not receive adequate profit, or the licensee does not get adequate service, or both.

- **Improper Performances**

  Licensee may not perform properly. For instance the licensee may not communicate adequately with licensor; or maintain proper quality of operations; or exercise due diligence in business matters.

  Licensor may give inadequate service or training to the licensee, may not pass along improvements, may not have adequate concern for the business success of the licensee.

  Licensor may not perform his required services in a timely manner.

- **Improper Understanding**

  Licensee or licensor may not thoroughly understand the coverage of the agreement. There can be a significant difference between the licensor's and licensee's interpretation of the contract.

- *Improper Competition*

  Licensee and licensor may turn out to be competitors, not partners.

- *Increased Liability Risk*

  Licensor may be exposed to increased product liability over which there is inadequate control or legal defense.

- *Unforeseen Problems*

  Insufficient testing done on a new product and problems encountered in production raise costs to licensee and/or licensor.

  Insufficient market experience of either licensee or licensor can result in sales difficulties. Perhaps the licensor put emphasis in the wrong market area or the licensee is trying to sell to the wrong customers.

Finding the right one.

There are a number of steps to be taken by a licensor to find a licensee or by a would-be licensee to find a licensor.

First comes the search for prospects. There are many sources of information. Sometimes there have been firms who have already made inquiries of the potential licensor. There may be potential licensor firms who are advertising their technology with technology broker firms. Some technology broker firms have computerized listings not only of technology available but also seekers of technology. In the United States and in certain other countries, trade associations can furnish valuable leads and references. Within the United States, various state departments of commerce can be helpful. Outside the United States, the U.S. Department of Commerce offices (or equivalent offices of other governments) can be very helpful (World Trade Data Service Reports of the U.S. DOC can be particularly useful). If there is a World Trade Center or affiliate office accessible to the prospective licensee/licensor, the World Trade Centers Association Data Bank can be of tremendous help in supplying commercial and corporate data. The nearest World Trade Center or affiliate, if not known, may be located by contacting W.T.C.A. Headquarters, One World Trade Center, Suite 7701, New York, N.Y., 10048, phone 212-313-4610. Chambers of Commerce, and certain United Nations offices, such as UNIDO can also furnish valuable background regarding those seeking technology and those who have technology to license.

Another, and perhaps the most useful method of all, is to work through a friendly firm that can be trusted for good business judgment and that already has contacts in the area. Commercial banks have substantial background of information on marketing, technical and financial subjects. The best approach to banks is through local offices with which the licensor or licensee has or is about to have an account or other commercial relationship. Through friendly firms and banks, it is possible to obtain financial references and general business background comments that might not otherwise be available.

After a search for prospects, a list of potential licensees or licensors can be drawn up and analyzed. A more detailed analysis can then be made of those firms that appear to be the best prospects. Once again, the establishment of the "select list" can be made considerably easier by working with a second cooperating firm with established communications in the area. Additional information on this subject is found in bibliographic references 3, 54, 58, 59, 60, 61, 74 and 86.

Licensor background.

A licensee seeking a licensor should obtain as much information as possible about a potential licensor. Except for details that may relate to know-how disclosure, any reluctance on the part of a licensor should be regarded as suspect. Judgments by the licensee in respect to license desirability should consider the nature and completeness of response to these questions. Note that for international licensing, the U.S. Department of Commerce has very useful information services, such as the World Trade Data Service, which for $75 will conduct a background check on a foreign firm and provide a report. The various country desks of both U.S. Commerce and State Departments can also provide information, as can the U.S. and Foreign Commercial Service of Commerce Department. As a checklist, the following information is desirable:

General:

- Full name and address of headquarters.
- Annual report (if available).
- Capitalization.

- Annual turnover.
- Annual profit before taxes.
- Total number of employees.
- Principal products, relative place in the market and profitability.
- Secondary products, relative place in the market and profitability.
- Locations for main and branch production operations and products made at each.
- Locations for main and branch offices and research and development facilities.
- Number of employees at each facility.

Specific:

- Design and manufacturing information on product or process proposed for a license.
- Manufacturing or use cost data on same.
- Profitability on same.
- What other products or processes of licensor have been licensed where, when, how successfully?
- Estimated capital and operation or production costs on licensed product or process.
- Estimated market for licensed product, sales history to date.
- Summary of materials, components and equipment required.
- How many licenses already granted on product or process where, when, with whom.
- What has experience been with these licenses already granted.
- Intellectual property protection available.
- License terms: Standard or negotiable; Duration.; Grant-back; Payments.
- What training is offered, and how is it presented? What has been the licensor's experience with training and where?

In preparing a prospectus, the licensor must be careful that he says enough to describe the subject, but not enough to reveal proprietary information. The licensor must also be completely factual. Certain information constitutes a know-how disclosure and should never be revealed until a license is signed and an initial payment made. If detailed analysis is required in this respect, a confidential disclosure agreement should be signed.

Licensee background.

Likewise, the licensor will want to know a good deal about his prospective partner. The licensor or his representatives should conduct a thorough investigation of the licensee's facilities, his areas of competence and his place in the industry of which he is part. Information such as Dunn & Bradstreet analyses and confidential bank reports are appropriate supplements to on-site interviews and facilities inspections. In the case of foreign licensing, U.S. Department of Commerce World Trade Data Service reports and U.S. and FCS information can also be of great value (See also previous section "Finding the Right One"). The licensor will also look to the licensee for information, such as:

General:

- Full name and address of headquarters
- Annual report.
- Capitalization.
- Annual turnover (total company expenses).
- Annual profit before taxes.
- Total number of employees.
- Principal products, relative place in the market and profitability.
- Secondary products, relative place in the market and profitability.
- Locations for main and branch production operations and products at each.
- Locations for main and branch offices and research and development facilities.
- Number of employees at each facility.

Specific:

- Experience with other product or process licenses. For what, with whom, how successful?
- Facilities available for licensed product or process.
- Personnel available for license operation and qualification of same.
- Estimated costs for new license program equipment to be purchased and schedule for same
- Market and sales predictions-timetable.

Licensor-licensee mutual background.

Mutual Suitability

When considering any relationship that imposes legal obligations for several years, it is wise to consider the general suitability of the partners. It is important that the prospective licensor and licensee explore their mutual compatibility. During the exploratory stage, the prospective licensee and licensor need answers to many questions, and the potential license partner should be prepared to furnish answers to the following:

- Is the proposed license of mutual advantage to both parties? Why?

- How much experience has the prospective licensor/licensee had in this business, how much in licensing, either domestic or international?

- Does the prospective licensor possess both the required know-how and the ability to make it available. Will he do so willingly?

- Will the prospective licensee be able to use the required know-how once it is received?

- Will the prospective licensor/licensee be a source of future innovation or a worthwhile partner in equity?

After all the questions have been asked and answered, after all the advantages and disadvantages have been considered, there is still a judgement on suitability that can only be answered by personal visit and acquaintance. Regardless of the distances involved no major license contract should be signed until both sides have visited each other and determined that the feeling of mutual desirability is shared by those concerned. Hopefully the get acquainted time can be taken during the "question and answer" period. A custom in many Oriental countries is to take an initial period to become acquainted, without spending time on the mundane commercial and technical details. This practice is a good one to follow when possible. In any case, the establishment of friendship and respect is most important. It is always easier to negotiate an agreement when the parties understand each other's needs, psychological, commercial and technical.

Chapter V

INTELLECTUAL PROPERTY RIGHTS

Part One, Chapter I, has a few words on the essential nature of intellectual property rights and the need for optimum protection of proprietary interests for licenses of any type. Table II gives a useful, fast summary of the protection available in the U.S. For a well considered license program, however, more details and further discussion of the subject is necessary. Part Two, Chapter V has been prepared to give that additional overview needed for a full appreciation of this subject. Even if a licensing effort is not planned for the time being, any business with any proprietary know-how at all should be aware of the protection available. The following summary covers:

- Patents, their importance and their use
- Trade Secrets, their protection and value
- Trademarks, the value of quality symbols
- Copyrights, their use for literature, art work and computer software
- Mask Works, the protection of semiconductor chips in the U.S.

The subject of computer software protection is, in itself, so important in today's world of high technology that it is given special treatment in Part Two, Chapter VI. For full appreciation of protection considerations Chapters V and VI should be read as one total subject. Proper, effective business planning, strategic and tactical, will include an ongoing consideration of intellectual property rights.

PATENTS.

Definition

A patent is a legally recognized form of protection for an invention that satisfies certain criteria of newness and originality. A patent provides its owner the right to exclude others from making, using or selling that patented invention for the life of the patent. Its subject matter can be:

- Composition of matter.
- Particular product or article.
- Apparatus or machinery.
- Process, procedure, or method.
- Living cells or combination of cells.

Patentability requirements will vary from country to country. Generally, to be patentable an invention must be new, un-obvious, of significant inventive level, or technical advance, and it must be useful. One patent cannot include more than one invention. The life of a patent will vary according to the country granting the patent (15 to 20 years for most). Through the use of the "Convention Year," the original filing date of a patent can be effective in most all countries when the foreign counterpart is filed within 12 months of the original filing date. This statement holds true for filing with the European Patent Office (EPO) as well as for individual European countries. Further postponement is possible for filing foreign counterparts with respect to cases filed as PCT cases (Patent Cooperation Treaty).

Special Note: It is possible for inventor Jones to have a valid patent on a new apparatus or process but still not be able legally to make, use or sell his invention because inventor Smith has a different patent that covers a special aspect of Jones' apparatus or process. In such case, each inventor may need a license from the other to make, use or sell the apparatus or process in question.

This matter of conflicting patents on a single technology can be extremely important. For example, Mr. Single Hand invents and obtains a patent for a telephone speaker and microphone connected at either end of a single handle, thus permitting one-handed use of a telephone. However, he finds that Mr. Loud Noyes has a patent on the use of a sound signal (bell, horn, buzz) to indicate an incoming call on the telephone. Thus, Mr. Hand cannot make a saleable phone without a license from Mr. Noyes under his sound signal patent, since any telephone without a sound signal is not as useful or saleable as one with a sound signal. Likewise, Mr. Noyes cannot make a "one-handed" telephone without a license from Mr. Hand. The possibility of patent conflict should be investigated by a competent patent attorney and provided for in any license agreement.

Patent Planning

Of vital concern to any patent applicant or owner are the internationally recognized patent conventions. These conventions offer certain advantages of patent application filing from one country to the next such as the "convention year" established by the Paris Convention. This 12-month period is generally available to an inventor starting with the time of first filing in the home country and offering 12 months in which to file in another country with the priority date of the home country filing. Most of the industrial countries of the world are signatories to the "Paris Convention."

In addition to the above, the relatively recent European Patent should be mentioned. By filing a single European patent application in only one of three official languages (English, French or German) it is possible to obtain a granted patent in each of the following European countries:

- Austria
- Belgium
- France
- Greece
- Italy
- Liechtenstein
- Luxembourg
- Netherlands
- Spain
- Sweden
- Switzerland
- United Kingdom
- West Germany

It is expected that other European countries will join this group as time goes on.

The principal advantage to the European Patent is the fact that filing in three or more of the above countries is generally less expensive by going through the European Patent Office (EPO) than by making individual country applications. The advantage offered by the EPO is one of cost (for three or more countries) plus simplification of filing procedure. The only reason for not using the EPO would be cost in respect to filing in only one or two European countries. Considerations of EPO filing may also be influenced by the fact that 1992 is the year in which the European Common Market is committed to conduct itself as a single economic unit.

For U.S. patentors the adherence of the United States to Chapters I and II of the Patent Cooperation Treaty permits the decision on foreign filing to be delayed by as much as 20 or 30 months respectively from the date of the original U.S. filing. For those considering the PCT route, it must be realized, however, that all of the countries of the world are not yet signatories of the PCT even though there are 43 countries listed as PCT member states.

It has been said that the economies of PCT filing are greater for those firms with a fairly large patent portfolio than for those who are concerned with the filing of foreign counterparts on only one or two patents per year. At the same time, the 20- or 30-month period before the final foreign filing date does offer a decision flexibility greater than the 12-month convention year that is automatically in place through the Paris Convention. The mechanics of filing via the PCT route are relatively simple and can be accomplished through the U.S. Patent Office with the payment of a filing fee (about $3,000) and indication of the countries in which filing is requested.

Also important is the fact that individual country patent laws still vary from country to country. Some grant patents with little or no examination for novelty, invention or priority. In other countries the subject of a patent application is automatically published after a period of time (usually 18 months) following first filing in the originating country with final patent examination and grant being delayed for several years. For certain technical/commercial operations, such early disclosures may not be desirable and should be properly considered for overall protection and strategy. In other countries prior description in advertising or technical publications anywhere in the world can be a bar to patentability thus making an early technical press announcement inadvisable until thorough patent strategy can be considered.

In regard to licensing, it may sometimes be desirable to initiate a licensing program on the basis of one or more patent applications. While such action is entirely suitable in many countries, the licensing under a patent application instead of a granted patent can be tricky. In some countries it cannot be done; in others it is valid retroactively *if* the patent is granted. In some countries, it is valid to license until the application fails and in others the license is valid only after provisional publication of the patents.

In planning a patent protection program, it is also good to remember that patents in markets where there is neither licensee nor intention of licensing still offer a psychological protection against copiers. While actual litigation, based on patent rights, may be too expensive, a good many executives justify wide patent coverage on the theory that the likelihood of ideas and designs being stolen or copied is greatly diminished by the would-be thief's fear of legal action. All of these factors must be considered in planning an adequate licensing program with patent support.

For proper patent planning an initial idea of the economics of maintaining patent properties in various countries, (patent taxes) should be considered. In regard to overall costs of patent filing, generalization is risky, but it can be said that patent filing costs will probably vary from about U.S. $1,000 to $3,000 per patent per country depending on the country and translation costs plus the extent of patent office action required. With respect to both EPO and PCT filing, costs will vary depending on the number of countries covered.

All in all, patent laws vary to such an extent that the advice of a good patent attorney, skilled in U.S. and international patent activities and licensing requirements is a vital consideration for any successful licensing program. This fact cannot be over emphasized. For instance Alan Conrad Rose reviews the details of some of the most recent U.S. Intellectual Property Law changes in Bibliography 91. Furthermore, the patent attorney should be brought in as early as possible to give advice at the beginning of the project.

Patent Importance — A Summary

Patents and patent rights can be of significant interest and value to any firm that depends on technology in any way whether it is new, "high-tech" R&D or an improvement of a standard product or production process. The importance of patents can be expressed as protection, promotion and information:

- *Protection* via an exclusive position gives an opportunity to recover development cost and obtain further reward through the proper use of the patent.

   Active Protection: to defend an important invention, in such cases the patent holder is willing to defend the position in spite of the costs of court suits.

   Passive Protection: probably will depend on the "nuisance" value of a patent and the potential for modest licensing, as a deterrent against those who would use the invention by infringing.

Defensive Protection: patent filed to protect against others obtaining a patent and thus restricting practice of the invention.

Protection Alternates: must also be considered in respect to patents. If the invention subject is difficult to "police" (i.e., determine infringers) it may also be reasonable not to patent, but to maintain invention secrecy and operate as a trade secret, without revelation through patents.

- *Promotion*: the opportunity to sell technology in product and process and thereby retain further profit and use in addition to the use of invention by the inventor.

Self-manufacture and selected licensing is one method of obtaining the greatest benefit possible by continuing to practice the invention while still making it available for use by others, to create multiple sources of supply, to make possible further advancement through technology of capable licensees to create extra income.

Manufacturing and general licensing is the accepted method of obtaining maximum profit from widespread use of an invention, while still maintaining control of quality and manufacturing methods. This system is often used in a field that requires general use of a patented process or large-volume production of a patented item.

Licensing only without use by the inventor is the most generally accepted method for obtaining some income from an invention that is not in the main interest or field of manufacturing of the inventor (prime method for using "fall-out technology"). This method of licensing is also used when the inventor is anxious to promote greater use of an invention with proper quality, while supplying an essential ingredient for use of the invention.

- *Information Source*: An effective and inclusive search of patent art in any given field can be used as a valuable source for technical information and background to be used in the planning and directing of research and development activities.

TRADE SECRETS AND KNOW-HOW.

Definition Of Trade Secret

U.S. Patent laws were first enacted by the U.S. Congress in 1790 and have been governed by federal legislation ever since. Trade Secrets law was founded in English common law long before the "thirteen colonies" sought their independence, and today it will be found in state laws rather than federal statutes.

Recently, the U.S. Uniform Trade Secrets Act has attempted to bring together the various trade secrets laws of the many states. It is hoped that this act will be adopted by most, if not all, states. The Uniform Trade Secrets Act defines a trade secret as:

> *Information including a formula, pattern, compilation, program, device, method, technique or process, that derives independent of economic value, actual or potential from not being generally known to, and not being readily ascertainable by proper means by other persons, who can obtain economic value from its disclosure or use, and is the subject of efforts that are reasonable under the circumstances to maintain its secrecy.*

Definition Of Know-How

Know-how can be defined as scientific, engineering or other technical or specialized knowledge that cannot be defined as a trade secret but has particular application to or use with a certain product or process. Proprietary know-how, while it may not be a trade secret, may very well have particular value in the manufacture, use or sale of a given licensed product or process and may, therefore, add significant value to a license (see Part Two, Chapters II and VII).

In common usage, know-how is a broad term, covering many kinds of knowledge and ranges from the highly specific to the very general. It is often used as a term describing either standard engineering knowledge applied particularly to the subject of the license or to special trade secret knowledge which is protected as such by the licensor. In certain countries, know-how is recognized, defensible industrial property. In other countries it is not. To be recognized as a trade secret, know-how must be unknown to others, restricted in its handling and clearly provable as being protected against casual availability. Know-how includes specifications or components for metal alloys, synthetics of many types, chemical compounds, petrochemicals and pharmaceutical products; it also covers all knowledge areas which can be expressed clearly in written engineering specifications, chemical formulas or the like. On the other hand, know-how also means knowledge of man and machine manufacturing operations or standards, also organization methods and procedures. The latter is elusive and vague and often defies precise written specification. In spite of such lack of definition, this latter know-how can be a major determinant of efficiency, and represents a large part of the know-how traded today in world commerce.

Protection Of Trade Secrets

With regard to trade secrets, there are advantages and cautions in their use, whether the secret technology will be privately maintained (formula for Coca Cola) or licensed to others. A trade secret can be any formula, plan or coordinated information used in a business for a competitive advantage if it is not generally known in the particular trade. Originally, trade secrets were the development of a business owner, plus, perhaps, a limited number of trusted employees or associates. With the expansion of industry and specialized knowledge in many fields, modern trade secret law has expanded to permit wide dissemination and use of trade secret information without the sacrifice of legal protection if, and only if, that trade secret status is maintained.

Protection of trade secrets is a combination of steps that should be taken within the owner-organization and measures that are appropriate with respect to independent contractors, suppliers, licensees and the like.(Bib. 20, 21, 22 and 23) The procedures to be taken include:

- Employment agreements and practices.
    Restrictive covenants.
    Post-employment restrictions.

- Hiring and discharge practices.
    Clearance of new employees from competing firms.
    Debriefing of employees on termination.

- Attention to employee morale.
    Broad and specific policies that can create either loyalty or dissatisfaction.

- Dissemination only to those with a need to know.

- Workplace security.

- Document and publication handling.

- Identification, classification and security of key documents, drawings, specifications.

- Clearance of articles, papers, etc. by employees and by others associated with the firm.

- Dealings with third parties.

- Contractual safeguards with service people, suppliers, cooperating firms and persons, licensees, etc.

Trade Secrets vs. Non-Proprietary Know-How

It is of utmost importance to define clearly the difference between trade secrets and non-proprietary know-how. Critically important and appropriate restrictions of the licensor upon the licensee are likely to be invalid, perhaps illegal, if those restrictions cannot be qualified as necessary to the maintenance of a trade secret or proprietary know-how classification. For example, the licensor may want to condition the license in a way to prevent use of the technology in competition with the licensor. These restrictions may be geographical or in a field of use. Or, the licensor may want to have the technology returned and its use terminated upon termination of the license. The above regard for the status of trade secrets in respect to antitrust and other restrictions must, of course, be considered thoroughly with qualified legal counsel. Further discussions can be found in bibliographic entries 21 and 22.

Trade Secrets vs. Patents

The question of which is the better choice, trade secret or patent, is a question that cannot be answered in general. Often difficult to answer, this question must be answered on a case by case basis. Factors to be considered include:

TRADE SECRET	PATENT
Trade secret has no limitation on its life. It is entitled to protection as long as secrecy endures.	Patent Life (U.S.) is 17 years.
Trade secret can legally be discovered or "reverse engineered" by others.	Patent gives its owner a full legal exclusive right of ownership for the life of the patent. On the other hand: a patent publishes the invention which may be a process or formula whose use is impossible to detect in the final product.
Trade secret status can be applied to protect non-patentable subject matter.	Patents must satisfy certain requirements of inventiveness, novelty, etc.
Trade secret costs may be maintained at the known level of required protection, but will vary depending on circumstance and will require the continued cost of maintaining secrecy.	Patents, are relatively predictable in cost, may be more expensive to obtain and can become very expensive, especially when filed in several countries.
Trade secret owner has worldwide rights. (Subject to various country laws.)	Patent owner has rights only where patent exists.
Trade secret licensor may have considerable latitude in restrictions which can legally be imposed upon licensors.	Patent licensors must take particular care not to violate antitrust regulations and/or to misuse the exclusive right of the patent.
Criminal sanctions, fines and/or imprisonment may be imposed under U.S. State Laws for the theft of trade secrets. In addition, the same remedies may be found for trade secret theft cases as are found for patent infringement.	Under patent infringement, the offender may be enjoined, required to pay damages (no less than reasonable royalty) and may even be held responsible for attorney's fees where the infringer shows "willful and wanton" conduct.

Trade secrets can be licensed, sold and transferred.	Patents are equally licensable, transferrable and saleable.
Regarded by some as lower in value since exclusive right is absent.	Exclusive right to make, use and sell and patent laws create greater value for some.

Duration Of Agreements

Duration of a trade secret agreement can be significant for both licensor and licensee. For instance, the U.S. Justice Department (Antitrust Guide for International Operations, January 26, 1977, Case F) has indicated that, "territorial restriction would likely be challenged if the length of the restriction (20 years) exceeded the time necessary for reverse-engineering of the technology, unless the parties could justify it as necessary to the technology sharing agreement." Duration is involved in both restraints on use and payment of royalties. For example, a licensee can be required to pay royalty on a license even after a trade secret has become freely available. Similarly, a license for non-secret know-how can require the payment of royalty for any specified period of time. In either case, if a time period (duration) is not specified, the royalty requirement could remain legally enforceable virtually forever.

A corollary to the question of duration is the use and maintenance of secrecy of trade secret know-how after the termination date of a license agreement. Various solutions to this question are possible and reasonable, depending upon the circumstances:

- Return all technologies and embodiments of same to the licensor.
- Cease all use of the technology.
- Continue license on a renewed basis with royalty requirements the same but reduced on a sliding scale over time to a minimum.
- Continue license with no royalty due but secrecy maintained.

In any case, it is obvious that the trade secret status is one to be carefully established and jealously guarded. The principal steps that should be taken to establish and maintain a trade secret have been outlined. At the same time, precautions against loss of the trade secret status must include:

- Publication in a patent that describes the trade secret.
- Public sale of a product that discloses the trade secret.
- Lack of security protection.

- Public demonstration.

Appropriate steps to insure trade secret status in respect to public disclosure should include:

- Confidential disclosure agreements with those to be exposed to the know-how.
- Stamping and marking of all material drawings, etc. that demonstrate the trade secret.
- Clear and monitored restrictions on any licensee using the trade secret knowledge.

With respect to duration, even of a know-how agreement, the case of *Aronson vs. Quick Point Pencil Company* (440 U.S. 257, 201 USPQ 1 (1979)) is most significant in the clear indication of why patent values and know-how values should often be separated. A contract was made in which an invention of Aronson was used by Quick Point with one royalty to be paid if a patent was issued on the invention and another (lower) royalty to be paid for as long as the invention was used if a patent was not granted. The court said that royalties should be paid indefinitely at the lower rate even though the secrecy of the invention was lost by its use as of the time the product went on the market. The moral of this story is that it is often very helpful to have royalties properly apportioned in accordance with the values of patents, trade secrets, know-how and engineering assistance.

Combined Use

For many firms a combination of patents and trade secrets offer the best solution for optimum protection. In the United States, patent protection does not start until the patent has been granted, leaving the period of patent pendency unprotected. The treatment of an invention or technology as a trade secret can offer protection not available prior to patent grant. Furthermore, a license established during this time could many times continue as a trade secret license even if the patent is not granted, as long as that license is drafted accordingly.

Perhaps even more important is the fact that many little details of manufacture or processing are of greatest significance for the best and most efficient operation of an invention or manufacturing procedure. These details often are not covered by a patent because they have not been perfected at the time the patent is filed. Often, applied know-how and special techniques make the difference between a profitable, efficient procedure and an effort which follows the patent and carries out the invention but cannot compete on the marketplace. Since trade secrets law requires far less uniqueness or inventiveness than patent law, these little details can be protected as trade secrets. And very often the technical manager will consider these assets as the most important part of the entire technology.

TRADEMARKS.

Definition

Chapter 4 of *Patent Law Fundamentals* by Peter D. Rosenberg (Bib. 19) gives an excellent definition of a trademark:

What a Trademark is:

> *A trademark is anything that is adopted and used to identify the source of origin of goods and is capable of distinguishing them from goods emanating from a competitor. As such, trademarks are subject to exclusive appropriation and are a monopoly of sorts.*
>
> *That different goods, be they the same or related products, bear the same trademark signifies to the public that the goods emanate from, or have passed through the control of, a common source, whether that source is the actual manufacturer or merely a distributor.*
>
> *Because consumers associate all goods bearing the same trademark with a common source, by placing the same trademark on different goods the trademark owner, at least by implication, certifies that the various goods are of like or equal quality. A trademark thus carries with it its owner's goodwill and reputation, and serves as a focal point for advertising.*
>
> *A trademark symbolizes and is often a shorthand representation of a source of origin. As such, trademarks serve as merchandising tools. Advertising involving an attractive or catchy trademark undoubtedly promotes sales.*

> *A trademark may consist of a word (i.e., a brand name)
> or a group of words (i.e., a slogan or a jingle), or a pic-
> torial representation or other symbol, or some other
> device (i.e., a configuration), or of a combination there-
> of. The color, pattern, or other dress of goods may serve
> a trademark function. Even musical sounds, as the NBC
> chimes, may constitute a service mark. The mere posi-
> tion of a label on a garment without regard to the con-
> tent of such label may constitute a trademark.*

Planning And Registration

Trademarks are another significant element for international protection
and licensing. In general, each country has its own trademark laws and
system for registration of trademarks.

United States:

In the United States, trademarks are protected by state and federal
laws, and may be registered at both the state and federal level. State
trademark registrations are generally processed and issued by the Office of the Secretary of State in each state. Trademarks may be federally
registered at the United States Patent and Trademark Office, which is
part of the United States Department of Commerce, Washington, D.C.

While unregistered trademarks may be protected under both state and
federal laws, federal registration of a trademark at the United States
Patent and Trademark Office on the Principal Register provides substantive and procedural rights which are not otherwise available to the
owner of an unregistered trademark or of a state trademark registration.

Prompt federal registration of a trademark is particularly important
since a federal trademark registration on the Principal Register issued
on or after November 16, 1989 provides the owner with a nationwide
"constructive use" date of the trademark as of the filing date of the
registration application. Such a registration should prevent a third party
from acquiring a common law right in the identical trademark, or a confusingly similar trademark, for related goods or services in a specific
trading area based on its use after the registration's filing date.

In the event the identical trademark or a confusingly similar mark is
federally registered by a subsequent user for related goods or services,

the registration may prevent a prior user from lawfully expanding his use of the trademark beyond the scope of his trading area which existed as of the date of issuance of the federal registration.

Without a federal registration, a person acquires common law rights in a trademark only in those specific trading areas in the United States where he and his licensees or franchisees were the first to use the trademark. Expansion of trademark use to a new trading area may be precluded if another person has already established in good faith common law rights in the same trademark, or a confusingly similar trademark, for related goods or services in that new trading area.

In order to obtain the broadest scope of protection available for a trademark which will be licensed or franchised, efforts should be made to seek prompt registration of the trademark at the United States Patent and Trademark Office once the decision is made to adopt the trademark.

Other Countries:

Ownership of trademark rights in one country does not determine trademark rights in other countries. For example, while a company may own exclusive rights to a trademark in the United States and a federal trademark registration, that company may be precluded from using and/or registering that trademark in another country as a result of another company's earlier use and/or registration of the identical trademark or a confusingly similar mark in that other country.

Many countries allow registration of a trademark before it has actually been used in those countries on the basis of the applicant's intent to use the trademark in the future. Also, in some countries, trademark rights may not exist in the absence of a trademark registration.

These factors represent a very significant danger since the registrant of a trademark in one country does *not* have to be the original owner or user of that trademark, or even the principal user in one or more countries. If this set of conditions appears to open the opportunity of trademark piracy or the unauthorized registry of trademarks, the assumption is correct.

Under some circumstances, an "International" trademark registration providing protection in multiple countries can be obtained based on the filing of one application with the United International Bureau for the

Protection of Industry Property, Geneva, Switzerland. However, neither the United States nor Canada is a member of this particular convention (the "Madrid Union"), and International registrations can only be obtained and owned by a company in a member country, such as Switzerland.

For a U.S. or Canadian company to obtain an International registration for a trademark, a foreign firm (affiliate or subsidiary) would have to be designated the owner of the trademark in those countries covered by International registration, and the application would be filed in the name of the foreign firm. If this is done, it would be preferable for the designated foreign firm to be a wholly-owned subsidiary. However, such an arrangement may not be wise since it puts the trademark into the hands of other ownership. For full control, it would be best to maintain ownership by the U.S. or Canadian company through individual country registrations.

Licensing Of Trademarks

It may be desirable to keep a trademark license separate from a patent or know-how license. Sometimes the standards of product quality in a given country will not be good enough to justify the granting of a trademark license, although the product itself may be satisfactory for manufacture and use under a patent and/or know-how license. In such a case, the reputation of the trademark as an identifier of quality products may be damaged by the use of the trademark in connection with a lower quality product. Here there is a clear advantage in having the trademark licenses separately from a patent or know-how license.

In the event a company is granted both a trademark license and a patent or know-how license, there is an advantage in having the trademark license separately terminable in respect to the technical or patent license. Most standard trademark licenses include a provision whereby the license may be terminated if the quality of the product distributed or sold by the licensee under the trademark does not meet the quality standards of the licensor. Often, the license will provide that the licensor must give the licensee written notice of termination, and that if the licensee is unable to cure the deficiencies in the product quality to the satisfaction of the licensor by the end of a period of time stated in the license, the license will be terminated. Following such termination, the licensee is not entitled to use the trademark. However, the licensee may continue to produce the product under the patent and/or know-how license.

On the other hand, a properly used and protected trademark will increase in value as time goes on. Thus, as the value of know-how decreases for a given license, as the patent approaches its expiration date, a good trademark may then be worth more than either know-how or patent. Under such circumstances, the continuation of royalties may depend upon the continuing strength and value of the trademark. Such circumstances might pertain when the quality standards of both product and trademark must absolutely be met in order to assure proper function. Final decisions as to whether to have a separate or included trademark license must be made on a case by case basis.

In some foreign countries, a trademark license must be recorded against the trademark registration by the appropriate governmental authority. Failure to record the license may result in the loss of trademark rights. It is therefore important that local laws with respect to trademark registration, use and licensing be considered prior to the granting of a trademark license.

Incidentally, it may also be a wise move on the part of a trademark licensor to insist on an arbitrary 60- or 90-day notice cancellation right. This right for the licensor can eliminate many difficulties in establishing proper quality or other standards. Such a right eliminates time and money consuming arguments on what is "reasonable" or "proper" or "suitable." The licensor has the final decision, and that is that. Such absolute control can be critical in dealing with a value as ephemeral as a trademark reputation.

A final caution is appropriate in respect to trademark licensing: Pay attention to franchising regulations. Part One, Chapter I, and Part Two, Chapter III, outline certain concerns in respect to trademark licensing vs. franchising. Attention to these cautions is essential.

Trademark Value

Trademarks are a vital, quickly recognized symbol of a corporation and its products and services. As such, trademarks should be protected and jealously defended throughout the logical markets or those parts of the world where the company or product may be recognized or found.

Improper use or handling of a trademark can result in its loss as an exclusive proprietary term. (Aspirin was once the trademark of Bayer.) A trademark should be used as a proper adjective followed by the noun describing the product, such as "KLEENEX facial tissues". The improper use of a trademark as a noun encourages the public to perceive the trademark as the generic name of the product, and not as a protectable brand name. Therefore, care must be taken in trademark registration and use by both proprietor and any licensee. Improper use, whether by mistake or deliberate misuse or use without permission, can cause the loss of trademark rights.(Bib. 30 and 31)

Incidentally, the tranlation of a good trademark or trade name from the English language usage to another language may present problems in product acceptance. Such problems are best avoided if they can be foreseen. For example, the sales of the Chevrolet NOVA were alarming low in Brazil. Then someone realized that "NOVA" in Portugese, the language of Brazil, means "NO GO". The Chevrolet NOVA was promptly given a different name in Brazil.

Trademarks can be an important aspect of a licensing program. They may be a useful but secondary part of a technical assistance manufacturing license, or they may be the basic essence and heart of a valuable license or license program. Regardless of position in a marketing or licensing program, trademarks should be properly recognized and carefully handled in order to obtain their maximum value and to offer their optimum recognition.

When licensing or planning to license a trademark in certain developing countries (such as Mexico, Brazil, other Latin American countries, India and others), care should be taken to study the local laws with respect to trademark registration, use and licensing. The regulations in some of these countries are such that it is possible to lose the right to use one's own trademark or at least to have any control over its use if certain regulations are not observed.

COPYRIGHTS.

The U.S. Copyright Law of 1790 was enacted to provide to originators of literature, art and music and to their publishers a legal protection against unauthorized copying (pirating) of their rightfully owned products. Subsequent developments have expanded the scope of copyright law to include many embodiments, including sound recordings and, of particular interest in licensing, computer software.

To describe the essence of copyright, the following example provides a good definition: If Jones took a trip through the New York City World

Trade Center and then wrote a book on his experience, he could obtain a copyright on that book. If Smith printed a copy of Jones' copyrighted book, or a portion of it, without permission, he would violate Jones' copyright and be liable for legal action by Jones to claim damages. On the other hand, if Smith took the same tour of the twin-towered World Trade Center that Jones took and subsequently wrote his own book describing the same things, he would not violate Jones' copyright. Smith would then be entitled to get his own copyright on his own book.

The Universal Copyright Convention was ratified in respect to adherence by the United States as of September 16, 1955. On this basis, foreign counterpart copyrights can be obtained by U.S. authors with essentially the same rights as in the United States. The "Berne Union" of 1886 is also in effect for most of the industrialized countries of the world, although the United States does not belong. Since Canada is a member, it is possible for a U.S. citizen to have a "backdoor" entry by simultaneous publication in Canada of his U.S. work. As opposed to individual copyright registration in each country, the Berne Union registry gives an automatic registration in all signatory Union members.

While it is not likely that there will be any significant licensing of copyrighted works of literature, music, etc., there are still corporate publications, demonstration, instructional and users books and the like that should be protected. Among other considerations, they still represent know-how.

Of great importance in the protection and licensing of corporate intellectual property is the protection of computer software through copyrights. In that context, copyright basics should be appreciated for their reference to software protection and licensing as discussed in Part Two, Chapter VI, "Computer Software — A Special Case."

Whether it be for literature (handbooks, etc.), music (advertising or publicity tunes and songs), pictures or computer software a copyright should be registered on any qualifying creative work. The cost of copyright registration is so low and the action so easy to take, that it does not make any sense for any company not to have that protection. It can be achieved by direct filing of very simple registration forms with the U.S. Patent, Trademark and Copyright office in Washington, D.C. It may be helpful to have the company's patent and trademark lawyer handle the matter. However, such legal help is not necessary in *every case.*

MASK WORKS AND SEMICONDUCTOR CHIPS.

The Semiconductor Chip Protection Act of 1984 helped to clarify many problems in this rapidly expanding technology. The following material has been excerpted from an article by Charles N. Quinn which appeared in September 1987 in *les Nouvelles*.(Bib. 77)

The United States has adopted a new form of intellectual property protection specifically directed toward protecting semiconductor chips. This new form of intellectual property protection was brought about by the Semiconductor Chip Protection Act of 1984, which added sections 901 through 914 to Title 17 of United States Code, the Title concerned with copyrights. However, new sections 901 through 914 are not copyright law sections and represent an entirely new form of intellectual property protection under United States law. Because these sections are not copyright law, court cases construing copyright law should not be used for guidance in construing the Semiconductor Chip Protection Act of 1984.

The key to understanding the new semiconductor chip protection now available under United States law lies in appreciating and understanding the definitions of a "semiconductor chip" and a "mask work" in the act. These two definitions follow:

- *A semiconductor chip product is the final or intermediate form of any product*

  Having two or more layers of metallic, insulating, or semiconductor material, deposited or otherwise placed on, or etched away or otherwise removed from, a piece of semiconductor material in accordance with a predetermined pattern; and

  Intended to perform electronic circuitry functions.

- *A mask work is a series of related images, however fixed or encoded*

  Having or representing the predetermined, three

dimensional pattern of metallic, insulating, or semi-conductor material present or removed from the layers of a semiconductor chip product; and

In which series the relation of the images to one another is that each image has the pattern of the surface of one form of the semiconductor chip product.

This new form of protection provides exclusive rights in both semiconductor chips and mask works. The protected rights in both the mask work and the semiconductor chip belong to the owner of the mask work. In other words, the owner of the semiconductor chip has no exclusive rights under this act; all of the exclusive rights relating both to the semiconductor chip and to the mask work belong to the mask work owner.

To obtain protection under the act, registration is mandatory. Registration must be made within two years of the first commercial exploitation of the mask work anywhere in the world. In other words, the "statutory bar" period so familiar to patent attorneys is two years. If registration is not made within two years of the first use of the mask work in a commercial context, no matter where that work is exploited, protection is lost forever in the United States.

The term of protection is for 10 years. The 10-year period is measured from the earlier of two dates. These two dates are (a) the date the mask work is first commercially exploited anywhere in the world and (b) the date the mask work is registered in the United States. It is important to note that the dates pertain to the "mask work" and that the registration is made of the "mask work." Registration is not made of the "semiconductor chip product," which the mask work was used to manufacture.

Finally, as noted above, one of the criteria for protection of a mask work under the act is that the mask work be covered by a Presidential proclamation. This portion of the act is intended to permit the President of the United States to grant interim protection to nationals of other countries, for chips which are not first commercially exploited in the United States, if the president finds that the governments of the countries in which these nationals reside are making progress toward enacting reciprocal legislation, providing chip protection for U.S. nationals whose chips are first exploited in such other country.

*****

Table II (page 10) summarizes the various forms of protection available for proprietary and intellectual property rights in the United States.

*****

Chapter VI

COMPUTER SOFTWARE — A SPECIAL CASE

Protection of intellectual property rights.

The origin and application of computer programs (software) have been widely discussed in respect to protection through patents, trade secrets, copyrights, trademark rights, and contract rights.

The Computer Software Copyright Act (Pub. L. No. 96517) was passed on December 12, 1980. It gives the author of a software program at least the protection of a copyright. Following the Supreme Court's decisions in *Diehr* and *Bradley*, the U.S. Patent, Trademark and Copyright Office has been more amenable to using patents on systems that include computer software as an element of the system. Software programs are additionally protected as trade secrets. At the same time, because of the needs for certain specific types of programs in various and unrelated industries, the maintenance of secrecy may be difficult. Some developers of software solve the piracy problem by applying an "automatic stop" provision into their programs, this "check point" coming into effect only when the program is being duplicated.

With all of the foregoing, it appears that the protection of computer software, one of the most significant industrial/social developments since the industrial revolution, is better defined under U.S. intellectual property rights law than any other national law. Myrick and Sprowl, writing in the *American Bar Association Journal*, (Bib. 24) concluded:

> *The Supreme Court appears to have resolved the conflict between law and technology in favor of granting patents to those who invent by feeding instructions into universal machines as well as to those who invent by assembling specially designed parts.*

However, patentability has been a very difficult case to prove for most software.

Alan C. Rose, partner in the firm of Poms, Smith, Lande and Rose, (Bib. 25) points out that in 1978 the Court of Custom and Patent Appeals (CCPA) rendered companion decisions (*In re Freeman* and *In re Walter*), which expressed a two-step test for patentability of a computer program. The first step is to determine whether the claims are directed to a formula, equation or mathematical algorithm. If so, it should be determined whether the claims, taken altogether, completely preempt the mathematical algorithm from use in all fields. An affirmative answer to the first with a negative answer to the second would indicate patentability. Mr. Rose concludes:

> *. . . if a claimed invention produces a physical thing . . . the fact that it is expressed in numerical form will not make the claim nonstatutory. To summarize . . . the presence of novel structural limitations or novel process steps where there is a physical change of state or quality tends to make a claim patentable.*

A good case for the simultaneous protection by both trade secret and copyright is made by New York attorney Roger C. Milgrim.(Bib. 26) He summarizes this subject as follows:

> *The advantages of doing so are not inconsiderable. First, protection of the software trade secret safeguards the underlying ideas through use of contractual licensing and related techniques. Layering on copyright protection as well provides protection from third-party recipients who have not signed agreements restricting use or disclosure. Moreover, the availability of statutory remedies, which in cases of willful infringement can go as high as $50,000, are a meaningful deterrent, as is the possibility of a judge ordering the offender to pay the plaintiff's attorney's fees.*

For a summary of protection on an international basis, see the *International Computer Software Quick Reference Table* (Bibliography No. 94).

Licensing considerations.

Because the licensing of software is so important and has developed so rapidly, the paper of Gerald E. Lester "Fundamentals of Computer Software Licensing" is reprinted below. This article does an outstanding job of setting forth the principal considerations for those who are considering software licensing. It was written for teaching an LES (U.S.A. and Canada) course. Additional and more detailed information may be found in Bibliographic references 27, 77, 78, 79 and 90.

This paper is directed to lawyers and non-lawyers who are new to the discipline of licensing in general and software licensing in particular. Since the paper was drafted in preparation for a 15 minute LES video presentation, the view of only the licensor has been adopted to address in a straightforward manner what I perceive to be key licensing concerns.

In the licensing of computer software from either the licensor's or licensee's perspective, it is necessary to understand (1) the subject matter being licensed; (2) the business objectives to be achieved; (3) why licensing is preferred over other forms of technology transfers such as an outright sale; (4) the intellectual property rights that are available to the licensor in the subject matter to be licensed; (5) the types and scope of grant clauses that may be used in the license to achieve the business objectives; and (6) the protections that may be included in a license to reduce any risks associated with the licensing venture.

Briefly, a computer software program evolves from the desire to perform a function. The method of achieving the function, referred to as an algorithm, may be described by means of a logic flow diagram which is used to guide a programmer in creating an ordered list of instructions. The instructions may be in a near conversational or high-level language such as Fortran, or in a more technical machine-conscious language. The high-level languages are referred to as source code, which is easily reverse engineered to discover the underlying algorithm. Through the use of a translator such as a compiler or an assembler, the source code may be reduced to a lower level machine language, object code, which is not as easily reverse engineered.

An ordered set of instructions in either source code or object code form is referred to as the computer program. The computer program in an object code or binary form may be stored in the memory of a central processing unit ("CPU"), and thereafter fetched instruction by instruction by the control unit of the CPU to be decoded and executed. The control unit also sequences the operation of the CPU in response to a microprogram or firmware written in an even lower-level language referred to as microcode. The microprogram is comprised of microinstructions representing elemental operations, and is usually embedded in a semiconductor chip internal to the control unit.

The computer programs that normally are marketed may be broadly categorized as system software or application software. System software includes operating system software such as Digital Equipment Corporation's VMS System, which enables a CPU to function and become a general purpose machine. Application software operates under the operating systems software to provide solutions for end user applications.

In marketing computer software, the owner may desire to exercise more control over software copies than can be exercised in merely selling the copies. Under a license agreement, the licensor may grant such rights and impose such limits on use as are allowed by his ownership interests. Generally speaking, restrictions on use are valid if they do not enlarge the rights granted to the inventor/author/owner under the patent and copyright laws, and if they are not unreasonable restraints of trade under the antitrust laws.

A license agreement grants a licensee the right to engage in conduct that otherwise may infringe the licensor's intellectual property rights. Although the patent, copyright and trademark laws are set forth in federal statutes, the license agreement is a legal contract that is interpreted in accordance with accepted principles of state contract law. It is essential, therefore, that the contract principles of definiteness be applied in defining the licensed subject matter and in stating the rights granted to the licensee. It also is recommended that the intellectual property rights under which the license is granted be defined. An example definition is as follows:

Intellectual Property Rights shall mean:

i) All rights, title and interests in all Letters Patent and applications for Letters Patent, Industrial Models, Industrial Designs, Petty Patents, Patents of Importation, Utility Models, Certificates of Invention, and other indicia of government issued invention ownership including any reissue, division, continuation or continuation-in-part applications throughout the world now or hereafter filed; and

ii) All rights, title and interests in all trade secret rights arising under the common law, state law, federal law and laws of foreign countries; and

iii) All chip mask work registration rights, copyright rights and all other literary property and author rights whether or not copyrightable; and all rights, title and interests in all chip mask work registrations, copyrights and copyrighted interests; and

iv) All rights, title and interests in all know-how and show-how whether or not protectable by patent, copyright or trade secret laws.

Upon defining the licensed subject matter ("LICENSED TECHNOLOGY") and the INTELLECTUAL PROPERTY RIGHTS under which the license is to be granted, consideration should be given to the type of license that shall be required to meet the business objectives.

License agreements generally fall into one of three categories: (1) exclusive license; (2) nonexclusive license; (3) sole license. Upon granting an exclusive license, the licensor is barred from using the licensed subject matter and from granting licenses to third parties. The granting of a nonexclusive license, however, does not bar either the licensor's use or the licensor's granting of nonexclusive licenses to third parties. A sole license is generally understood to raise no bar against the licensor's use of the licensed subject matter, but rather to raise only a bar against licensing third parties.

For clarity in a license agreement, it is strongly recommended that the license type be defined to remove all doubt as to what is intended.

The following summary of license issues is not intended to be exhaustive. Rather it addresses regularly occurring problems in the software licensing discipline:

1. Be specific as to the forms and embodiments of the computer software program that is being licensed.

2. In the grant clause, be specific as to the intended use, place of the intended use, and the time period during which such use is to take place. A licensor usually will want to control the number of copies that may be made, and the distribution of such copies.

3. Add a set of negation clauses following the grant clause to address those uses that are not intended. Negation clauses clarify the scope of the grant clauses, and preempt any unintended implied licenses that otherwise may be construed from the grant clauses.

4. Set royalty fees to be paid by the licensee only after conducting a market survey and determining the cost of introducing the product into the marketplace.

5. All copies of the licensor's computer program should be required to carry legible notices of the licensor's copyright, trade secret and trademark rights.

6. The protection offered to a licensor by the intellectual property laws is only as good as the ability of the licensor to detect a misuse. The licensor should consider including an audit provision in the license to allow inspection of records and verification of copy distributions.

7. Consideration should be given to the rights of the parties in the event of a termination of the license.

8. In view of the increase in concern over a licensor's product liability exposure, a limitation of liability clause, a limitation of warranty clause, and an indemnification clause indemnifying against third party suits arising from the licensee's use of the computer program should be given careful attention.

9. Because contract laws vary from state to state, the law under which a contract is construed may be critical. Thus, a choice-of-law provision should be added that calls for the application of the law of a state with which the licensor is familiar.

* * * * *

Chapter VII

AGREEMENT TERMS

ESSENTIAL AND NOT SO ESSENTIAL

A well written license often appears to the business person to be over-burdened with legal provisions and protective devices. In some cases this opinion will be correct. Entire negotiations have been badly damaged by overprotecting, legalistic agreement drafts. With a tendency in many countries toward the "two-page license" or a very general "statement of understanding," some people react strongly against severely worded or multiple-page agreements. However, a poorly written agreement with inadequate protection can be worse than no agreement at all. The following terms are generally found in licenses involving technology and the application thereof. It is not the purpose of this summary to render opinions on the legality or the necessity of these provisions or to indicate provisions that are unnecessary. It is hoped, however, that the comments will indicate the importance of many terms relative to the license as a business instrument. In addition, it should be emphasized once again that the licensor and licensee through counsel in matters of patents, taxes, national and international law must be familiar with all the pertinent laws. This statement applies regardless of the countries involved. A knowledgeable negotiator should be familiar with the laws pertaining to both parties.

As an aid to alert the negotiator of international agreements on potential misunderstandings, LES International, the parent of LES (U.S.A. and Canada), has developed the *International License Negotiating Thesaurus*, a special listing of words and phrases often used in patent and technology license negotiations. This listing is available through LES (U.S.A. and Canada), Inc. (A3 as noted in Bibliography No. 95).

There are, of course, certain statements and terms that are required.[1] Some are particularly appropriate for specific countries and/or specific situations:

- Recitation of parties, full name and location.

- Recitation of intent.
- Recitation of other parties or corporate connections as appropriate.
- Effective date and place for contract.
- Signature date.

In addition to the above, the following comments are directed toward certain standard terms and reflect a businessman's attitude and experience:

License Grant is clearly the most important aspect of any license. Properly written and backed up by the proper definitions, the license grant will establish clearly for all those concerned exactly what is to be licensed and what rights are being extended to the licensee by the licensor. An unclear or improperly understood license grant clause is a guarantee for problems and disputes between licensor and licensee.

Definitions of key terms should be clearly and succinctly written, and used sparingly. Properly written definitions save arguments and possible arbitration proceedings or litigation. Be sure that all critical terms are clearly defined and understood. Among terms which should be defined are:

- Licensed Product.
- Field or Territory.
- Subsidiaries.
- Improvements.
- Net Sales.
- Items Peculiar to the License Subject.

Exclusive or Sole License category can be an essential element for determining license limitations and establishing requirements for other elements in the license. A grant of exclusivity is a grant of all rights on the licensed subject within the territory licensed. A *sole* license is one that establishes the licensee as the only licensee while the licensor or proprietor of the technology retains the right also to exercise or practice that technology within the licensed territory.

Field of Use: It is usually proper to license a patent to one licensee for one use and to a second licensee for a different use, providing that the fields of use are, indeed, separable and noncompetitive. A good example of such a licensing operation is given in "Overview of Licensing and Technology Transfer" by Homer O. Blair, published by North

Carolina Journal of International Law and Commercial Regulation, Vol. 8, No. 2:

> *As a practical matter, it is often easier to define the technology involved by a field definition because technology may be useful in a wide variety of different fields that are not related. For example, a number of years ago, Itek developed technology for use in photographic processing. The technology was licensed to different companies in the microfilm field, the medical xray field, and the industrial photographic field. The equipment used to process xrays is quite large because the normal medical xray film is over a foot wide. The equipment used to process microfilm, on the other hand, is quite different. The markets are different and the companies involved in these businesses had no interest in branching out into other areas of business. Each licensee, however, wanted an exclusive license in its field so that Itek would not license the competition.*

Territorial Rights in a license may be best specified in respect to patent or trademark coverage.

Duration for any license, in respect to royalty payments, is as long as possible for the licensor and as short as possible for the licensee. The life of existing patents is a term often specified. Licenses can also be made for a given term with automatic renewal conditions effective unless termination notice is given. Obligations and rights intended are often as important as royalty payments for both licensee and licensor. This fact can be critical when one or more patents expire, along with the concurrent royalty obligations. Are there continuing obligations and rights intended by the licensee or licensor? Such continuation should be described and defined.

Patent Coverage, provision for future patent inclusion, rights of original patentor to licensees patents, all of these provisions are important for any license that involves patents.

Patent Infringement Notices and *Patent Defense* provisions are often desirable features to protect against later disagreement or misunderstanding.

Patent Indemnification and a guarantee against infringement of third-party patents are features often requested by licensees. They should be regarded with considerable apprehension and care by licensors. With varying patent laws in different countries and present proliferation of patents throughout the world, it is extremely risky for a licensor to undertake any assurances of this sort. If it is essential or proper to give some guarantee or support in these areas, the licensor should be careful to limit the liability to a point of reasonable commitment, lest it exceed the value of the license. From the licensee standpoint, maximum or unlimited protection is most desirable.

Patent Warranty: If possible, the licensor should disclaim any warranty as to the validity or utility of the licensed patents, certainly with respect to foreign patents. The reason for this policy position is that it is difficult to impossible to predict the judgments and actions of foreign patent courts. Also, it is difficult to determine absolutely that no other conflicting patent coverage exists in another country. If some sort of warranty is essential, it should be very carefully spelled out and any payments under warranty limited to a percentage of the royalty return.

Trademarks are often licensed separately. Their use should be covered thoroughly, with the licensor's right to control the nature and quality of the goods sold under the trademark ensured by stringent inspection procedures and an arbitrary cancellation privilege for the licensor if the products do not satisfy the licensor's standards. For example, in the event the licensee's products fail to meet the licensor's quality standards, the licensor may unilaterally cancel the trademark license by providing the licensor with written notice of such cancellation 60 or 90 days in advance. It may be that the trademark and its reputation is the strongest part of the license. Under such circumstances, the major license, and royalty obligations, might appropriately include the trademark for the length of time that it is valid and renewed when appropriate. Conversely, it should also be specifically stated what trademark use or privileges are not included in the license, thus protecting against misuse or unauthorized use.

Trademark Defense and notices of third-party infringement are vital to any firm with a trademark. If a trademark is registered, it must have value. If a trademark is not defended, it immediately loses its value. Provisions in this field should be drafted accordingly.

Quality Requirements or *Diligence Provisions* are often included in licenses of all types. They can serve some purpose of emphasis on good intentions. They may be virtually worthless in proving compliance with agreement terms, except when a warranty is given or unless specific control mechanisms are built into the agreement.

Royalty, Know-how Payments, Technical Service Fees are necessary in any license that is designed as a profit-producing business arrangement. Lack of such payments may cause regulatory government bodies to search for hidden compensation outside the provisions of the law.

Exchange Control provisions should always be present in any agreement involving parties headquartered in different countries. The danger of currency blockage or exchange limitation is always present with international licensing.

Accounting and Reporting provisions are not only necessary, but also should be enforced. When licensor and licensee are good friends and in close rapport, the formalities of accounting and reporting may be "overlooked" or treated casually. Such treatment is a bad practice. Whether used or not, it is also a good idea to provide for the licensor's right to inspect the licensee's books of record.

Taxes Each license should clearly state who pays what taxes.

Technical Assistance is essential for know-how licenses and is expected for most patent licenses involving elements of know-how. The licensee is well advised to be sure that such assistance rights are adequately provided. Conversely, the licensor should be careful that the technical assistance required does not exceed the proper coverage of the license, or the extent of compensation for such service.

Guarantees and Warranties: If possible, the licensor should disclaim any warranty as to the accuracy or usefulness of his know-how and the quality of the goods that can be made by using that know-how. When the licensor does not have full control of those using the licensed product or process, it is difficult to be certain that the job is being done right. If a warranty must be given, it should be very carefully spelled out, together with provisions for remedy or damages in case of breach. If any warranty is given, the provisions on definitions, technical assistance and coverage become critical. Of course, the effectiveness of technology transmission becomes the key to avoiding breach of any quality warranty on the part of both licensee and licensor. Equally significant is the adequate definition of what is or is not a satisfactory product or result. A detailed discussion of this subject is justified for many process licenses or turn-key plant contracts.

Warranty protection and assurance can be useful to both licensee and licensor. A licensee must have some assurance that the technology he is buying has the utility he anticipates. The licensor must have some means of protection against improper and inadequate application of the technology. The purpose of any valid license is to transfer from one party to the other a useful technology or industrial property right. Appropriate use of this property implies both adequate transfer of knowledge and sufficient application of effort to apply the knowledge. A proper warranty provision can offer a method of determining whether the licensor's transfer has been adequate and whether the licensee's performance has been correct and sufficient (Also refer to Bibliography No. 96).

Improvements and Grantback like technical assistance are often considered valuable to technology transfer licenses. Many times it is desirable to specify not only the inclusion of improvements, but also the extent of same. Grantback refers to the rights of the licensor to the developments of the licensee. The granting back of licensee developments to the licensor can be very important. Generally, grantback is desirable, and it should always be equitable.

Visitation of licensee to licensor and vice versa is normally expected in any working license for transfer of technology. To avoid misunderstanding and even awkward liability situations, visitation rights should be carefully defined, including:

- Times to be convenient.
- Duration of visit.
- Frequency of visit.
- Rights of host to require return of a visitor who becomes undesirable for one reason or another.
- Rights of host to refuse entry to persons who are undesirable from the host's perception.
- Requirements of host to provide safe working areas.
- Liability in case of injury.
- Fees and per diem charges.
- Licensor rights to inspect operation without invitation.

"Most Favored Nation": is a term applied to a clause stating that the licensor will modify an existing license to equal any more favorable

terms granted later to another party on the same subject. Such a clause is to be avoided if possible, being accepted by the licensor only when necessary. Such a term has the effect of limiting the ability of the licensor to negotiate different terms for another license on the same technology when the circumstances of the other license may be very different. If such a clause is necessary, it should be limited as much as possible, i.e., to apply only to certain monetary payment provisions.

Arbitration/Forum and Dispute Resolution: Provision for arbitration of disputes is highly desirable, particulary for international licenses. Often the arbitration clause is limited to the location and rules, i.e. International Chamber of Commerce, American Arbitration Association, I.C.C. or U.N. rules, Governing Law, etc. While these considerations are valid, the first question, in case of disputes, is: "Where will they be adjudicated?" Usually, the licensor will want the courts of his country to have exclusive jurisdiction because he knows them and knows what to expect. For the same reasons the licensee wants his courts to have exclusive jurisdiction. Often the fairest compromise is arbitration in a third country. Before making a decision on this point the parties must know whether either or both courts will accept the exclusive jurisdiction of the other, or will recognize arbitration. If, for example, the licensee's courts will not recognize an ouster of jurisdiction in favor of another court or arbitration, the licensor is left with the choice of (a) not making the license, or (b) accepting the licensee's forum. The I.C.C. rules are generally acceptable, but they are incomplete in certain respects, leaving some questions more or less to chance. American Arbitration Association is today specified in an increasing number of cases. To be correct in every way, this clause should provide who the arbitrators shall be (nationality, language and education or professional qualifications), how they shall be chosen, where they shall sit, and what rules of evidence and procedure they shall follow. Very often the place of arbitration is chosen for the rules of procedure, e.g.: "in the city of Zurich under the rules of procedure of the Canton of Zurich." Other rules commonly used are the I.C.C. or the U.N. rules.

The foregoing is obviously directed principally to international licensing. At the same time, certain aspects are important to domestic licenses by reason of differences in laws between provinces or states, as well as the desirability of selecting arbitration rules. It should also be noted here that various developing countries and communist countries have special rules and customs with respect to resolution of disputes.

Governing Law: Licensor country or licensee country or a third country can be chosen for application of substantive law and/or as a forum and for enforcement. Such preestablishment may be desirable to establish a proper basis for dispute resolution. However, there is a general, unfortunately mistaken, assumption among both some U.S. businessmen and some lawyers that knowledge of another country's laws is not essential because, through a "Governing Law" provision, the law of the licensor's country may be made to govern. While it is true that it may be possible to choose the licensor's law for the general interpretation of the license agreement, one cannot avoid the application of at least that portion of the licensee's law that its courts consider to be in the domain of public policy. Unfortunately, "public policy" covers many vital areas such as antitrust, exchange control, taxation, security, patents, trademarks and import-export controls. Moreover, the licensee's law on industrial property may make highly advisable certain particular provisions on warranties, termination and royalties. Too often, the choice of licensor's law is an exercise in self-delusion. Thus, if the forum court will be in the licensee's jurisdiction, it is better to accept the licensee's law and make sure that the licensor is fully protected under that law.

The foregoing statement pertains especially to the interests of the licensor. It is also important that the licensee be assured of adequate protection, especially if the governing law is to be that of the licensor or of a third country. If arbitration is agreed upon (a desirable move) care should be taken on both sides that the arbitrators and the governing law are matched in understanding.

Language: The choice of language can be of great importance and may depend on the choice of forum and law. For example, if the forum is a Spanish court or a board of Spanish arbitrators, the agreements might best be in Spanish. Many U.S. licensors, however, who have worthwhile technology, have proficiency in only one language. In that case, they may be justified in requiring that, for their protection, the language of the license should be that with which the licensor management is familiar, regardless of the familiarity of the legal counsel involved. Incidentally, bilingual agreements (agreements in which two languages are considered to be equally legal and effective) create more problems than they solve, both in negotiation and as a source of later disputes.

Waiver or excuse from one or more conditions of the agreement as mutually agreed by both parties, should be considered. In any such clause it should be clearly stated that no single waiver can be taken to be effective for subsequent events not specifically covered.

Modifications or Changes: No change in any license should be made effective until it is made in writing and formally notified to both parties as provided under *Notices* (see following page under *Notices*). This fact is so important that it should be stated in the body of the contract and not in a separate letter. Then, failure to observe the requirement would be a breach of the contract.

Force Majeure is the clause that permits changes in the contract when conditions of the contract change through no fault of either party. A force majeure clause eliminates some arguments. However, the wording and meaning must be very carefully handled. Many countries will not accept the definitions commonly approved in the United States for events beyond control such as "Act of God," "strikes," etc.

Approval of an agreement is often required by licensee governments. It should be incumbent upon the licensee to obtain all necessary approvals, with any penalties accruing to the licensee if a necessary approval is not obtained. In addition, it is often desirable to specify a time within which the approval must be obtained.

Licensor governments may restrict the technical information that can be transmitted. If a sensitive area is being covered, the licensor may be well advised to provide that the licensor cannot be in breach if prevented by government regulation from furnishing all or certain elements of the licensed technical information. Likewise, the licensee may wish to have provisions changing royalty obligations or other requirements if all required technology is not available.

Notices and technical correspondence are often sent to different offices of licensee or licensor. Confusion, misunderstanding and even the accusation of failure to provide certain information may result from incorrectly addressed notices and/or technical communications. Therefore, it is essential that each party knows the address to which official notices and specifically defined technical information must be sent, in addition to routine correspondence.

Sublicense Rights refers to the right of a licensee to sublicense or transfer the licensed technology and rights to same to a third party. Sublicensing rights can be very important to both licensee and licensor.

Assignability: This provision is a very useful protection device for both licensor and licensee, especially the former. Each party is likely to want to have control over the other party's ability to transfer or assign the license to a third party.

Bankruptcy: The conditions for continuance of the license in case of bankruptcy ("winding down" in British terminology) of either licensee or licensor should be covered as an "insurance" provision. Both licensor and licensee should be protected in the right under license in case the other party should be subject to bankruptcy proceedings.

Notice of Breach of any term of the agreement should be given to the party in breach promptly (within 30 days of the time that it is discovered). Normally, a period of 30, 60 or 90 days is then given to cure the breach, following which, if the breach is not cured, the license may be considered to be terminated. The termination may be made subject to arbitration, or other predetermined remedies can be applied.

Termination reasons range from automatic at the end of a time period to various circumstances of breach by either party. Termination on notice of a period of days (30, 60, or ?) is also a good provision to have as an alternative to certain undesirable circumstances that may not be preventable, especially in the case of trademark licenses with respect to quality requirements. Adequate description of termination conditions is essential, as is a thorough understanding of their meaning by both parties.

Schedules refer to a review of details, appendix material and ancillary details which should be included as part of the agreement (such as training conditions, etc.), but which are not logical parts of the contract terms. All of this detail material can appropriately be made a part of the agreement by specific inclusion as a scheduled item at the end of the contract. Another way of including a review of applicable standards, specifications, training requirements, warranties, etc., is to have a "Technical Agreement" that covers all the technical points agreed upon, and which is included by mention as a part of the controlling "Commercial Agreement."

Summary.

In the words of Tom Arnold of Arnold, White & Durkee, Houston, Texas (Bib. 57):

Suffice here to say that the various clause concepts are as keys upon a piano. Each may be played loudly, softly, staccato or with lingering resonance; and each may be played in solo melody or in chords with the others in infinite variety; they constitute a piano upon which infinite varieties of transactions can be played.

And the playing of them well, requires some careful attention to the skills and strategies of negotiation. . . . For the man with the imagination to figure out and use both his own and his potential partner's legitimate needs and greeds, and to figure out how to satisfy them on both sides, will produce good contracts whereas others will fail. And oftentimes, it is the burdens of your own side's restraints that are harder to work with than those of the (opposing) negotiator.

* * * * *

FOOTNOTES:
[1]See Bibliography 93.

Chapter VIII

SPECIAL NATIONAL RESTRICTIONS

It is not the purpose of this book to detail all the considerations for licensing and joint-ventures as controlled by special national regulations. However, it is appropriate to call attention to the several sources of information on such restrictions and to point out that knowledge of these restrictions may either open the way for profitable agreements or determine valid reasons for not entering into an agreement.

General cautions.

In the field of licensing and joint-ventures, one of the countries most publicized for its regulations has been Japan. Shortly after World War II, this nation established the Ministry of International Trade and Industry (MITI). Today, many people credit MITI with substantial responsibility in the growth of the Japanese economy. Many other countries have tried to use the same system some with more success than others. In all cases, however, the result is the same for the licensor going into a country with such regulations. The additional restrictions limit the type of agreement and extent of profits that can be obtained through licensing.

This sort of restriction is prevalent in certain developing countries, in many communist countries and in nations that feel they must take control of industry to assure maximum benefit to their overall economy. The licensor in a so-called "technically advanced" country is cautioned to examine all such regulations that may apply, as well as the possibility of further restrictions. While these limitations need not prevent the licensor from making a suitable arrangement, they certainly indicate a need for serious study and possibly a definite limit in the overall technical commitment.

Prior to negotiation, the licensor should review thoroughly the regulations and restrictions of the licensee's country. These laws and limitations may have a serious effect on terms to be negotiated.

Information is available on certain countries in *The Law and Business of Licensing* (Bib. 1). The various publications of Business International, Inc. cover the subject of national regulations and restrictions in various news items and in certain special reports, particularly the publication *International Licensing and Trading* (Bib. 12). Other publications that can be very useful have been issued by the Hong Kong and Shanghai Banking Corporation (Bib. 29) and Price Waterhouse & Company (Bib. 28). Fund for Multinational Management Education (FMME) in New York City conducts various seminars on different countries and maintains available reference publications based on these seminars. United Nations Industrial Development Organization (UNIDO), P.O. Box 300, A1400 Vienna, Austria, has considerable information available on regulations of developing countries through its Technological Information Exchange System. And last, but by no means least, the U.S. Department of Commerce and Department of State, Washington, D.C. have considerable information available through their various country "desks." It is suggested that these information sources be investigated prior to first entry into any country with a license or joint-venture contract.

Communist countries.

Technology offered by the USSR, certain Eastern European Block countries and The Peoples Republic of China (PRC) has been interesting and useful to certain companies in the U.S., Canada and other non-Communist countries. At the same time, those countries have a genuine desire to acquire technologies not presently available at home. The USSR and East European countries have useful patent systems. The PRC patent law became effective April 1, 1985. Its coverage is similar in many ways to those of other communist countries. Coverage of past patentable inventions, also certain chemical and pharmaceutical technology, must still be covered in the license contract in the PRC.

Licenses can be made on the basis of patent coverage, patent plus know-how, or know-how alone. Payments can be made in various combinations of lump-sum fee, fixed annual fee, running royalty or combinations thereof. Generally speaking, however, lump-sum fees or fixed annual fees are preferred, and many times it will be necessary to incorporate a countertrade arrangement into the deal. Each country has one or more specialized trading companies specifically responsible for the field of licensing such as Licensintorg for the USSR, Licenzia for Hungary and CNTIC for China.

With all this expressed interest, it must be remembered that the communist system is one of state-regulated enterprises in R&D, in manufacturing, in distribution. Each industry or field of endeavor has its own ministry, enterprises and committees for manufacture of products and study of special subjects as well as its own research and development centers. In order to establish a meaningful contact, therefore, it is necessary to determine the proper organizations, enterprise or committee for contact in the technology of interest. In any case, licensing efforts are likely to be time-consuming and frustrating. Experience of those who have concluded licenses in Eastern Europe and/or China indicates that one needs both technical competence and monumental patience. The "Three P's" of dealing with the communist world are still: Patience, Patience, and Patience.

It is not the purpose of this review to give a detailed report on the subject of licensing to the communist world. However, there can be genuine opportunities in licensing "in" and "out" with these countries. As is obvious, while this text is being written, the many political and economic changes in Eastern Europe are likely to have significant, though presently unpredictable, effects on this entire situation. Further information on these areas of interest are available through the U.S. Department of Commerce; the U.S. State Department; Business International, Inc.; and other organizations and offices in contact with the communist countries. Past experience still emphasizes the need for the "Three P's". Do not forget them.

Developing countries.

In terms of technology needs, developing countries often need equity and/or manpower support (management and technical assistance), as well as a direct license without equity. Governmental bodies and private organizations have created useful contacts between those who "need to know" and those who have the knowledge. Typical of this work are the programs of UNIDO and IESC (International Executive Service Corps, P.O. Box 10005, Stamford, CT, 06904, U.S.A.). "Good citizenship" practices by the licensor can strengthen its position in many developing countries. The motives for such action can involve direct profit and an interest in social and technical development of an area.

Some developing countries offer tax advantages and favorable investment regulations when a licensing project promotes a further development that has been established as a need for the country. Such a project could thus be profit-oriented and keyed to a social development program. Capitalizing know-how to establish an equity position can be one advantage for a licensor. Favorable tax treatment or even a tax holiday for a given period of years may be negotiable if the project is important for the country.

Some countries, however, present problems of local government regulations. Examples are repatriation of funds, payment of fees and royalties, percentage of equity permitted, management control, export requirements. These aspects should always be investigated and negotiated as necessary. Admittedly, there are developing countries that are regarded as being unstable politically or as being unfriendly in a business and/or political sense. For these reasons, a proper political risk analysis should be made of the political and social patterns of the country, predicting, insofar as possible, the stability and accountability of the proposed host country. U.S. Overseas Private Investment Corporation (OPIC) in Washington, D.C. provides country information kits covering all types of data on conditions, laws, regulations and customs on more than 100 developing countries. The OPIC phone number is 1-800-424-6742.

* * * * *

Chapter IX
NOTES FOR NEGOTIATING

Negotiation is 70% preparation and 30% knowing what to do. The side that seems to be smarter may just be better prepared. The following comments are a series of observations of the author and many other licensing professionals.

*****

Negotiation has been written about in books and papers and has been the subject of numerous seminar programs.(Bib. 34, 35, 36, 37, 38, 50) For the licensing professional, the ability to negotiate successfully is essential. The licensing professional in international business must know how to deal with different cultures, foreign business practices, and sometimes strange habits, along with the natural differences in personality found with all people. For further details of negotiating, see the publications listed in the Bibliography.

The "Fairness Doctrine" is of utmost importance for a successful license (see Part One, Chapter I, Definition of a good license). The final negotiated agreement must balance the values of the license subject and the needs of all parties in such a way that a "win-win" situation results. (Both sides win.) This achievement is best reached through proper preparation, sufficient knowledge of the subject, and an appreciation of the interests, needs and backgrounds of all the negotiating parties. To reemphasize, good negotiation is 70% preparation.

Preparation.

Adequate preparation for a license negotiation implies a thorough study and analysis for the proposed agreement. Such a study should consider:

- The types of license available and desirable.

- Advantages and disadvantages of the proposed license.

- Corporate objectives and planning.

- The technology (process, product) to be licensed.

- The potential licensees or licensors for the desired technology.

- Important factors for a license.

- Specific forms needed or desired.

- Compensation costs, operation costs and other financial requirements.

- Protection of intellectual property rights.

- Joint-venture possibilities.

- Legal restrictions.

- Warranties and guarantees.

The study and analysis should be completed before negotiation starts. The following summary is a reminder of the headings and principles under which preparation should be made:

- Purpose of License: Be sure to know what all negotiating parties want to achieve.

- Subject of License: A full, accurate definition of the license subject must be available, one that describes adequately without giving up valuable know-how. (Is a confidential disclosure agreement needed? If so, is it ready?)

- Evaluation of License: In considering the purpose, try to establish values of the license for all parties.

- Parties to the License: Study the proposed parties, determine their needs, their probable hopes, potential contribution to the license, national characteristics or prejudices, organizational restrictions (especially in regard to communist or developing countries).

- Team Work: For a major project, there should be a negotiation team, that carries the project from beginning to end. The composition of the team should include persons who can speak for the company in regard to the following interests:

  > Licensing or Joint-Venture Leader.
  > Technical.
  > Commercial.
  > Legal.

If possible, there should be both an "optimist" and a "pessimist" in the group. In other words, the team should have a pessimist who can say, "I do not think we should take this action because. . . ." The optimist can then counter with "Yes, but I think we can make it work right if we can have. . . ." These assignments can be useful in developing certain negotiation objectives.

At the same time, the licensing leader must be the only person to make commitments or give definite judgments. The above listing includes a lawyer, although in many foreign negotiations the lawyer should not initially be a part of the negotiating group. Foreign business people are sometimes "put off" by the presence of a lawyer. Thus, the legal side should not be physically represented until actual contract wording is being discussed. Notwithstanding the above, a lawyer should always be a part of the team that studies and reviews the license proposal.

- Location Arrangement: If it is possible to decide where the negotiation will take place, select a comfortable location with business-like atmosphere. Assure privacy, comfortable temperature, good lighting, good seating arrangements, adequate table facilities, available writing material, blackboard, easel, etc. Coffee, tea, and soft drinks should be considered for the morning and for mid-afternoon. Do not leave any arrangements to chance.

Entry readiness.

After a thorough preparation, the following should be checked to be sure that the negotiating team is indeed ready:

- Homework: Have all items under "Preparation" been completed?

- Have prepared for use as needed:

    Outline Terms.
    Confidential Disclosure Agreement.
    Letter of Intent.
    Complete Agreement (not to be used at the start).

- Analysis of the other party's probable needs.

- Summary of the other party's probable methods.

- Review of the other party's negotiating principles, practices and personnel, as far as they can be determined.

- Conduct a dry run with the full team based on all known factors and assumptions.

- Be sure your company policy is understood by all team members in all aspects.

- Know your limits of flexibility. Don't be greedy, and don't be charitable.

- Be adequately rested going into negotiation.

- Be sure that all members of the negotiating team are "properly" dressed (i.e. respectful of local conditions).

- Be sure that all members of the team are fully informed of local customs, prejudices, specific personal prejudices of other party.

Negotiation.

Negotiation is the exchange of ideas with others with respect to values which are variable. When values are absolutely fixed, negotiation becomes persuasion, and that can be much more difficult.

For Preliminary Session: For any major contract never expect to accomplish complete negotiation in one meeting, perhaps not even during the first visit of several days. The first session is the "get acquainted round." It is possible that the only accomplishment at first will be the establishment of good relations, a most vital first step. At most, expect the following:

- Start with good news.

- Exchange basic information.

- Check out original assumptions (if possible), including the needs of the other side, collective and individual.

- Establish reasons and desires for the parties to reach an agreement.

- Test for flexibility of the other side.

- As an initial step, it may be appropriate to try for an agreement in principle — establish that both sides do want to reach an agreement. Everyone should win something.

Strategies and tactics.

Strategies should be based on the analysis of the situation, needs of parties and the strengths and weaknesses perceived. Situation analysis should be carried out before and after each negotiating session, and strategies adjusted if necessary.

Often, the best strategy for negotiating with people from other countries and cultures is *not* to spend a lot of time preparing to counter anticipated arguments and presenting the situation as seen from your own business viewpoint. Rather, the first strategic decision should be how to position the proposal, how to "package" the proposition, to appeal most to the other side. This approach can range through technical assistance considerations, training programs and marketing consultation.

As a part of the approach strategy it may be wise to consider whether the basic negotiating stance should be competitive or cooperative. For example, the Soviets will always approach the negotiation table on a competitive basis. Many times it is the competitive approach that wins the more favorable deals. But, many developing countries, and others, respond better to an approach that is basically cooperative. In all cases, remember that the initial approach *must* be one of mutual respect, friendly cooperation and trust. These are magic words, and they should be used (or their equivalents) in every first meeting. This posturing is virtually a required ritual for the first session of many license negotiations.

Tactics are the techniques used by the members of the negotiating team (not necessarily the same for each member, e.g., playing the optimist, pessimist game). Individual tactics may involve:

- Use visual aids where possible — pictures, movies, product samples, graphs but watch out for cultural problems. Adapt the visual aids to suit the local conditions.

- Present the subject so as to answer the other party's emotional needs of security, comfort, friendship, self-esteem and esteem of others.

- Ask good questions. Determine ahead of time where you would like more information, try to get background in every way possible. Make sure that questions are sensible and useful, not frivolous or inconsequential. The best time for some questions may be when you are away from the negotiating table, with the opposite party in a social situation, such as at meal time.

- Be a good listener. Try to let the other side do most of the talking. You are not learning anything when your mouth is open. Take notes while listening. Clarify unfamiliar terms. Don't interrupt with commentary.

- Be aware of cultural practices that may or may not signal a message, i.e.: Arab desire for closeness (breathing on you). Also be aware of cultural "don'ts." (In Arab countries, don't show the bottom of the foot, such as with crossed legs.) In all countries, take your time cues from the other party, and don't refuse hospitality unless it is necessary to do so for personal or moral reasons (coffee, tea, slivovitz or (?)).

- If the other party has a wrong idea, or must be corrected on an important matter, be diplomatic in correcting and try to leave the other person with a way of changing that still saves face. ("Perhaps you were not aware of these facts . . ." "This new situation has just recently been known . . .")

- Give face whenever possible. All people enjoy the esteem of others, and it is always helpful to compliment, to treat as equals, to recognize accomplishments and abilities when this can be done smoothly and diplomatically. The reverse is also true. If you want to upset the negotiations, the best way is to contradict, criticize and question the abilities of the other party. Avoid an appearance of the latter unless you have a specific tactical reason for doing so. Basically, causing a disturbance is not a good idea.

- Go behind the scenes. Make special efforts, without being obvious, to be informally acquainted with the other side. Very often negotiations can be stalled by a local constraint, which will not surface in a formal negotiation session, but which can be solved by informal discussions. In some countries, the formal negotiation is merely a session for developing the final form for what has been worked out ahead of time.

- When there are opinion differences, try to "use" the ego of the other party as opposed to challenging the ego. (Example: "Perhaps you could explain your reasons for . . ." instead of, "We cannot accept your position on this matter.")

- Formulate negotiating problems in such a way as to lead the other party to solutions favorable to your needs.

- Price high and concede slowly; do not appear anxious to settle "at any price."

- Compensation:

  He who aspires too little,
     is rewarded with little

  When the price is too high,
     the customer leaves.

  Use good cost analysis when
     it is helpful.

- Avoid overkill on any subject.

- Determine negotiable points ahead of time. Try to evaluate potential trade-offs in contract terms. Don't concede points too easily. Make sure that the concessions you get are really valuable and are worth the concessions you are giving. Consider having certain requirements in your proposal that you are willing to give up in order to gain concessions on other points from the other party.

- Flag the difficult points for later reconsideration and proceed to the next area of discussion. Achieve overall agreement in principle and then solve the difficult problem areas.

- Avoid an indefinite time frame. Not setting a deadline can lead to no agreement at all.

- Be careful of lightning-quick decisions. Sleep on it overnight.

- If the other party has legitimate derogatory facts about your product, process or company, present them first yourself in the best possible light to defuse the other party's argument.

- Be aware of the other party's nonverbal signals, intentional and unintentional (body language), and recognize their significance.

- Use deliberate body language to express opinions when appropriate. Otherwise, avoid body language and facial expressions that give an undesired tip-off to your feelings.

- Good-guy bad-guy techniques can be useful. One member of the team states a proposal or a hard position. A second member then states a modified or softer position (which might be acceptable, but could still get "more" than a straight argument of facts).

- "Sucker Punch" is a technique that can be used successfully. But watch out for it, and be skillful in using it. Usually, a "sucker punch" is a statement or question to which the other party quickly reacts (often without thinking) with a response that reveals information that might not normally be available. (Example: "When we consider your labor rate at $X, then the cost will be $WXZ." Quick reply: "But our labor rate is not $X; it is $Y!")

- Be alert to dirty tricks, physical discomfort during negotiation, half truths, falsified evidence. If this is found to prevail, do you really want an agreement?

- Maintain a team's united front in the negotiation and save disagreements for the caucus room. Make sure that disagreements within the team are not informally passed on to the other side during evening social periods or at other outside contacts. Also be careful about private team discussions in public places (restaurants, bars, elevators, waiting rooms). There are likely to be unidentified listeners who understand what you are saying.

- The advantage of not having the President or other top company official present for negotiations, is that the chief negotiator can always fall back to that reference for a final approval on a difficult point.

- Keep good negotiation notes and records along with the original project file, and refer to them during private strategy sessions.

- Take time to think. If necessary, request a caucus or recess for your team. Big and little breaks are essential to thinking through all the aspects of an ongoing negotiation session. Sometimes it is even useful to go to the bathroom for a moment's break.

- Lone-wolf negotiations are undesirable. Don't do it against a skilled team. If it is necessary to act as a single negotiator, try to do so "one-on-one." In any case, *be well prepared*.

- Be prepared to walk away from the entire negotiation, if necessary.

- If you are terminating negotiations, make a clean break with goodwill on both sides. Part company as friends, because a year later your situation may change, and it may be possible to reopen negotiations. If so, you will want to be welcomed at the negotiating table not challenged as an opponent.

Performance.

Above all, remember that *every* negotiation is conducted on three levels: (1) subconscious (cultural background, personal preferences, etc.); (2) emotional (needs, prejudice, feelings) and (3) logic and reason. Try to avoid the reaction of "Don't confuse me with facts. My mind is already made up."

Sometimes, a party will come to a negotiation determined to take every possible advantage, fair or unfair. If this attitude cannot be changed, it must be dealt with, and a good negotiator will have done enough "homework" to determine the best "pressure points" to use on the op posite party. He will be able to judge the best moves, appropriate pressures and the right time to walk away. Remember, a bad agreement may be worse than none at all.

* * * * *

PART THREE

Stories of licensing success

From Milwaukee to Melbourne
and
From work benches to audio systems

"There are almost as many objectives for licensing as there are licensing agreements"

John A. Quelch
Harvard Business Review
May-June, 1985

Chapter I

LICENSING IS NOT JUST "HIGH TECH"

Licensing is not restricted to "High Tech". Many people think about the romance in the new technologies of computers, software, electronics and biotechnology. However, the world still operates with very ordinary "Low Tech" products and processes. Some of these are brought to commercial reality through licensing. John Moorehead, President, Technology Search International, Inc., is involved with the day to day licensing of many technologies. In two, short, real-life stories, he describes the successful commercialization of a new travelling lawn sprinkler and a home mechanics' auto ramp. Neither case is high tech; both demonstrate good business use of licensing. In each case, fictitious names are used.

Royalty is paid in product.

"Waterit," a U.S. company, produces quick-disconnect hose fittings from injection molded and extruded plastic parts. Its product line is sold throughout the United States with mass merchandisers, such as Sears and K-Mart. It has roughly 300 employees, and its annual sales are about $35 million.

A few years ago, Waterit became aware of a special lawn sprinkler design by "Mowit," a Scandinavian manufacturer of lawn mowers. Waterit learned that Mowit was unhappy with its local injection molder and also wanted to reach the U.S. market.

Mowit and Waterit got together and established a commercial and technical license which suited both. For $35,000 Mowit transferred to Waterit the tooling for making the sprinklers, along with full rights to the U.S. market. Royalty to Mowit is paid in finished sprinklers made by Waterit, transferred at an agreed price. Mowit also has the right to purchase additional sprinklers at an agreed price. Mowit covers the Scandinavian and other European countries for their market, and Waterit covers North America. Both parties are happy with a situation that perfectly suits their needs.

* * * * *

Metal stamping shop works with individual inventor. Both succeed.

Proving the old adage that any idea is a good idea, if you can use it, the Wecandoo Company found success by working with an inventor who had a good product idea, a patent and rough tools, but no manufacturing facilities. Wecandoo is a 25-year-old metal stamping shop with 115 employees, and an annual turnover of about $20 million, all on job shop work. The management of Wecandoo was anxiously looking for a good product that would fit its facilities, offer a steady base income and would not require a large sales force. Fortunately, they found an inventor, Mr. I.M. Ready, who had "the right product" and no manufacturer.

A few months earlier, Mr. Ready had seen his initial licensee go bankrupt for business reasons not related to the special invention and he had nothing but a cancelled license and a large box of tools that might or might not be useful. The product was a unique auto ramp for use by home auto mechanics. Mr. Ready had a utility patent on the ramp and a design patent on a special container for packing and shipping and/or storing the ramp.

The agreement negotiated covered a $25,000 initial payment to cover technology transfer and residual tooling, plus a royalty of 5 percent on the sales of the ramp for the life of the patent. Wecandoo spent another $25,000 on additional tooling and shop preparation and established an excellent business. Product sales are handled by a system of sales representatives who answer under contract to the President of Wecandoo. The sales representatives sell to automotive specialty supply companies. The market has been analyzed at $1.5 to $2 million. Wecandoo is delighted with the results and so is Mr. Ready.

* * * * *

Chapter II

CONCRETE BLOCKS
THAT LOOK LIKE CUT STONE[1]

A license program that is a principal source of income
By Robert W. Dean, Jr., President
Designer Blocks, Inc.

In early 1980 I was Sales Manager for Best Block Company, a time when the construction industry was in the depths of depression in Milwaukee. I was trying to apply some of the marketing theory I had learned while earning my MBA at The University of Wisconsin at Milwaukee. The theory was product differentiation. The idea was that good companies differentiate their product line from that of their competitors. I was searching for a product that would differentiate our product line from the competition. I was thinking about some buildings that I had seen that were laid in stone in an offset, random pattern, and I thought to myself why not split block in an offset pattern. That idea is now the essence of Designer Blocks technology.

What is the Designer Blocks technology?

Blocks utilizing our technology are made in pairs. This is accomplished by removing a division plate in a mold box. In place of the division plate we install a core bar with spikes attached to it to make small holes between the pair of blocks. The blocks are hardened or cured. Soon after, the blocks are taken by conveyor to the automatic splitter. In order to make our blocks, a set of offset splitting knives are installed. The offset is 0.75". The small cores separate the sections and allow for controlled splitting at different planes. The result is the random pattern that I was searching for, a cut-stone texture. Basically our patent, which was granted in 1982, is for splitting blocks on different planes along the face of the block.

Who was the incubator? What is the relationship?

Let's step back a bit to the time when I went to the owner and president of Best Block with my idea about the new block and also . . . with the idea for a new company. Now, we hadn't made a block and here I was discussing national promotion. It was a very critical time. I thought I had something hot and the management of Best Block Company sensed it, but most importantly they encouraged the new idea. It's easy to imagine how they could have reacted. . . . like "we'll take possession of your idea now." But somehow, in their infinite wisdom, they knew that would stifle me and the idea. Besides that, these fellows believed strongly in free enterprise. So we set up the framework for a business that has benefited all of us. The product has been extremely successful for Best Block. The owners and president of Best Block Company became stockholders in Designer Blocks, and I got the opportunity to develop my idea.

How did we find our licensees?

The primary source for information about the concrete block industry is a trade association called the National Concrete Masonry Association. This association holds a major convention each year which is attended by 2,000-3,000 people. I was informed by my patent attorney that the patent would issue about four weeks before the convention. We purchased exhibit space at the convention and scurried like crazy to put an exhibit together. At the convention I met with other suppliers who suggested the best prospects in the various regions. I also reviewed the program to see who chaired committees, served on the executive board, etc. to get an idea of who the leaders in the industry were. We also advertised in the program that this was a newly patented product. So, many of the leaders also sought us out because they knew how important it is to be first with new products in their respective markets. Others were interested in simply tying up the new idea.

At any rate, ours was the first new product in the industry in several years and we were able to generate a lot of interest at the first convention we attended, even though the industry was in a pretty severe recession. As of May, 1988, Designer Blocks has licensed 56 concrete block manufacturers in the United States, Canada, Australia and Ireland.

What are the key terms of our license agreement?

- We offer an exclusive license to manufacture and sell our products in an exclusive territory. We evaluate each market separately but on average the market would be a 150 mile radius, closer in the East and wider in the West. This relates to the distance that one can economically ship block.

- We provide the equipment the licensee needs to make the blocks. This equipment is leased by us but maintained by the licensee. The idea here is that if the license terminates, we want the equipment back. We also want to make it easy for the licensee to get started.

- We charge a minimum monthly royalty in combination with a per-unit royalty that kicks in after the minimum is reached. This provides us with steady cash flow, discourages someone from trying to tie up the license and also addresses the concern about counting units.

- The licensee is given the exclusive option on new designs.

- The contract term is three years and is automatically rolled over for additional three-year terms if both parties wish to continue.

How do we support our licensees?

One thing is for sure. We support our licensees more than I ever imagined we would! I think one misconception that those new to licensing have is that you sign people up and sit back and collect money. If you sit back, you won't be collecting long. Our support is as follows:

- We offer our licensees technical support. We provide a manual with step-by-step instructions for manufacturing our products.

- Our biggest effort, however, is made in marketing support. First, we provide a manual showing how to sell and promote the Designer Series blocks.

- We offer our licensees a variety of brochures and a set of slides showing a wide variety of applications for our product.

- We coordinate national advertising such as through Sweet's Architectural Catalogue.

- Three times a year we direct-mail our *On Site* newsletter for architects. We imprint the licensee's logo, do the mailing, and collect the reply cards.

- We also send letters continually to prospects developing new projects. For these letters we subscribe to a service that provides the leads.

What have I learned and what would we do differently?

- Licensee performance is rarely as good as a licensor would like. I expect the licensees to concentrate more on our product than they think they can. In slow markets I may encourage sublicensing.

- I think the *exclusive* license was the way to go, but there are drawbacks. Only one company in a territory carries the banner for you. Some buyers are adverse to the exclusivity.

- Our company is changing out of the entrepreneurial stage into more of an established business. Our challenge now is to maintain the network that we have built.

- Finally, I am noticing that the relationship with the licensee changes from a partnership in the beginning to more of a traditional customer relationship as time goes by.

* * * * *

FOOTNOTES:
[1]Paper presented in Milwaukee, Wisconsin, May 10, 1988, at licensing seminar, sponsored by the Wisconsin members of LES.

Chapter III

A BUSINESS BUILT UPON ACQUIRED TECHNOLOGY

By G. Parks Souther, President
Parkson Corporation

Parkson Corporation was founded in 1960 as a supplier of evaporation equipment to the chemical process industries. In 1964, it was acquired by Parker Pen and in 1967 A. Johnson & Company, Inc. purchased it from Parker Pen. (A. Johnson is part of the Swedish Axel Johnson Group based in Stockholm.) At this time, Parkson's sales were less then $1 million per year and the company was unprofitable.

I joined the Company in 1970 with the mandate to look for additional products for Parkson to market and sell. I have a Chemical Engineering background and had spent eight years at Dow Chemical in new product/market development work.

We spent a year evaluating products which could be licensed, and ultimately licensed a compact gravity sedimentation device, the Lamella Gravity Settler, for the separation of solids from a liquid. Such a device had significant cost/space advantages over conventional clarifiers which are routinely used in water and wastewater treatment.

We began marketing the product in 1971 and by 1974 had passed the break-even point. In 1976, we licensed the Magnum Press, a solids dewatering machine and in 1978 the Dynasand Filter, a continuous backwashing sand filter. All three licenses were with the Axel Johnson Institute for Industrial Research, Nynashamn, Sweden, another member of the Johnson Group. However, they were independent from us, and we had to argue long and hard to obtain these licenses.

These three products gave us a base business in the water/wastewater treatment market of $10-15 million per year, but we wanted to continue to grow. (The evaporation product line was divested in 1975.) In 1980 we licensed a Japanese bar screen, the Aqua-Guard, and in 1982 a rotating screen, the Roto-Guard (from Sweden), and the Oxycharger, a static aeration device from a U.S. textile firm. In 1984 we continued to expand the aeration business with a license for the Wyss Flex-A-Tube aerator. The licensor was an Ohio resident who did not want to build his own firm to exploit this invention. In 1985 we licensed the Biolac System from a West German inventor.

Currently (1987), we are continuing our search for additional products. Parkson has grown to be a very profitable company with sales over $25 million per year through the licensing of cost-effective products to our marketplace. We could not have afforded the time and expense of developing our own products in the early 1970s. It is interesting to note that firms that dominated the market when we started, but did not introduce new products, have pretty much faded from the scene.

* * * * *

Chapter IV

GROWING WITH THE TECHNOLOGY[1]

The story of company growth through an informal licensing program
by Mr. Tony Andraitis, President
EMI Corporation, Jackson Center, Ohio

In 1968 I started the Plastics Equipment Division of Erico Products, a multi-division industrial equipment company serving many industries. Management of Erico had decided that plastics would be the material of the future and that equipment to manufacture plastic parts should be designed, engineered, manufactured and sold by Erico. My job was to market these products.

Our first year was rough. With only a few products, our sales were about $100,000, roughly $900,000 below forecast. The Chairman of the Board for Erico said, "Okay, Tony, do what you have to do to get new products in your line. They should be better and more cost effective than competitive products. We will stand behind you with the finances."

As of June 1969, all we had was a list of new products that were needed by our customers. After prioritizing these products, we contacted outside sources which had good design, engineering and manufacturing capabilities. Our basic program was this:

- We have a good idea for a particular product. We are confident we can sell it to the plastics industry.

- Can you help us in design and manufacture of a final product.

- We feel the selling price for this product should be "X" dollars.

- Our gross profit should be "Y" dollars.

- Our sales forecast is "Z" units per year.

- We want you to make a fair profit manufacturing this product.

- Are you genuinely interested in working with us on the development of these products.

The answer was usually "yes." As I think of our accomplishments back in 1969, and the early 70s, what we were really doing was licensing in without a formal contract. The manufacturer (licensor) charged us (licensee) on a per part basis for their technology and development costs. In return they had the exclusive rights to manufacture the product or products for us and naturally they would sell the product or products only to us.

For us the arrangement worked well. There were only a couple of times when things didn't work out. One such case involved a product that we sold in large quantities to a major automotive supplier. For some reason the company we had the informal agreement with decided to bypass us and sell direct, thereby keeping for itself the extra money which was our margin. Unfortunately for that company, the management did not know how to market the products profitably, and they had considerable difficulties. We never had to resort to any litigation. The company in question simply gave up. We eventually shook hands and each went in different directions. After much difficulty, we established an agreement with another supplier. Today this particular product is one of our leading products, but we all had many sleepless nights during that time. I will admit this type of problem is the largest pitfall in the informal licensing in of technology (i.e. licensing without a written contract). (Editors note: Arrangements such as this should be avoided at all costs.)

The 1970s were rewarding to our company. Our growth continued, our customer base expanded and new products kept coming out. We had sales agents throughout the United States, four direct salesmen, and we were fast becoming a recognized supplier of accessories to the plastic injection molding industry. New products were the key to our growth.

In 1972, our customers were telling us that there was a need for belt conveyors to be especially adapted to injection molding presses. There were hundreds of conveyor manufacturers then and still are, but we had to find one that was flexible enough to work with us, listen to us and accept the application requirements. The company we chose was a small, successful company in Ohio. The timing of the product introduction was perfect, and the technology we received from the conveyor manufacturer was excellent. The engineering know-how and experience saved us months of R&D. And most importantly, we were able to penetrate the marketplace with the first belt conveyor especially designed for plastic processing within three or four months of our initial meeting. With the exception of a few hold harmless agreements, this arrangement was again one of the "informal" licensing agreements.

In 1980 I had my first experience with a formal licensing contract. A customer of ours developed a product called a shut-off nozzle. He had applied for a patent and the patent was still pending. The customer wanted us to take over the patent application and pay his patent attorney about $5,000. The resulting patent would then become our property. Our customer would do all the manufacturing and we would pay him a royalty on sales with some very high minimums. We would be responsible for defending the patent. My feeling, however, has always been that the greatest liability for a small businessman in owning a patent is defending that patent. After several months of negotiating, it was agreed that the customer would retain the patent and manufacture the product. We would then sell the product. We made an informal agreement on that basis. Through the past five years the customer has made a very handsome return on the manufacture of the product. We have made a good return on the selling of the product. The customer has updated and improved the patent through those years, and two years ago we purchased the patent for a price in excess of $100,000. My point here is that patience paid off for both of us.

To continue the EMI story, we bought out our conveyor supplier in 1979, and in 1983 Erico sold the plastics equipment division to me and a few other key employees. We then had our own company and have continued the same philosophy as in the past.

In 1987 we were approached by S.C. Johnson & Son, Inc., of Racine, Wisconsin, to license-in its technology on two products which it had developed and felt were saleable to the plastics industry. S.C. Johnson had developed these products to improve the profits for its in-house operations. Patents had been granted on the products and Johnson now wanted to license-out the technology. After an initial general meeting at the Johnson facility, a second trip was made to discuss the products, their engineering and their function. The next meeting was scheduled to be at our facility within six weeks, and we believe the Johnson people were impressed with our operations. Both parties then started to work on subjects such as sales forecasts, royalties, minimums and how to defend the patents. Correspondence followed that meeting and a formal licensing in agreement was signed. This action was a major step for EMI as it was the first formal licensing in agreement we had made with a large company. Today we are very pleased to have these new products. The assistance, upgrade of design and information from S.C. Johnson, the licensor, has been outstanding. Acceptance of the products by our customers has been good, and we are proceeding with great enthusiasm.

If you are considering licensing in technology, you must be sure that the technology or product is saleable to the marketplace. Can it be manufactured and brought to the marketplace and sold at a fair profit to you? Can the person or company licensing out be sure that your group will do justice to the technology and that they can make a fair profit? If all of these questions can be answered "Yes," then you probably have a good reason for licensing-in.

* * * * *

FOOTNOTES:

[1]This paper was presented to the licensing seminar of the Wisconsin Group of LES in Milwaukee, Wisconsin, on May 10, 1988.

Chapter V

SOLVING THE PROBLEM OF DAVID VS. GOLIATH[1]

How a small business stepped into the world
of licensing; income is 7% of revenues
By Thomas Nunes
Technical Director, Advanced Circuit Technology, Inc.,
Nashua, New Hampshire

Printed circuits built of bendable, twistable plastic film and copper facilitate the production of a host of electronic systems from satellites to the household telephone. In 1976, spurred on by a spark of innovation and a jolt of entrepreneurial spirit a group of young, determined New Hampshireites set out to manufacture a unique form of flexible circuits. Dubbed "Sculptured Flexible Circuits," these unique devices reduce weight, facilitate assembly, and make possible today's ultracompact electronic packages.

In the mid 1970s electronic interconnection technology was relatively stagnant. Accepted techniques included discrete wire, parallel conductor ribbon cable, and flexible circuits. The most expensive factor in using flexible printed circuits had been that associated with termination hardware attached pins, expensive connector systems, and/or other expensive "add-ons." Rational deduction yielded the conclusion that it would be economically feasible and practicable to incur higher raw material costs in the fabrication of circuitry when that increase resulted in significant savings by eliminating additional hardware and equipment and/or a savings in manufacturing labor for the manufacturer.

The idea of Sculptured Flexible Circuits (SFC), distinctive flexible circuits that acquire, transport, and redistribute electronic signals without the need for additional pins or connectors, created the impetus for forming Advanced Circuit Technology, Inc. (ACT). SFC are literally carved out of copper by ACT, using conventional chemical milling processes. Three-dimensional chemical milling permits termination devices to be manufactured as integral parts of each circuit. A typical SFC may have rigid pin-like fingers to receive signals, flexible conductors to transmit them, and raised lands with octagonal holes to terminate the interconnection. Reliability is increased because the circuit and interconnection hardware are made from one piece of copper.

When ACT began marketing this new product, one of the first problems encountered was the reluctance of prospective customers to buy a new device available from only a single source. Paranoia also set in — a Goliath might "steal the idea." A new, inexperienced company couldn't afford to defend its patents against a large multinational corporation. ACT needed a second source to manufacture our products, one that might be willing to share the expense of protecting our patents. Furthermore, ACT might reap added benefits by having another company manufacture with the ACT process. Licensing was seen as a potential answer to our prayers.

Novices to licensing.

As novices to the world of licensing, the question was, How to select a potential licensee? A strategy began to unfold: go to the major customers of ACT and ask whom, besides ACT, they would like to see manufacturing our products. These recommendations were narrowed to a select group of three. Each company was scrutinized using a host of objective and subjective criteria. Armed with letters of introduction from customers, ACT set out to sell its first license. With patience, a little bit of luck, and a lot of grit the ice was broken and a license sold to a company that on the surface appeared to be a major competitor. This licensee was selected due to an excellent reputation in the industry as well as technical competence. Fear of competition in the domestic market was outweighed by needs for a second source and someone to share the burden of potential patent defenses. A tidy technical transfer sum and an attractive royalty schedule sweetened the pot.

Now that ACT had a domestic second source to help proselytize (and sell) the benefits of our technology, inquiries started to come in from Europe and the Far East. ACT was too small to afford an export sales staff that could work with customer engineers in the far reaches of the universe. How could product be exploited overseas? Again, the licensing lamp was lit. It was the ACT belief that carefully selected manufacturers overseas would be better able to market products that require continuing, one-on-one liaison between product designers and customer engineers.

Initially, the decision was to seek three licensees in Europe, two in Japan, and one in Canada. As other countries and regions developed their electronics industries, the plan was to enter into those markets. For example, ACT has recently sold a license to an Indian firm and has targeted Taiwan, Hong Kong, Korea, Israel, Australia, the Peoples' Republic of China, and Brazil for future licensing efforts. In the process of working with our Japanese and German licensees, ACT was also able to sell nonexclusive licenses in Singapore and Taiwan.

Alternatives to licensing also were explored, including joint-ventures. Analysis revealed that joint-ventures are the only practicable alternative to licensing that would help to build the market for ACT products outside of North America. ACT has entered into one joint-venture to produce one of the products of our R&D, and others are being seriously considered where the potential return warrants the investment of time, money, and our technologies.

In each of the ACT agreements care has been taken to craft provisions that create a family of manufacturers producing the same products. Members form a kindred bond resulting in their providing support to each other. Licensees each have developed manufacturing, handling, and packaging techniques. By mutual consent, that knowledge is shared with ACT and the other licensees, increasing profitability, and improving product quality and reliability. ACT licensees possess a common bond, technology, and a common burden of producing quality products. Experience has demonstrated a willingness to exchange ideas, experiences, and knowledge through correspondence, and in a new forum the ACT annual licensees' meeting. The licensee's success is truly ACT's success. We learn from each other.

Organizing for the work of licensing.

In the process of marketing licenses, negotiating them, and servicing our licensees, it was necessary to look at the license program organization. As with many growing high-tech companies, ACT appeared to be in a constant state of reorganization. One of those structural adjustments linked R&D, Licensing, Product Development, and Model Shops under one umbrella organization dubbed the Advanced Technology Group.

An identifiable licensing function was established to find new licensees, service and monitor the efforts of existing licensees, and otherwise market new technologies that were constantly being developed.

Make no bones about it, licensing is time consuming and sometimes tedious. Anyone in a small business contemplating getting into licensing should ask lots of questions, especially from others who have experience in licensing. Many small businesses have difficulty learning how other small to mid-size businesses have employed licensing in strategic planning.

Licensing is not really something companies usually advertise. It's also expensive. If a company guesses that licensing will cost an amount X, one might be prudent to double or triple the amount. Foreign travel is expensive. So are the Telex, telephone, courier and other charges one encounters. And, oh, those legal fees!

Frustration also enters into licensing. There is nothing more tedious than waiting for the answer on the end of a Telex. Will they buy, or not? Do they need more information. Have I learned enough about the particular cultural values, mores, etc. to properly deal with the people in that country? Have I assessed their needs adequately? Did I overprice the technology? Underprice it? Why won't he give me an answer?

Plan for it and try it.

Why get into licensing in the first place? A small to mid-size business contemplating a licensing program needs to carefully examine whether its product is one that effectively lends itself to the process. Is there potential for 100% or more growth per year? Is the product one that needs "in-country liaison" to deliver quality product? Will you have problems meeting customer demand? If your answer is yes to these questions, consider trying licensing.

Most small businesses cannot afford to hire a corporate attorney and/or a licensing executive. How do you get started? If you're the president, sales boss, or technical manager, talk to someone who has done it. Businessmen (and women) love to discuss their prowess and acumen. Pump their brains. In addition, several reputable firms provide consulting services and act as license "brokers" bringing together those who would sell with those eager and willing to purchase. Of course a fee/commission is charged. But these companies are often the key to making a deal.

Make licensing an integral part of your strategic planning. It's as important as your marketing, production, R&D, or other corporate functions. Maintain credibility by maintaining an effective intellectual property program. Look at licensing as a long-term commitment: one cannot view licensing as a means to achieve short-term goals. There is income in licensing, but it's over the long haul, not the short run.

Licensing is not the exclusive province of large business. There is plenty of opportunity for small and mid-size businesses. Be prepared for lots of hard work. But, the results are well worth the effort in terms of remuneration as well as the opportunity to meet and engage in business with people throughout the world.

* * * * *

FOOTNOTES:

[1]"Licensing and the Small Business," from *les Nouvelles*, June 1986.

Chapter VI

POOLING BRAINPOWER

Unforseen advantages of a service program over the years.

An example of international cooperation, licensee service and coordination was described in the August 10, 1970, issue of *International Commerce* (now published as *Business America* by U.S. Department of Commerce). Allied Tube and Conduit Corporation, the firm whose experience is outlined in this account is still carrying out an active program with strong licensees in India, the United Kingdom and the Netherlands:

"We cast our bread upon the waters and received a bakery in return." That's the way A.J. Raymond of Allied Tube and Conduit Corporation, Harvey, Illinois, describes his firm's experience in licensing its process to overseas manufacturers.

In fact, Allied received such a wealth of process-improvement information from its overseas licensees that President Ted Drengel decided to create a continuing technical dialogue with them through annual research conferences. "This way we multiply our research staff in direct proportion to the number of companies to whom we grant a license," says Raymond.

He admits, "The first meeting of the clan is a lot like a newly married couple inviting all the in-laws over to the house for dinner. To avoid international heartburn, every course must be prepared in advance. Leave nothing to chance.

"A first and most important decision is site selection. Just because they're your licensees, don't limit yourself to holding the conference in your general office. They have no doubt toured your facilities many times during contractual negotiations anyway."

Raymond visited each licensee 11 months before the conference to discuss with their management and research directors what project reports each would present. Project lists were drawn up for each company and mutually agreed upon. Research was assigned based on the needs and experience of the licensee.

Another important step is to make the host licensee jointly responsible for the success of the venture, according to Raymond, who also maintains that, "One of the most important by-products of the first meeting of licensees is that they get to know one another and get along together. So, the social aspects should not be played down."

Allied's first conference spanned four days. During the two days allocated for technical seminars, 12 research papers were presented. Of these, three were delivered by Allied's research staff and nine by the licensees.

The afternoon session of the final day was used to announce 48 new research projects to be shared among the licensees and Allied. Reports on these projects will be presented at the second international conference in the spring of 1971.

Looking back on the first conference and planning the second, Raymond commented, "It was a real international brainstorming session."

Eighteen years after this article was written, Mr. David Shott, Vice-President of Operations for Allied Tube, says that, while the format of license conferences has changed somewhat, the basic results are still the same. According to Mr. Shott, even though royalty returns are always important, some of the most valuable results of their program are non-monetary the exchange of new ideas, shared trade secret manufacturing know-how, opportunities for special equipment and a generally better understanding of their industry market on a worldwide basis.

* * * * *

Chapter VII

A CASE HISTORY: 'WORKMATE'[1]

By M.J. Roos

*How the patent system and licensing provided protection
and financial returns to the inventor of Workmate, a collapsible workbench.*

There is little doubt that the invention of Workmate arose from the fact
that Ron Hickman, the inventor, was, and still is, an ardent do-it-yourself enthusiast. He wanted to be able to do simple woodworking jobs in
a home that had no workshop.

By 1968 Hickman was convinced that he had a product (a collapsible,
portable workbench) that was patentable and would have great practical utility. He therefore had the first provisional British patent specification filed and approached various British manufacturers including
Black & Decker, Stanley, Record, Burgess, Polycell, Salmens and
Marples. In most cases he managed to obtain interviews at a fairly
senior level and made a full presentation of the hardware then available,
and demonstrated the jobs it could do. In all cases the idea was
rejected. In many instances the reason given was that it had no potential.

As a result of these failures to find licensees Ron Hickman decided to
produce the bench himself. The manufacture of the parts was con-
tracted out but the assembly and marketing were done by a small team
recruited for the purpose. The original Workmate appeared in 1968,
and within four years sales had increased to 14,000 units a year, mainly
by mail order.

The success of the product prompted the inventor into developing the
Mark II version. This design, which had further features, including alternative heights, and a system of swivelling pegs in the vise beams for

clamping awkward shapes, was being completed when Ron Hickman was approached for a license in the U.K. and Europe by Walter Goldsmith, then general manager of Black & Decker in the U.K.

Once the license agreement was consummated, Black & Decker decided to manufacture the Mark II design virtually in the form the inventor had developed, and tooling for this purpose was installed in its U.K. factory at Spennymoor.

The market launch was in 1972 and was an immediate success. For several years demand outstripped supply. Production lines for supplying the European market were set up in Eire, Spain, Germany, and Italy. Later, under a further license covering America and the rest of the world, production also started in Canada, U.S.A., Mexico, Brazil, and Japan.

The licensing arrangements with Black & Decker have been governed by three agreements covering different territories, initially two for the U.K. and Europe, and later, a third for North and South America and the rest of the world. Certain specific aspects of the licenses may be of interest.

The royalty was settled at a flat rate of 3% of net sales value. Bearing in mind that at the time of the negotiations, Workmate was already showing signs of being a revolutionary product, and that significant patent protection was likely to be obtained on many aspects of the product as a whole, the author advised Ron Hickman at the time that the 3% figure would be too low.

The author considers that this view has been borne out in practice, since, despite efforts by competitors in many countries to enter the very lucrative market, Black & Decker has maintained a virtual worldwide exclusivity which the author still believes justifies a royalty of 5%, if not higher.

Ron Hickman's view, even in hindsight, is that he took the correct approach to the royalty in view of his hopes for high-volume production. In addition, for what was a relatively untried product, he also received quite substantial advance payments, and of course the financial return actually produced by the 3% royalty has been considerable.

The U.K. and European agreements provided that the royalty percentage of 3% was split into two tranches of 1-1/2%. One of these tranches was payable for know-how and copyright, and was unaffected by the patent position. In the agreement covering America and the rest of the world, the same 3% royalty applies, but this is tied completely to patents and is paid as long as any patent protection is in force, either in the country where the product is manufactured or where it is sold. The three agreements with Black & Decker included substantial advance royalty and minimum royalty terms.

The U.K. and European agreements included an option permitting Black & Decker to take an assignment of all rights under the agreements for a lump sum based on a factor multiplied by the best year's royalties. This option was exercised in 1977 by Black & Decker. Accordingly, it now owns the original U.K. and European patents outright. In North and South America, the Far East and in Australasia, Black & Decker continues to pay the 3% royalty.

During the subsistence of the U.K. and European agreements, Ron Hickman maintained the right, and indeed was obliged, to sue infringers, the cost of (and any profit from) the litigation being shared between the licensee and licensor. This left the inventor in a position of being able to administer patent litigation himself, as for example occurred in the United Kingdom. Most importantly, because of this, the inventor was in a position to defend the inevitable counterclaim of invalidity. This right of the inventor to defend his own patents and hence to keep secure his royalty position was a significant advantage but nevertheless an extremely expensive burden.

When it came to negotiating the license for the rest of the world, the inventor passed the initial right to sue, and hence the control of the litigation, to Black & Decker, his licensee. In any event, this has proved perfectly satisfactory. For example, during the course of extremely expensive, but completely successful, litigation against Sears, Roebuck and Emerson Electric in the United States, the licensee and inventor have, as joint plaintiffs, put forward a forthright defense to attacks on the validity of the patents.

Infringement proceedings under Workmate patents, and in one or two instances under unfair competition laws, have stopped the sale of competitive workbench products twice in the U.S.A., once in Canada, three times in the U.K. (on one occasion with actions against 10 defendants), once in South Africa, twice in France, three times in Germany, twice in Japan, once in Italy, and once in Denmark. In only two countries, U.K.

and U.S.A., have the infringement proceedings resulted in full trials, both going to appeal.

The close cooperation achieved by Ron Hickman and the author, and their advisors all over the world, since the first British provisional specification was filed in 1968 has been a most rewarding experience, not simply in financial terms for the inventor, but in the sense that the patent system has been used to the full to extract from it a monopoly for the inventor's designs which, at least at the time of drafting this article, has withstood virtually all attacks.

* * * * *

FOOTNOTES:
[1]Many home workshop enthusiasts are familiar with the "Workmate," a folding, portable workbench sold by Black & Decker. Not many realize that it had its beginning with an individual inventor, British do-it-yourself enthusiast, Ron Hickman. Mr. Hickman, working with a London law firm and, ultimately, with Black & Decker, achieved a worldwide market position for his invention through licensing and the all-important defense of patent rights. First, however, he had to prove that his invention was, indeed, a marketable product. This experience story is taken from a more detailed account which appeared in the June 1983 issue of les Nouvelles. The author, M.J. Roos, is a member of the law firm of Kilburn & Strode, London, England. Mr. Roos and his firm handled the patents and legal matters described in this account.

Chapter VIII

LICENSING INFLUENCE IN CORPORATE STRATEGY[1]

The growth of a company through licensing in and out.
By William S. Campbell
Executive Vice President, Consumers Packaging, Inc.
Toronto, Ontario, Canada

Those of you who are not involved in the packaging industry probably have not heard of our company, Consumers Packing Inc. I still have a little trouble with it myself. We were Consumers Glass Company Limited for 69 years and changed our name on July 1 (1986). To put us in perspective, we are Canada's 222nd largest public company by sales and 128th largest by earnings. We changed our name to give effect to our change in our corporate strategy. For us it became increasingly apparent that we were no longer just a glass-container company but a packaging company. This is a subject I will discuss later because licensing has played a major role in our change from a manufacturer of glass containers (product offered) to a broad-based packaging company dedicated to supplying our customers' market needs.

Consumers Packaging is a multinational company with operations in Canada, the United States, and the United Kingdom. We operate 12 manufacturing plants, employ more than 4,000 people, and we have annual sales of approximately $350 million. Our products include most types of glass bottles and jars, plastic-thermoformed containers, plastic bottles and plastic closures.

Our first experience in the field of licensing took place in the early 1960s when a comprehensive technical assistance agreement covering glass containers was signed with Brockway, Inc. of New York, the second largest glass container manufacturer in the United States and one of the world's most advanced technologically. The original agreement has been renewed and modified a number of times over the years and remains in force today. We have just celebrated the 25th anniversary.

We did little "out" licensing until the late 1960s when we helped form Glass Containers Limited in Sydney, Australia. A key part of the foundation for this new enterprise was based on a technical assistance agreement, or licensing agreement, that provided the Australian company with all of our manufacturing technology and capability. This enabled the new company to be launched successfully and highly profitably and to capture a significant percentage of the Australian market for glass containers.

We continued to utilize the vehicle of licensing technology into the early 1970s but these programs were basically opportunistic in nature. We did not have an overall plan of operations in this area although some very interesting and highly profitable license agreements were made.

As you might expect, not all were winners, and any senior management must, or should, recognize this. The obvious trick is to be more right than wrong. It is equally obvious that this is easier said than done!

As we moved through the 1970s, we realized that a growing company of our size had to rely upon our licensing program more and more to compete effectively in the Canadian and North American marketplace. Our competitors, by and large, are corporations much larger than we are with sales many times greater than we have. We simply did not have the resources to devote to the rapidly advancing world technology of packaging. Accordingly, we consciously developed a planned approach to actively seek new technology, new products, and new methods for our future success through the process of licensing and technical agreements. Accordingly, again, we committed our resources to produce and process development and improvement. These are areas where we have a proven track record of considerable success.

The most essential requirement of any comprehensive licensing program is the total commitment of the senior management with support in strategic terms from the Board of Directors. I stress this because no amount of effort will drive a licensing program without total commitment and support.

I particularly address these comments to those of you engaged in the corporate side of your organizations. You can have the best licensing

program known to man but you will be, at best, only marginally successful without the commitment of senior management. If you don't have
this, you should make it your number-one priority to obtain it.

To those of you who are young-at-heart, I would add that if you cannot
demonstrate the value of, and therefore earn, this commitment, you
should consider, seriously consider, if licensing is your responsibility, a
career change or job change. In my view, at best, only marginal success
is possible unless the key people want it to happen.

To the consultant and lawyers I would give the same advice. If the commitment is not present from senior management you should find a new
client. You'll end up with fewer headaches and more rewards.

Within Consumers Packaging we have such a commitment. To us,
licensing is an integral part of the development and implementation of
our corporate strategic plan. It has become involved and intertwined
with our corporate development and acquisition program and is an active component of the profit and sales growth objectives of our corporation.

We have determined that our company will meet the market needs of
our customers and future customers by positioning ourselves to fill as
many of those needs as makes good business sense for our company.

Consistent with this strategy we set as one of our goals to expand further
into plastics packaging. We did our industry survey work and our
market research. First, and the first here is absolutely essential in our
view, we licensed a technology from Japan to produce a barrier, or multilayer, plastic bottle. We had this agreement in-place before we made
the first of two acquisitions that have made us the largest supplier of
plastic bottles in Canada. The technology from Japan was an important
base. It was an essential part of our business plan that, when in-place,
enabled us to construct a 60,000-square-foot plant addition to produce
a new product, for us, designed specifically to meet the market needs of
a large number of our customers.

That is one example. In fact, our licensing program reaches across our
entire product line, from glass containers, to closures, to thermoform-
ing, to sheet extrusion, to plastic bottles. All are touched by the wonder-
ful world of licensing.

Through the years we have gained a sizable amount of experience in licensing. We have had a problem or two from time to time, perhaps comparable to that statement made by a fellow industrialist who said: "Behind every problem there are probably 1,000 opportunities to make a mistake."

We have made a few mistakes, but not too many, and we have tried to apply our knowledge base to each new agreement as it comes along.

Let me give you a quick assessment of our company's present situation.

In glass containers we have a broadly-based technical-assistance agreement with a world-class company supplemented by a few specific license agreements to cover specialized areas of the glass-making process.

We are also a founding member of the International Partners in Glass Research. This is a partnership of our company and glass-making companies from the United States, Australia, United Kingdom, Germany, France, Japan and the glass machinery manufacturer, Emhart. We have set up a pool of funds for basic research at various universities and research organizations directed at ways of developing glass containers that will be both lighter and stronger. This will make a highly interesting licensing story at some future time.

In plastics, we have five process-related agreements that include both know-how and patents. The licensors are Brockway, Inc., Monsanto of St. Louis, O.N.O. of Auneau, France, Toyo Seikan Kaisha of Tokyo, Japan, and Metal Box of Reading, England.

In our opinion, these licensing agreements have enabled us to produce high-performance, high-technology plastic packaging, and place us in a lead position of world-class technology.

It is an interesting mix. Brockway is a good-sized U.S. company that is an acknowledged world-leader in glass containers, technology and know-how. They, too, produce plastic containers although this is a relatively new packaging area for them.

Monsanto is a large chemical and resin producer based in the U.S. with operations in many parts of the world along the with downstream operations.

O.N.O. is a small private French company that has world-class technology in the area of co-extruded, multilayer plastic sheet.

Toyo Seikan is probably the world's largest packaging company with all that goes with being that size. The company is innovative, progressive and a very, very powerful force in its market and in world markets.

Metal Box is a world-class packaging company. Probably about number three in sales, it has a very large R&D budget. It employs about 500 persons at its R&D center, 280 of whom are professionals. There are more than 60 microbiologists on staff, complete kitchen and packaging facilities, and a truly outstanding ability to develop and innovate new products and new processes.

All of these companies are first-class partners. They view us in the same way.

We also have numerous product agreements that have either a strong know-how component or patent protection and come to us from various homes. We have a great mix of size and geography when we look down our list of licensors.

Several of these licensing agreements are comparatively new and they have helped in the pursuit of our new strategy to change the type of company we are. That is one of the reasons we changed our name earlier this year to Consumers Packaging Inc. from Consumers Glass Company Limited. We are now a broader type of packaging company than we were in the past, and we will continue to broaden our capabilities and product lines to this end in the years ahead.

Let me close with one last thought. We have learned an important vital fact through our licensing program and that is this:

If you have established a solidly-based licensing program that is active with full management support, you can have a major impact on the strategic direction of your entire company. As an aside, you most assuredly will be in a position to license out.

* * * * *

FOOTNOTES:

[1]This case study on how a successful licensing program impacted a Canadian corporation was originally presented at the 1986 Annual Meeting of LES (U.S.A. and Canada) and later published in the December 1986 issue of *les Nouvelles*. Mr. Campbell's title is given as it was in 1986. In 1988 Mr. Campbell retired from consumers Packaging, and in February 1989 he died of cancer.

Chapter IX

UNIQUE INVENTION CHANGES AN ORDINARY PAPER BAG INTO WORLDWIDE USE AS A HEAVY DUTY SACK[1]

How a major worldwide licensing program was organized.
By Dudley B. Smith
Former Manager of Licensee Services
Clupak, Inc.

Clupak is an uncreped kraft paper much the same as ordinary kraft paper except that added toughness and flexibility have been "built in." A patented mechanical process has crowded and pushed the fibers together while the paper was being formed.

The advantages of paper treated by this process include toughness a better ability to absorb energy and withstand impact; flexibility a better ability to conform to irregular shapes; and tear resistance the fibers are held together by a better bond. For example, when Clupak is used in multiwall sacks for shipping cement or fertilizer, fewer plies and less basis weight of paper can be used since Clupak is tougher and stronger. In other words, multiwalls made of Clupak can be sold for less money to the cement company yet these same sacks will give better performance in terms of less breakage in transit.

Let's go back in time and explore the background and events which led to the setting up of our licensing program. Sanford L. Cluett is the inventive genius responsible for the cloth shrinkage process which is known to the public through the extensive promotion of the Sanforized trademark. Back in the 1940s, he also conceived the basic idea for manufacturing extensible paper with initial experiments on a two inch-wide laboratory test model.

By way of orientation, Mr. Cluett is a Vice President of Cluett, Peabody and Company, the makers of Arrow shirts and men's wear and the owners of the Sanforized trademark. Cluett Peabody was not and is not engaged in the paper business. It thus was natural that Cluett Peabody should seek out a reputable paper firm to advise it as to the possibilities of this new process after it became evident that the process was patentable in a basic manner.

United States and foreign patents having been applied for, an agreement was worked out between Cluett Peabody and West Virginia Pulp and Paper Company. This agreement provided that Cluett Peabody would license West Virginia under the patents, turn over all know-how then available concerning the process, and provide the consulting services of Mr. Cluett. West Virginia, on the other hand, agreed to assign an R&D team to bring the process to commercial realization. Both parties agreed that if anything came out of the endeavor, the fruits would be shared equally.

After a great deal of work, and approximately three years and $2,500,000 later, West Virginia reported commercial success in the kraft field with the process. It also reported the availability of additional patent applications arising from development work of West Virginia Pulp and Paper and from the work of Beloit Iron Works in the construction of the first large-scale extensible paper machinery. This development stage was achieved by the Fall of 1957.

It was at this point that an important decision faced West Virginia and Cluett Peabody. How best to exploit commercially what appeared to be a major breakthrough in paper making. One of two paths could be followed. The first path would lead to exclusive utilization of the invention in the United States by West Virginia, thus opening tremendous new markets for its sales people with a possible additional profit from foreign licensing in those countries noncompetitive with West Virginia. This path might also lead to larger export markets for West Virginia since foreign patents could maintain, at least for a time, exclusivity in foreign countries to which West Virginia might export extensible paper.

The second path was one well known to Cluett Peabody through its experience licensing Sanforized. It called for setting up of a combination, domestic international licensing program, nonexclusive, with all interested paper mills throughout the world invited to practice the process in return for royalty payments.

A primary consideration was the availability of licensing know-how. After all, licensing is just another way of doing business but it's one where the availability of business know-how can be important. In this case, licensing know-how was available from Cluett Peabody. Sanforized is successfully licensed in 35 countries and Arrow in 7 countries, the former program now being almost 30 years old and still going strong.

Another factor was the market available for the paper to be made under license. Market research, the United States Department of Commerce, and trade associations both domestic and foreign provide invaluable assistance in working up projected sales figures. To answer the question of whether international markets could best be served by export or by local licensing, the experienced export department of West Virginia Pulp and Paper was of help.

The question of potential patent strength, country-by-country, also was a factor. Patents covering a process are excellent to control local manufacturing in an international licensing program and it appeared that the pending patents would allow such control.

Additional factors in the choice of exclusivity versus unlimited licensing include an estimate of the commercial life span of the development. This raises the questions of whether research might further develop the process for use on additional types of paper, who pays for research, and whether additional patent protection could be expected to result from such research. In our case, it was decided that the parents could establish a separate licensing entity which in turn could pay for additional research. Such research would probably generate new patent applications to better protect the ability to carry on a licensing program.

The final decision was made to license the development rather than practice it on an exclusive basis. The answers to such questions as "what royalty rate will the industry pay," "can a trademark be used to coordinate marketing" and "what additional research may be advisable in view of licensing markets available worldwide" were left to be answered as the first attempts were made to license other paper companies.

In 1958, a separate joint-venture corporation, owned half by West Virginia and half by Cluett Peabody, was established. The first task facing the infant corporation Clupak, Inc. was to obtain a draft of a license, which it was hoped would be acceptable to the paper industry while still allowing sufficient safeguards and the generation of sufficient royalties to make the program worthwhile to the parent companies. In general, West Virginia provided the technical and the paper industry know-how, Cluett Peabody the licensing know-how.

Briefly, the Clupak license sets forth a list of patents and trademarks country-by-country upon which the licensing structure is erected. It sets up quality standards which, when followed by licensees, will allow the trademark Clupak to be applied to the extensible paper produced by licensees. The royalty is calculated on the basis of the number of tons of extensible paper produced and there is a minimum royalty for the first three years.

The license for each country allows Clupak paper to be produced only in the country where the licensee is located, but sales are allowed worldwide. The license is nonexclusive.

In addition to the grant of a license under patents and trademarks worldwide, Clupak, Inc. of course agrees to disclose to the licensee all its know-how, technical information and techniques relative to extensible paper. The licensee, in addition to paying a royalty, agrees that if its work under the license generates additional patentable subject matter that could not be used without infringing existing Clupak patents, such patents will be made available to all other licensees worldwide. Clupak, Inc., in turn, agrees to take legal action against third parties who may infringe and to keep all licensees up to date on any new technical developments relative to extensible paper. These are the main substantive provisions of the license and, armed with the first draft of this license, a simultaneous approach was made to several of the largest producers of kraft paper in the United States.

The statement that the first draft license was negotiated with several paper companies oversimplifies what actually took place. This is for the reason that the initial license negotiations actually consumed the better part of four months. They called for many many meetings of Clupak, Inc. legal, technical and executive personnel with their counterparts in the prospective licensee companies. First off, of course, the licensees wanted to be satisfied that the process was sound in terms of cost accounting and available markets. Next, the licensees had to be satisfied that if they signed there would be no overlap of interest with their own pending R&D programs. Each word in each sentence of a multipage draft was examined and reexamined. These matters were helped immeasurably by the fact that West Virginia itself was by this time on line producing and selling Clupak paper in commercial quantities while the negotiations with the other prospects were under way. This created competitive pressures. The necessity to compete with the new successful product was a number one moving force behind the acceptance of the license.

In discussing the administration of a licensing program, we have elected to examine the organization of Clupak, Inc., in terms of function rather than along strictly departmental lines. Such a functional breakdown yields four main classifications under the president, namely, Licensee Services, Legal Function, Research and Technical Functions and Foreign Licensing.

The licensee services unit provides technical, marketing and promotion aids. Technical licensee services, for example, include the passing along from the licensor of technical and engineering know-how, the policing of trademark quality standards, the start-up of new equipment in the licensee's plant, troubleshooting for the licensee by licensor technical people, and the examination of new technical developments. Suppose, for example, that our development work or the experience of one of our licensees reveals that a new maintenance procedure on the extensible machinery is advisable. Our technical people would in the typical situation pass this know-how along to all of our licensees through personal contact and the issuance of a technical report. This requires, of course, that our technical people be in almost continuous contact with their counterparts at each licensee paper mill. Each time a new licensee starts up an extensible unit or, when an old licensee starts up a new unit, Clupak, Inc. technical personnel are on the spot.

In the field of marketing and sales, Clupak, Inc. also serves its licensees. For example, our technical people have published many articles concerning the process and the paper in trade publications. These are disseminated widely to licensee personnel as part of our service. Clupak, Inc. also holds seminars and meetings in which the salesmen, production people and engineers of our licensee companies sit in with their counterparts at Clupak, Inc. Here we exchange operating experience, marketing information, new uses for Clupak paper, the coordination of advertising programs, the availability of samples, and the like.

Since the only thing we actually sell are licenses, our advertising is somewhat indirect in that it is aimed at helping our licensees sell their Clupak paper. We seek the advice of our licensees as to particular products that should be advertised, case histories of successful applications of the paper, and the like. In all cases we attempt to use a broad approach that promotes the use of the Clupak trademark and advise prospective purchasers of bags, sacks, wrapping paper, etc. of the virtues of Clupak and of the many companies that produce this unique paper. We also cooperate with licensees at trade shows, help them set up their booths, help work up handouts at conventions and the like. In short, the promotion function does everything possible to promote the sale of Clupak paper.

Our advertising and promotion has a secondary purpose. For example, we carry on a direct-mail campaign with prospective new licensees around the world. If we receive an inquiry from the XYZ Paper Company in Australia, they are added to our mailing list. From then on, XYZ Paper Company receives copies of all of our advertisements, pamphlets, the trade articles, the pictures of trade shows in which Clupak was featured etc. This, in effect, is a marketing effort for Clupak, Inc. to gain new licensees.

The legal function at Clupak, Inc. is carried on in two areas, patent and general legal work. Our patent attorneys have a corresponding counterpart in each of 115 foreign countries. When Clupak, Inc. has a new patent application in the United States, market surveys are checked and perhaps 30 or 40 of the most important foreign countries are selected. Our general attorneys, on the other hand, must clear the draft of our license with a general attorney in each country where we propose to license the practice of the process.

The research function of Clupak, Inc. overlaps somewhat with the technical function. We have a vice-president who is in charge of research and technical services. He has several engineers working for him. One of their functions is to advise on new areas of research we should enter, how best to carry out our existing research program, and on management questions growing out of improvements in machinery, the process, and converting techniques for Clupak paper. They also must supervise research agreements we have with various companies.

All correspondence with prospects and existing licensees in foreign countries is funneled through one executive. Obviously, however, he must have help on technical matters from the engineers, on legal matters from the lawyers, and on promotion and advertising from that department. It is the dual function of the foreign licensing executive to gain new licensees in foreign fields and to promote the sale of Clupak paper by existing foreign licensees.

As a licensing program matures, it becomes necessary to have personnel resident in foreign countries. In Europe, we have a field man who acts as a contact man for the executive in New York in charge of foreign licensing. This field man visits paper mill managers, explaining the process and otherwise doing the spade work to gain new licensees. As Clupak, Inc. gains additional foreign licensees, it will also be necessary to base technical people in foreign countries for licensee servicing just as Sanforized does today. These technical people will perform the start-up, trademark "policing," and technical know-how functions which are performed by their counterparts in the United States.

An international licensing program can speed your market penetration. That is, ten licensees in ten countries usually can cover a market more thoroughly and faster than can a single manufacturer who attempts to cover other areas through export. Furthermore, licensing can reach markets which are otherwise blocked by customs barriers. Another consideration in favor of licensing in certain situations is that a minimum of capital investment and personnel is required.

There is a saying that "two heads are better than one" and certainly a dozen heads are better than two. This leads to the conclusion that licensing can lengthen the life of a technical development. Where one company attempts to maintain exclusivity, it must depend solely upon its own R&D program plus that which they purchase directly to keep them "out in front." With a licensing program such as Clupak, Inc. practices, new developments are made available for all to use. We expect that this program will further broaden markets and speed the market penetration of all licensees.

* * * * *

FOOTNOTES:
[1]While this experience story took place in the middle and late 1950's and early 1960's it is both interesting and instructive. It tells how a unique invention improved an ordinary paper bag and was developed into a worldwide application of very heavy duty sacks, all through a carefully planned license program. This experience story was used by Mr. Dudley B. Smith (currently President, Dudley B. Smith, Inc.) in an AMA licensing seminar in 1960. It is still a useful example of international licensing.

Chapter X

HOW A LICENSING PROGRAM BECAME THE BASIS OF A COMPANY WHOSE 1986 REVENUES EXCEEDED $29 MILLION[1]

Commercializing the Dolby System
By Ian Hardcastle
Vice-President
Dolby Laboratories Licensing Corporation
San Francisco, California

Ray Milton Dolby was born in Portland, Oregon, in 1933. He grew up in the San Francisco Bay Area. He began working for Ampex Corporation, one of the earliest manufacturers of magnetic tape recorders in the U.S., when he was 16. He later was responsible for developing a major part of the electronics of the world's first practical videotape recorder.

After his graduation from Stanford University in 1957, Dolby attended Cambridge University in England, where he worked on long-wavelength X-rays and received a Ph.D. in 1961. In 1963, he took up a two year appointment as a United Nations advisor in India.

Dolby had for many years been a keen amateur recording engineer and was aware of the degradation of recording quality caused by the noise inherent in the process of recording audio (or video) signals on magnetic tape. It was while he was in India that he began to think seriously of ways to reduce this noise without causing other degradations in the quality of the recording. This thought process resulted in the ideas that formed the basis of the Dolby A-type, B-type and C-type noise reduction systems, various Dolby video noise reduction systems that have never been exploited commercially, and a wealth of alternative and innovative ways of realizing these systems practically.

Returning to England in 1965, Dolby set up his own laboratory in London to investigate and explore his ideas relating to noise reduction and other topics. The company was called "Dolby Laboratories" and was incorporated in 1968. Although the company had its center of gravity in England for its first 10 years, it has always been an American company.

In 1965, a working unit of the Dolby A-type (A for audio) noise reduction system was produced. This system was designed to deal with a wide variety of audio noise reduction applications, especially with the noise problems of the tape recorders used in recording studios to record the master tapes from which phonograph records are cut.

In January 1966, Decca records in England concluded that Dolby A-type noise reduction did what Dolby said it did, and ordered nine Dolby A 301 A-type noise reduction units, the first of which was used in Vienna in May 1966 to record some Mozart piano concertos played by Vladimir Ashkenazy. In November that year, Decca released the first record that had been mastered using Dolby A-type noise reduction, Mahler's Second Symphony conducted by Sir Georg Solti.

Word spread that Dolby's noise reduction system actually worked, and the record industry gradually started to use it, first of all only on classical recordings and then, as multitrack recording spread, on more and more different types of recording.

Dolby was urged to develop a noise reduction system for consumer-quality tape recorders. Practical development of what was initially called "The Simplified Dolby System," and some time later was called Dolby B-type noise reduction, began in April 1967. The K.L.H. Research and Development Corporation in Cambridge, Massachusetts, which was developing a consumer-quality tape recorder and wanted to give it a major performance advantage by using noise reduction, successfully persuaded Dolby to begin this project. An agreement in principle to license K.L.H. to build B-type circuits into its tape recorders was signed in May 1967.

At the time the agreement was negotiated, the word "Dolby" was becoming known by the public but it had not been widely registered as a trademark. Nevertheless, rights to use the Dolby name in addition to the "S/N Stretcher" trademark ("S/N" means "Signal to Noise (Ratio)"), which Dolby used on all A 301 noise reduction units, were included in the license, together with the necessary quality control requirements.

A middle five-figures initial payment and a royalty of 4% of the ex-factory price of each tape recorder sold were agreed upon. Dolby insisted on a fairly substantial initial payment to give him at least some return for developing the Simplified System in the event that K.L.H. decided to stop making tape recorders soon after it started to make them.

A license agreement, giving K.L.H. a right to make tape recorders incorporating Dolby B-type noise reduction, exclusive until November 1969 (later extended to March 1970) and nonexclusive thereafter, was finally signed in April 1968. In addition to the license agreement there was a consultancy agreement covering the provision of technical support for the licensee.

The K.L.H. Model 40 tape recorder was launched in June 1968, to enthusiastic critical acclaim, which reflected well on the product itself and further enhanced the reputation of Dolby noise reduction and public awareness of it. Serious production did not begin until almost the end of the year. The product did not sell well mainly because of production difficulties and acute reliability problems. Dolby's insistence on a large initial payment turned out to be wise precaution: K.L.H. made less than 2,000 units of the tape recorder for which the "Simplified Dolby System" was designed.

Dolby caused considerable excitement in October 1969 when he demonstrated a compact cassette recorder with external Dolby B-type noise reduction to the Audio Engineering Society Convention in New York and to several U.S. high-fidelity manufacturers. He also travelled to Japan that year and discussed licensing with several companies there.

The first company licensed in Japan was Nakamichi Research, Inc., with whom licensing discussions were started in November 1969. Nakamichi specialized at that time almost exclusively in O.E.M. business and was ideally placed to exploit the demand for high-fidelity cassette recorders from the U.S. and from Europe. It was already making advanced cassette recorders and a product with Dolby B-type noise reduction, an open-reel recorder for K.L.H., the Model 41.

In the second generation agreement, the initial payment was reduced to $5,000, but separate agreements were required for tape recorders, amplifiers and receivers, and add-on noise reduction units. The royalty rate was 2% for tape recorders, amplifiers and receivers, and 4% for add-on units. The agreements, which also included rights to the trademarks "Dolby" and the "Double-D" symbol (first used by Dolby

Laboratories in 1969), were still in the form of a license agreement and a consultancy agreement.

In the rest of 1970, four new licensees signed the second-generation license agreement. Apart from Hitachi, these were all audio specialist companies. Also in 1970, Dolby employed a Japanese company, Continental Far East, Inc., to act as Tokyo liaison office to help deal with its licensees in Japan and the considerable number of companies that expressed interest in becoming licensees, a service that C.F.E. still performs.

The summer 1971 Consumer Electronics Show saw three more events that helped establish Dolby B-type's acceptance as the main consumer tape noise-reduction system. The first event was a demonstration to the press and licensees by Dolby Laboratories in cooperation with radio station WFMT, Chicago, of the use of Dolby B-type noise reduction on FM radio.

The second event was the joint announcement by Dolby Laboratories and Signetics Corporation that they had agreed to cooperate in the development of a special integrated circuit for use in the Dolby B-type circuit. As there is no point in designing special integrated circuits unless there is the prospect of selling them in the hundreds of thousands, this announcement further directed people's attention to the mass market potential of Dolby noise reduction.

The third event of the C.E.S. was the announcement by Dolby Laboratories of simplified licensing arrangements and a new, lower-cost royalty structure for its license. There was now to be a single license agreement granting patent, trademark and know-how rights and covering all consumer audio product categories, so multiple initial payments were no longer called for. Instead of a fixed percentage of the product selling price, always a tricky thing to define, the new royalty structure was based on the number of Dolby B-type circuits sold per calendar quarter, the first 10,000 being at 50 cents each, the next 40,000 being at 25 cents, and all above 50,000 being at 10 cents each. These basic royalty rates are tied to the U.S. Consumer Cost of Living Index, which this year (1983) multiplies these rates by 2.406. The new rates were intended to indicate to large potential licensees that were still sitting on the fence, the potential mass-market application of Dolby noise reduction.

In the middle of 1971, Dolby Laboratories set up a formal quality control program for its licensees' products. The quality control program has been successful in preventing products with substandard performance from reaching the market, thereby maintaining the quality image of products marked with the Dolby trademarks.

The events of 1971 turned out to be effective in communicating Dolby's message to the consumer audio equipment manufacturers and tape duplicators. In 1971, nine companies signed license agreements, including the company that has now the largest production rate of products with Dolby noise reduction and the company that often has the second largest production rate. In 1972, the number of licenses signed was 12 and in 1973 the number was 13. The companies that currently have the 10 highest production rates had all signed by the end of 1973.

Throughout his negotiations with the various consumer electronics companies, Dolby stuck to his objective of getting them to adopt his standard noise reduction system under his standard licensing terms. Dolby was able to convince prospective licensees that (a) standardization on the Dolby B-type noise-reduction system would further stimulate the record industry to produce B-type encoded prerecorded tapes; (b) that the wide availability of cassette recorders and prerecorded tapes all with the same Dolby B-type noise reduction would establish confidence in the mind of the prospective purchaser of a cassette recorder and (c) once consumer confidence in a new product category is established, the long-term growth of the market can be assured.

By the end of 1974, Dolby had 47 licensees including almost all the major manufacturers of consumer hi-fi audio equipment, and Dolby thought that there would be little need to negotiate many more new license agreements. This proved incorrect, since many new consumer applications of Dolby noise reduction opened up.

It is now used in such diverse applications as car stereos, music centers, portable radiocassettes, VHS video recorders and headphone stereos, and in each new field of application there were new specialist companies that needed to be licensed. New centers of production outside of Japan and Europe also opened up, all requiring individual attention as far as licensing is concerned. Dolby Laboratories now has about 160 licensees, of which about 100 are actually active. Dolby noise-reduction circuits are currently being produced at an annual rate of about 40 million, grossing about $9 million per year for the company (about half the company's income); about 160 million are manufactured in about 35 countries. The various Dolby trademarks are registered in over 85 countries.

The license agreement currently used for all applications is little changed from the third-generation agreement of 1971. New technologies are added to existing license agreements by using side letters. At the beginning of 1982, the royalty structure was changed to add royalty brackets that reflect the considerable increase in licensees' production volumes over what was envisaged in 1971.

The 10-cent bracket now only extends up to 250,000 processors, and an 8.5-cent bracket (250,001 to 1,000,000), and a 7.5-cent bracket (1,000,000 up) have been added. Also, playback-only processors such as are found in headphone portables and car stereos are counted as 0.75 of a processor for the purpose of counting royalties.

Dolby noise-reduction systems now account for about 95% of the sales of complementary noise-reduction systems in consumer products: Dolby Laboratories, Inc. is still a private company owned by Ray Dolby. Dolby has recently vacated the presidency of the company and is now its chairman. This new position will give him more time to devote to what he really enjoys doing — inventing.

* * * * *

FOOTNOTES:

[1]This story has been taken from a more detailed account in the December 1983 issue of *les Nouvelles*. It traces the development of the Dolby System from the first ideas of Ray Milton Dolby in the early 1960's to the present-day total market presence in the field of recording studios, records, tape recorders and players. As reported in the New York Times, Sunday, November 29, 1987, the latest development/invention of Dolby Laboratories' "Spectral Recording" (Dolby SR) is "Mr. Dolby's answer to digital recording." The result of six years' concentrated, personal work by Ray Dolby, the Dolby SR is alleged to be the equivalent or superior to digital in recording studios. How the competition turns out will be determined only by time.

Chapter XI

INVENTOR SUCCEEDS WITH A

DEVELOPMENT LICENSE[1]

By Robert Goldscheider, Chairman
International Licensing Network, Ltd.

An invention with large commercial potential required substantial additional engineering and investment to become marketable. The inventor had sunk his life savings, and those of this family and friends, into building a working prototype. He had tried to raise venture capital from investment bankers and was uniformly turned down · This, incidentally, had been a time-consuming and exhausting experience, requiring the preparation of detailed financial projections, which were essentially meaningless but which nevertheless seemed to be part of all these exercises.

The inventor was then introduced to a major company that had cash and engineering facilities, but which badly needed to diversify its product line. The solution turned out to be eminently satisfactory to all concerned; it might be described as a "master license." Under this arrangement, the inventor received a substantial cash payment in six figures for an exclusive, worldwide license to his invention, with the right of the licensee to grant sublicenses. The inventor was also retained as a consultant, at a generous amount, in return for at least half his professional time, to oversee further development work. The licensee agreed to provide specified facilities and engineering personnel, plus a minimum defined cash investment, during the first three years, as part of a detailed development program jointly worked out by the parties. If the licensee, itself, decided to sell the resulting products, it would pay specified royalties to the inventor. If, as was expected, the licensee would grant a series of nonexclusive sublicenses (under arrangements where it would also sell components and intermediates to the sublicensees), the resulting royalties would be divided on a 50-50 basis with the inventor.

As a result, the inventor has seen his brainchild become a reality. His old debts were satisfied from the down payment; the consulting fee enabled him to live well while he completed his work with the use of engineering assistance and facilities better than he could otherwise have hoped for, and his income from the sublicenses since concluded has made him a very wealthy man. The master licensee has also had an excellent return on its investment. It was able to put to work existing personnel and equipment which were being under utilized and it now has a new area of operations into which it has profitably diversified.

* * * * *

FOOTNOTES:
[1]This story is related by Robert Goldscheider in the 1982 Technology Management Handbook. The only editorial comment that seems appropriate is that an invention must have true significance and potential in order to be taken on at a development stage, otherwise it is very difficult to sell to potential licensees until it has been reduced to a commercial state. At the same time, the episode points out clearly what may be possible through licensing of a truly significant invention concept.

Chapter XII

THE STORY OF THE EASY OPEN CAN END

A worldwide licensing program benefits
licensees, licensees, and an entire industry.
By Edward P. White, Chairman
KEW Associates, Inc.

There are many interesting stories attached to the commercialization of the U.S. invented Easy Open Can End known by such names as "Pop-Top," "Pour Top," "Easy-O," etc. One is the successful international promotion through a program of licenses with more than 75 different firms outside the United States. This revolution in the rigid container industry is a story that began with cooperation between a small business and a large corporation.

Can sheet, a high quality, thin gauge aluminum sheet product was developed and perfected by Aluminum Company of America (Alcoa) in the late 1950s. In connection with its major development program for new products made with can sheet, Alcoa initiated a special product development program that combined the work of its own R&D facilities and the work of E.C. Fraze, the owner of Dayton Reliable Tool Company, a small, high-quality, tool and die shop in Dayton, Ohio.

This partnership was based primarily on an agreement for secrecy of development. Supplementing the legal papers of the confidential development program was a basic feeling of trust that cemented the working relationship between small, independent businessman, E.C. Fraze, and a multinational corporation, Alcoa.

The invention that came out of the Fraze-Alcoa program was the integral rivet tab attachment. The invention covered the method of forming a rivet from the metal of a can end, applying a tab and "heading" or fastening the tab with the formed rivet. All of this work was performed at production speeds of several hundred pieces per minute. As the inventor of the integral rivet attachment, Mr. Fraze held the primary patent position. Alcoa knew the market and the packaging development potential. On that basis, Alcoa took two exclusive licenses with Fraze, both with rights to sublicense the manufacture, use and sale under the Fraze Easy Open End patent and all subsequent related Fraze patents. One license covered domestic United States, and the other (the "Foreign License") covered all countries outside the United States. The domestic U.S. license covered Fraze patents held by Fraze and licensed by Alcoa along with the Alcoa patents which evolved from the program. The number of can makers in the United States is relatively small, but with an aggregate production volume that is staggering. The domestic licensing program was fairly straightforward, though requiring a significant amount of time to administer and service.

Under the foreign license, Alcoa paid for all foreign patents filed in this field by both Fraze and Alcoa. Since the development program was ongoing, there was the expectation of many more patents to be filed. That expectation, incidentally, proved to be correct. Patent costs were paid out of royalties collected from Alcoa's foreign licensees, and the remaining royalty income was split 50-50 between Fraze and Alcoa.

During the period between early 1960 and early 1980, more than 75 international sublicenses were established throughout the world. These sublicenses were all on the basis of standard terms, the same rates for all. Potential licensees were contacted through Alcoa's U.S. packaging industry customers, foreign industry contacts, friendly banks, and all possible references. A substantial network of cooperating licensees was created. Meanwhile, approximately 50 patents of Alcoa and Fraze were filed in 30 or more different countries. Both Fraze and Alcoa had net profit of royalties totalling several million dollars. The world market for aluminum can sheet was expanded substantially, with a significant part of that market going initially to Alcoa's U.S. sheet-rolling facilities and later to Alcoa's foreign subsidiary facilities, which were created during that period to fill the expanding market. Furthermore, the machine tool business of Mr. Fraze, Dayton Reliable Tool Company, obtained significant foreign sales of equipment to manufacture the Easy Open Ends, and Mr. Fraze found himself to be in considerable demand as a consultant on packaging industry tooling. In addition, many other machine tool builders also profited from that same business as did the other manufacturers of aluminum sheet. Obviously, the world's can manufacturers expanded their profits as a result of greater sales of improved products.

A successful license program was profitable for all concerned and established an entirely new segment of the world packaging industry. An inventor and a small Dayton, Ohio, tool company became a worldwide supplier of precision tools to the packaging industry, and a major U.S. aluminum company established itself as a worldwide supplier of can sheet with production facilities in the United Kingdom, Australia and Japan. In addition, this development also became a source of expanded business and profits for other machine tool builders and other aluminum sheet producers throughout the industrialized world.

* * * * *

Chapter XIII

HOW AN AUSTRALIAN FIRM INTRODUCED
ITS ROLLING DOOR
TO THE WORLDWIDE MARKET[1]

By Don Spry
General Manager
Byrne and Davidson (Overseas) Pty. Limited

My subject is roll-a-door, the principal product of the Byrne & David-son Industries Group, Revesby, N.S.W., Australia, and the history of its introduction to a market which is now worldwide.

Roll-a-door belongs to the generic group of doors or shutters that can be rolled up for storage and rolled down to provide shade, privacy or security.

The concept is not new. Rolling shutters existed 60 or 70 years ago in such countries as Italy, Greece, Iran, France, and Austria. B&D roll-a-door is essentially a highly developed version of the old concept, which had not, to our knowledge, been applied to a simple garage door.

Our R&D program has gone on for more than 20 years, with many changes to meet customer preferences and the ever-increasing cost of materials. With the product weight basically in steel, it was important to reduce the total amount of steel used. This has been done to the extent that the weight of a roller door is about one-third of the original concept and about two-thirds of the weight of the roll-formed slat-type shutter which is so common around the world.

It was also vital to have the proper use of materials, in some of the smaller components. For example, we needed nylon for strength, polypropylene for wear and lubrication. From a patentability point of view, what is offered and what can be successfully held under patent?

Because the overall concept is no longer novel, our patent potential now relates to elements of the door and we hold a number of patents in various parts of the world on specially adapted and improved components.

Nylofelt is one of our special components. It is a combination of material to achieve sound reduction with minimum friction and maximum durability. The change in the running strips of the door became one of the major steps in producing a quiet and easy operation, and lifted the product into the acceptability of a much greater range of consumers.

A great deal of our R&D went into producing specialized machinery for production of components and assembly of the product. However, one is not only dealing with the product in its own right as an item of technology, but one is also dealing with a valuable package of specialized equipment to retain the cost-effectiveness throughout manufacture. It is not sufficient to have a cost-effective product, by design, if it is not equally cost effective in manufacture.

Having scored a lot of success on the Australian market, we looked to the possibility of trying the product in other countries. First approaches were to those countries where the style of home and standard of living was similar to those in Australia and New Zealand. South Africa fell into that category. Our thoughts were toward the residential door rather than the industrial version, because we felt that much more impact could be gained with the type of marketing that we knew and had tried successfully, namely the garage door transformation.

After the residential garage door design was perfected, improvements were made to the industrial model so that the same degree of cost-effectiveness was available. In this category even greater weight reduction was achieved. As a matter of fact, it was in the industrial field that we worked our way into the U.S.A. and U.K. markets, and even today we concentrate in the United States of America on commercial and industrial application. Even though we have reached hundreds of thousands of doors sold in the United States of America, we have not made a move in the residential market.

Our opening moves in Western Europe serve as a good example of our approach to international licensing. At no stage did we go in cold, nor did we rely on introductions to companies through the Department of Trade and Resources representatives in that country. They certainly help, but they cannot be expected to do your work for you.

Our first step was to advertise three or four times in a local newspaper with business readers. This action usually resulted in 20 or 30 replies from companies of varying sizes and capacity. We would also draw a profile of the type and size of company that we were seeking. It needed to be a manufacturer of building products with metal processing facilities, and certainly for a product like ours, good distribution outlets in their own country, and preferably in some of the adjacent countries.

Our reply letter to these prospects called for details of the company in terms of sales turnover, product range, representation in the distribution field and views on promotion. You will appreciate that we were not looking for the most skilled manufacturing company in our particular case, because there are literally tens of thousands of them in Western Europe. More importantly, we were looking for a company with adequate manufacturing facilities, and with first-class promotional and selling capability and recognition.

Most European companies present themselves very well in second reply, and from that point we were able to grade them from A-plus down to C-minus in terms of priority and suitability. By subsequent correspondence, we worked our way through the "A" and "B" people, giving them enough information on door manufacturing equipment costs and processing costs which we asked them to compare with what we knew and they knew to be typical selling prices of a good quality product in their country.

In discussing manufacturing costs, one has to reveal a certain amount of confidential information, but if you do not do this it is difficult for the executives at the other end to see the money factor. The best one can hope for is a letter agreement to confidentiality. After three or four months of this type of discussion and preliminary negotiation, appointments were made to visit the top executives of the companies down to B-plus, using the assistance of Trade Commissioner staff if interpreters were needed, and to assist in setting up the appointments.

The rest of the sequence would be fairly straightforward, but we learned over the years to provide for second meetings to discuss the material that was offered at the first meeting. We usually managed to stay around the area to allow for yet another meeting if it looked as though this could finalize the deal. With varying rates of success and lots of disappointments, we have managed to set up manufacturing under license in 17 countries, including some of the unlikely countries such as Nigeria, Spain, Greece and Bahrain.

From a marketing point of view, even in the familiar scene of the United States of America, United Kingdom, South Africa and New Zealand, one is dealing with executives who might not appreciate the particular approach we take to the Australian market, where we use the local idiom and the local scene to advantage. Therefore, our presentation package contains some material that speaks for itself and is reasonably impressive to executives in a wide variety of backgrounds.

To help in this area, I take along a videocassette that introduces Australia as a country with vast potential. It also demonstrates the attractiveness of our product and sells some of the functional advantages and features. It indicates in a fairly subtle way that we have sophisticated equipment to produce the product and this is a vital component in the package. It then leads to our recent development of an automatic operator, which is designed for use exclusively with our door and which has attracted a lot of attention in various parts of the world.

Byrne and Davidson offers an exclusive license to manufacture to B&D's designs and specifications, including improvements, and to sell the end product in an exclusive home territory with possibly some non-exclusive adjacent territories. A supplementary license is offered for B&D control-a-door or other B&D products. The license places a number of restrictions on the licensee. One is to preclude any export to countries outside the exclusive or nonexclusive territories. This provision becomes a problem in some countries.

The agreement makes it clear that B&D shall provide, subject to payments, all the designs, specifications, calculations and details of equipment necessary to manufacture and service the product, and automatic access to all additions, modifications and improvements or developments. Ownership of the property and copyrights is retained by the licensor. The agreement also stresses that access to other B&D products is not automatic and must be negotiated by supplementary or additional license.

There are the usual rules on confidentiality and adherence to standards of materials and workmanship. Our standard agreement sets out the desired royalty percentages and provides for a technical or information fee on execution of this agreement. There are important restraints on the manufacture and sale of similar type doors with a similar function, and the continuity of manufacture after cancellation of an agreement. Access is given to usage of the trademark B&D Roll-A-Door, for the product identification only, and not for company identification.

We also have a proviso regarding ownership and control of the licensee company, which is required to satisfy some fairly basic standards, particularly in the event of change of ownership. This provision is important after one has negotiated an agreement with a company of a particular style and energy that appeals in the first instance, and suddenly is changed by different ownership. Such an occurrence can be a major problem. We felt we needed some protection to retain the initiative.

Anyone experienced in negotiating or arbitrating licenses in certain South American and Asian countries will agree that there is a lot of room for conflict with some of the tight laws governing the sale of technology in those countries. If you have a good product that can be marketed on a very broad base, then the agreement has to be a tough one, with a price. This price is arguable, depending on the philosophy of the country involved.

There are a large number of problem countries and the question must always be whether the amount of effort and cost involved in establishing a licensee is eventually worthwhile. One can negotiate successfully with a manufacturing company on the other side of the world and then go through the mind-bending program of amendments and obtain eventual approval. One word of advice. It is vital that the laws and limitations of the country involved be clearly understood at the outset. Where we have recognized this and steered the negotiations accordingly, there have been fewer delays and a better overall result.

Frequently in the "difficult countries" the licensee comes back to the licensor with the good news that the agreement has been approved by his government and then quietly mentions the bad news, that new percentages and restrictions are specified.

If I could sum up our attitude as far as market expansion is concerned, we are certainly selective and we do not believe in expending unlimited time, money and energy in some of the difficult countries.

We will continue to carry out a research effort on most countries and then selectively approach the market of that country with an attractive package, part of which might be in the form of supply of highly tooled components, or provision of specialized tooling for a consideration. If a company has an in-depth R&D program, then this package becomes more attractive because there is always the expectancy of new components, new materials and new methods, as a bargaining factor.

I have not said a lot about patents, but undoubtedly this is an important property area, in some countries more than others. We tend to stress the importance of energetic marketing of a good product as being the best protection for that product. Some of the traditionalists, e.g. the Japanese and Chinese, place great emphasis on patents. These need not be the centerpiece of a technical know-how agreement, but they certainly add to the value of the package.

It would not necessarily be in the best interests of the licensor to structure his agreement around a patent only, unless he is prepared to accept a lump-sum, with no ongoing benefits. The supreme value of a technical know-how agreement lies in its ongoing value to the licensor and the fact that it is far less likely to die on its feet when a patent is successfully challenged or superceded.

* * * * *

FOOTNOTES:

[1]Taken from paper presented at the March 1981 Annual Meeting of LES Australia-New Zealand and reprinted in the March 1982 issue of *les Nouvelles*.

Chapter XIV

STEEL WIRE MANUFACTURER FINDS
REASONABLE RETURN FROM
INTERNATIONAL LICENSING NETWORK[1]

Planning and Technology Section
Australian Wire Industries Pty. Limited

Australian Wire Industries (AWI) is a wholly-owned subsidiary of BHP
(Broken Hill Proprietary Ltd., a major Australian firm in mining and
steel production) and manufactures a wide range of steel wire ranging
from basic low carbon wires such as those used for welded mesh in concrete reinforcement to highly-processed wires for such products as
springs, tire beads, tire cords, and prestressed concrete tendons. AWI
also produces wire products such as ropes, netting, barbed wire, nails
and welded fabrics.

These products are either supplied as uncoated steel wire or as galvanized, oil-tempered, bronze-coated, brass-coated, coppered or plas-
tic-coated wire. Last year, AWI produced 580,000 tons of product. The
company holds the major share of the Australian wire market and also
exports on a worldwide basis, although its primary markets are within
the Pacific basin.

As a producer of steel wire and wire products, AWI ranks as one of the
five largest companies in the world in terms of volume. This is, of
course, of some significance when we come to consider the development and marketing of technology in that, among other considerations,
AWI has the capacity and resources to mount a fairly substantial effort
compared to most of its counterparts around the world. It has its own
research and engineering departments and can call upon the various research facilities within the BHP Group.

AWI has developed international technological leadership in hot-dip galvanizing of steel wire. Varying thicknesses of coatings are required for different market applications, determined usually by the degree of corrosion resistance needed. Light zinc coatings are achieved by tight-wiping of the wire with a pad of asbestos or some similar material after the wire emerges from the molten zinc. We call these standard galvanized wires.

The next range up in terms of coating thickness are heavily galvanized wires which require three to four times the coating mass of standard galvanized wires. The problem with the traditional methods of producing such wires from AWI's point of view was that running speeds were very slow if a satisfactory surface quality was to be achieved.

The traditional methods are known, broadly, by the term "Oiled-Charcoal Wiping."

It was the desire to produce heavily galvanized wire at much faster speeds and therefore greater productivity that led AWI into a major technological breakthrough in the industry.

In the mid-1960s extensive research work was undertaken in Newcastle combining gas atmospheres with beds filled with various heavier-than-charcoal materials. An important key to the whole exercise was discovered by careful analysis of a variety of results.

The conclusions ultimately reached were revolutionary. The new process appeared theoretically capable of wire speeds 10 times those of the traditional process and, given operational constraints elsewhere in the galvanizing process, speeds up to four times greater appeared quite feasible. This was in the context of previously considering gains of 20% as "breakthrough."

The process was developed within the technical department of AWI's Newcastle Wiremills, and there was a considerable period devoted to proving the process commercially. Since 1968, the basic patent for "improvement method of and apparatus for wiping galvanized wire or strip" has been applied for and granted in nine countries.

In the period of marketing the technology, which began seriously in 1970, 10 licensees have been established in the United States of America, Canada, the United Kingdom, France, Japan, South Africa and New Zealand.

While promoting the technology, AWI held detailed discussions and negotiations with 60 to 70 overseas companies, in many cases at their home location. This statement gives an indication of the considerable promotion costs involved in the marketing of the technology. On the other hand, AWI has earned revenues of several million dollars to date, with considerable future income still in prospect from existing license agreements and prospective new agreements.

By 1972 the technical aspects of the process were occupying considerable resources, two full-time and five part-time officers. Three major aspects of successful marketing of the technology became apparent in this period.

First, there was a need to understand more clearly the basic science of the process. Simply put, we knew it worked, but *exactly* why did it work? Knowing this, as we know it now, strengthened our patent establishment and made the application of the process in different environments and circumstances a great deal easier to manage.

Second, the major breakthrough in wiping put pressure on the capabilities of other aspects of the line such as wire steadiness at higher speeds, effective forced-water cooling and so on. It was necessary to upgrade these aspects to gain the full benefit from the technique while giving opportunities to strengthen the security of our proprietary rights through the development of associated patentable technology. Four such patents have been established extensively overseas in up to 24 countries.

Third, we had to combat what we considered to be exaggerated claims being made by some potential licensees with respect to the capabilities of the traditional oiled-charcoal process. This pointed to shortcomings in our data base and led to a program of controlled tests. Consequently, a better knowledge of the existing techniques was developed in building the technical case of the new technology. In particular, it was found that many claims for the conventional technology — for instance, standard deviations of the coating mass — were rationalizations of general observations rather than conclusions drawn from the analysis of actual data.

The ability to wield this technical strength at a crucial period in marketing the technology underlines the advantage of AWI being a major practitioner in the relevant industrial arts and being recognized as such overseas.

A factor that should be particularly stressed is that by the 1970-1973 period, AWI had made a total commitment to gas wiping in its own heavy galvanizing operations. Today, AWI produces a total of approximately 45,000 tons of wire from the process each year on installations in Newcastle, Sydney, Geelong and Perth. This total commitment also allowed the emphasis on patent protection in license negotiations to be somewhat reduced in favor of the technical expertise and assistance AWI was able to bring to potential licensee.

During 1974, there was a perceptible abatement in the marketing of the technology. This situation reflected the problem of incorporating the objectives and activities of technology marketing with those of a functionally-oriented organization, the prime purpose of which is the production and marketing of a tangible industrial product.

In the early days, the organization for these activities was clearly "ad hoc." Three distinct objectives are apparent from that period:

- Ensuring that individual contracts were profitable.

- Better understanding developments in the wire industry worldwide.

- Establishing AWI's reputation as a leader in wire galvanizing technology.

In later years, another objective has gained importance:

- Maintaining an effective licensing network for the long term.

Lately, increasing importance has also been seen in a fifth objective:

- Maximizing the exchange and "feedback" in the licensing network.

It is worth saying a few words about these latter objectives, which were not apparent earlier.

To establish an effective licensing network, one needs to dispel the myth that patents are a cast-iron safeguard to a monopoly situation.

First, if the techniques being patented are of value, imitators are almost certain to spring up. Given that the products we are dealing with are very similar to products produced in large quantities throughout the world, it is reasonable to assume that parallel development work will be going on in other places. Consequently, an effective licensing system will not be built without the commitment to monitor and defend the integrity of the system.

Second, we are seeking to build a long-term relationship with our licensees. We believe the more the licensee benefits from the technology and is happy with it, the more benefit is likely to flow to AWI through customer loyalty, royalties and the attraction of new licensees.

Conversely, if we are not closely in touch with our licensees, practices may develop that bring the technology into disrepute. Therefore, we seek to be:

- Consistent in the terms we seek from one licensee to another, and to relate those terms to performance and benefits derived.

- Supportive to the licensee in passing on new developments and advice on a regular basis.

- Inquisitive about the licensees' progress, market situations, and experimentation with the process.

To achieve all these objectives consistently there was a need for structure in the organization of our technology marketing the "ad hoc" approach would no longer suffice. Our solution has been to create what might be termed a "business unit" within the function of Planning and Technology. Although members of the business unit have outside responsibilities, their roles with respect to technology marketing are defined. The business unit works to an objective plan, with budget targets and a programmed set of activities.

This structural arrangement covers technology transfer overall and includes purchase as well as sale of technology.

Specific features of agreements.

First, it is important to define precisely the specific subject matter of the technology transfer. In our agreements, we tie this down to the wiping area of the galvanizing line. In practice, it will be necessary to advise the licensee on other aspects of the operation of the galvanizing line to obtain the full benefits from the process, but this advice is essentially gratuitous. What we are offering is a unique and commercially-successful approach to the wiping of the wire. Moreover, we do not guarantee the licensee successful operation of the line. There is the evidence of our own extensive operations to demonstrate that a line set up correctly will bring the benefits we are claiming.

We build into our agreements the condition that an AWI expert attends the commissioning period of the process when it is put into commercial operation on the licensee's plant. At such time, advice to the licensee inevitably extends beyond the strict wiping area of the galvanizing line. Our motivation is to make sure, insofar as it is in our power, that the commercial operation is commenced on the best possible footing. This is analogous to the sentiment behind a TV commercial for one health club that occasionally disturbs my evenings: "If you don't look good, we don't look good."

As a general comment, we relate the terms of our license to the benefit that the licensee will receive in his own particular situation with the caveat that those terms must be consistent with our existing licensing agreements and that the body of benefit flowing to AWI must be significant enough to make the license worthwhile from our point of view. These points are made quite clear as soon as we enter serious discussions with a potential licensee. Consequently, the inducement for both parties is to maximize the total benefit flowing from the use of the process and, as a general principle, it is important to have an agreement that is fair and reasonable to both parties.

Generally, we have adopted the principle of nonexclusivity in our license agreements. The concept of exclusivity may not induce the licensee to work the process to maximum benefit. Nonexclusivity, on the other hand, is more likely to provide such an inducement. Moreover, exclusive licenses may be an encouragement for nonlicensees to seek means of circumventing the patents. There may be situations where exclusivity is appropriate, but we would regard them as very exceptional.

Last, provisions are built into the agreements for mutually passing on improvements to the techniques concerned. As I suggested earlier, we see this interchange as a major ongoing benefit of being involved in technology marketing. To be successful, there has to be a perception by both parties that such exchanges are to their own benefit. We find that regular service visits to licensees assist in facilitating this interchange as well as confirming our position as an actively supportive licensor.

Conclusions.

AWI has found technology marketing a demanding but highly-rewarding activity. The rewards arise in a number of ways. Despite the costs involved in promoting the technology and maintaining an effective licensing network, there is a reasonable return on our efforts. We have developed a widespread network of contacts and a flow of marketing and technical interchange which, in the long run, is probably of more importance than the direct financial returns. We estimate that all our licensees combined now produce at least twice the amount of relevant product that AWI does, yet there is no evidence that AWI has lost sales of its own product as a result.

* * * * *

FOOTNOTES:
[1]Taken from paper presented at the March 1981 Annual Meeting of LES Australia-New Zealand and reprinted in the March 1982 issue of *les Nouvelles.*

Chapter XV

THE PROGRESSION OF A CORPORATE PARTNERING[1]

Contract research grows into a
multiple company partnership through licensing
By Andrew L. Ney
Partner, Ratner and Prestia, P.C.

In 1963, while the DuPont Company was in the metals business, it was developing an alloy that DuPont personnel believed could be applied to fabrication of high-strength fasteners. The alloy was still in the technical development stage far from being ready for commercialization.

DuPont contacted the contract research group of SPS Technologies of Jenkintown, Pennsylvania, a highly respected manufacturer of aircraft and automotive fasteners and other industrial equipment, to evaluate this alloy. SPS's contract research group accepts various assignments. In some instances, it functions like an independent testing laboratory evaluating designs and developments of others, whether or not in the field of fasteners. Other times, the SPS contract research group is hired to render design, development or engineering services, again within or outside the fastener field. The assignment from DuPont was to test and evaluate the alloy. SPS received the assignment because of its reputation as the technical leader in the fastener field. The most readily identifiable application of the alloy was for fasteners.

Relationship.

The initial relationship between SPS and DuPont was simply that of a testing facility and client. For a fee the client received from the testing facility comprehensive data regarding the alloy being tested. DuPont owned the data.

Early testing was to evaluate the mechanical properties, such as tensile strength and ductility, of test specimens furnished by DuPont. In time, SPS fabricated fasteners from the sample material coming from DuPont and tested these fasteners. Thus, the SPS testing was on two levels: general properties of the alloy and specific capability to be a fastener material.

With time, the SPS-DuPont relationship changed. SPS began collaborating with DuPont in the development of the alloy. There was no longer a fee coming to SPS and there were no strings attached to SPS's involvement. SPS continued to evaluate the material and offered advice to DuPont on how to overcome problems and enhance the chances of commercial acceptance of the material. For example, SPS encountered a great deal of difficulty because of variations in the properties of the alloy resulting from different heats that were being melted in small batches. This fact was reported to DuPont. SPS indicated that, at least for high-strength fastener fabrication, the alloy could become commercially viable only if it could be made on a large scale to have truly consistent properties. Thus, while SPS was testing the material, it was working with DuPont at developing melting and fabrication methods.

From its testing, SPS found that the DuPont alloy had the required attributes of aircraft fastener material:

- Great fatigue strength.

- High ultimate tensile strength.

- Superior corrosion resistance.

As SPS realized the potential for this alloy developing, it began telling its airframe and aircraft engine customers about it. With DuPont support, SPS provided test data and sample parts.

I have gone into this detail about the SPS-DuPont relationship to emphasize the closeness of the association and the cooperation between the two companies. There were frequent meetings at which detailed information was exchanged. As I already indicated, much of this took place at a time when no strings were attached to SPS's participation. Undoubtedly, this highly-effective relationship was a factor in subsequent dealings between SPS and DuPont.

At the time the DuPont alloy was developed to the satisfaction of Du-Pont and SPS, DuPont decided to withdraw from the metals business. As part of this withdrawal, DuPont decided to sell all of its rights and interests in the alloy, which by this time had been named Multiphase. DuPont invited a few specialty steel fabricators to make bids. SPS requested the right to bid for the Multiphase alloy in competition with these specialty steel fabricators. Although SPS has a steel mill in Sheffield, England, which, for the most part supplies raw material to SPS fastener operations, SPS is not considered a specialty steel supplier engaged in trade sales. Nevertheless, SPS asked if it could participate in the bidding because, by this time, SPS could identify the potential of the Multiphase alloy to aircraft fasteners. In view of SPS's prior involvement with DuPont in the technical development of the Multiphase alloy, Du-Pont invited SPS to present a proposal. DuPont placed only one condition on the proposals — an up-front payment of a specified amount. Otherwise, the bidders were free to price and format their offers in any way.

SPS arranged with Latrobe Steel Company to have Latrobe become the source of the alloy if SPS was the successful bidder. Latrobe was a supplier of raw material to SPS and had been a supplier for quite a while. SPS had good experience with Latrobe and the personnel of the two companies were familiar with each other. SPS agreed to grant Latrobe exclusive melting rights upon SPS acquiring the rights to the Multiphase alloy. With the terms of the Latrobe license fairly well established, SPS presented its proposal to DuPont and advised DuPont that Latrobe would be the melting source of the Multiphase alloy.

DuPont chose to accept SPS's offer. SPS acquired United States and foreign patents and patent applications, manufacturing know-how, marketing information, and the Multiphase trademark. Although ownership of the patents and other property passed to SPS, the form of the payments from SPS to DuPont was fashioned after an exclusive license. Besides the down payment, the license provided for royalties on sales and for annual minimum royalties starting with a certain number of years.

SPS bought technology to fill a product line need. The technology was unproven commercially, but SPS could identify and quantify a need for at least one business segment and judged this alloy to be able to fill that need. DuPont, SPS and Latrobe had good reputations and there had been a very favorable relationship between DuPont and SPS and between SPS and Latrobe prior to the negotiation and consummation of the deals.

After the acquisition by SPS of the Multiphase alloy assets, Latrobe was given technical information and assistance available from SPS and DuPont to melt the alloy. The exclusive license granted by SPS to Latrobe permits sales of the alloy to anyone for non-fastener applications and to fastener manufacturers who have first been licensed by SPS to manufacture and sell fasteners from the alloy. Over the years, SPS has licensed three fastener competitors.

The first license was granted to a competitor who had taken an exclusive license which SPS had dismissed too quickly. SPS later took a license from this competitor to make the proprietary fastener from titanium. When SPS determined that it wanted to fabricate this fastener from the Multiphase alloy, SPS licensed the competitor to make this fastener from the Multiphase alloy and had the license extended to permit SPS to manufacture and sell the fastener from the Multiphase alloy.

SPS granted the second license to a competitor to broaden the promotion of this alloy with airframe and aircraft engine customers.

The third license was granted to satisfy a customer requirement for multiple sourcing. All three licenses granted by SPS to the fastener manufacturers included trade secret and technical assistance provisions because a special knowledge is required to fabricate fasteners from the Multiphase alloy. Besides having to meet the needs of its licensees, SPS wanted to assure that the products made by our licensees would be of such high quality as to support the acceptance and broadening applications of the alloy.

The royalty income from Latrobe sales for non-fastener applications is analogous to licensing by-product technology for the purpose of deriving licensing income. The fastener manufacturers were licensed to obtain greater acceptance of the product and satisfy multiple sourcing requirements.

I will not go into great detail about SPS's efforts in promoting the Multiphase alloy for fastener applications. It will suffice to state that much time and effort went into engineering evaluations of potential applications, distribution of technical reports to potential customers, and general advertising. SPS slowly penetrated the aircraft fastener market with this new alloy. Nevertheless, in the early 1970s, SPS owed DuPont a substantial balance on a minimum royalty. One of our fastener licensees also owed us a substantial balance on a minimum royalty. The acceptance of the Multiphase alloy for aircraft fasteners didn't happen as fast as SPS had anticipated. A significant contributing factor was the drop in aerospace business. SPS then approached DuPont to renegotiate the minimums to reflect a change in circumstance which had not been anticipated. DuPont granted the request. SPS also renegotiated the minimum with its licensees.

SPS and its fastener licensees have been very successful with Multiphase alloy fasteners. Sales have grown nicely and the products yield SPS a good margin. The licensing of fastener manufacturers has been a happy compromise between satisfying the customers' demands for multiple sourcing, yet not diluting the situation for SPS and its licensees.

Meanwhile, Latrobe has been active promoting the Multiphase alloy for other applications. Because it cannot supply all forms of mill products, Latrobe has arranged for one company to supply the Multiphase alloy in wire form and another to supply the alloy in flat rolled form. The Multiphase alloy is now used for medical implants and heart pacer cases in the United States and abroad. Latrobe has worked hard with medical implant suppliers, surgeons and medical standards groups to promote these uses. In addition to creating royalty income, these developments have resulted in a new business for SPS. Because of SPS's familiarity with the alloy and its metal working capability, SPS now makes medical implant devices for a company in the implant business.

Other new applications of the Multiphase alloy are in gas wells where sour gas attacks metallic components. The corrosion resistance of the Multiphase alloy makes it especially useful for tubing in gas wells and as cable material for holding instrument packages which log the structures of the wells, some of which are 25,000 feet deep. Here again, Latrobe expended a significant amount of time and effort in promoting the alloy for these uses. Yet another new application for the Multiphase alloy is as industrial spring material in chemical pumps.

Not long after SPS acquired the Multiphase alloy assets, it was recognized that, as good as it was, this alloy would not satisfy certain applications of aircraft engine fasteners. It became evident that for these applications, a new alloy was needed which had higher temperature resistance and could be hot forged, rendering it less dependent on cold working, at least for the larger-size fasteners.

With the need identified and the envelope of the solution to the problem quantified, SPS and Latrobe embarked upon a joint development program. The agreement under which the two companies operated defined the respective responsibilities and the rights to results flowing from the program. SPS again was collaborating with a metals company in the technical development of an alloy. The joint development program involved continuous alloying efforts by Latrobe, testing by SPS, and exchanges between the two of technical information relating to product specifications, alloying and forging and other manufacturing procedures.

In advance of commencement of the program, SPS and Latrobe agreed to fashion rights to any new alloy developed under the program after the arrangement in the SPS-Latrobe Multiphase alloy license. After three years, the program bore fruit. The product of the program satisfied the predetermined requirements and it has been a commercial success. As with the original Multiphase alloy, sales of fasteners made from the new alloy have grown nicely and the margins on these fasteners are good.

I have given you the highlights of a 16-year success story. While from time-to-time there were difficulties, the overall activity went very well.

* * * * *

FOOTNOTES:

[1]Excerpted from the article "Ingredients for Success" by Andrew L. Ney as published in the December 1979 issue of *les Nouvelles*.

PART FOUR

In Conclusion

"In our rapidly changing industrial world, licensing is not an end in guaranteeing technological advancements, profits, and a better quality of life. Rather, it is a means in helping the business world move through a period of rapid industrial change and in attracting those companies in the best position to turn intellectual property into profit.

Dr. Douglas E. Olesen
Executive Vice President and Chief Operating Officer
Battelle Memorial Institute

IN CONCLUSION

According to news reports, California Biotechnology has licensed its experimental system for nasal delivery of drugs to Eli Lilly and Ayerst for insulin and to Ortho Pharmaceutical, Division of Johnson and Johnson for a contraceptive. Greens Alive, Inc., of Aurora, Ontario, Canada, offers under license its system for rapid indoor production of lettuce at exceptionally low prices in northern climates. According to the *Wall Street Journal* of November 9, 1989, IBM has licensed memory-chip technology to Micron Technology of Boise, Idaho, a departure from past practice of not licensing such technology — the move having been made to combat Japanese competition. Research Frontiers, Inc., of Woodbury, N.Y., is reported (1989) as having signed licenses with Japan Steel Works, Ltd., and Central Glass Company, Ltd. for the use of Research Frontiers' technology in making architectural glass that controls sunlight transmission. The license territory is Japan. Designer Blocks, Inc. has 56 licensees in the United States and Canada plus one in Europe and one in Australia all for a unique way to make special design concrete blocks.

Clearly, if a small or not-so-small company has worthwhile product or process technology, it can very likely use licensing, joint-venturing or franchising as a profitable part of its business plan. Similarly, a firm looking for new products and expanded markets can fulfill its objectives through the same business techniques.

Planning for short term is "tactics." Planning for the long term is "strategy." The successful businessman must use both. Facing this dual need, however, the busy CEO, manager or business owner often finds himself in the position of the Florida farmer who was up to his waist in alligators and had difficulty in remembering that his original goal was to drain the swamp.

We hope that this book will demonstrate ways in which licensing can be used on both short-term "alligators" and long-term "swamps." Chapter I includes "Twenty Questions, Doubts and Fears" about licensing as expressed by different business owners and managers in a variety of industries. We hope that Parts One, Two and Three of this book will have helped the reader find answers to most of those questions. We have attempted to show that, in its broadest context, a license can cover a simple patent, know-how, trade secret, copyright, trademark or co-promotion agreement. It can be used to bring in new technology or gain more profits from your own technology. Or it can be a joint-venture, strategic alliance or corporate partnering if you need to expand efforts, establish an equity presence in a new market or combine the talents of complementary operations. Or it might be one or more franchise agreements to set up or to acquire new outlets based on a proven business line.

Some of these licenses can offer an immediate answer to the "alligator problem" of tactics. Other licenses are directed toward long-term goals of product diversification, expanding technology uses, and entering foreign markets. These may be the answer to the problem of "draining the swamp." Tactics or strategy, licenses have a versatility of purpose and profitability that is equalled by few business methods. Whether it is the right step for you at a particular time will depend on circumstances of market, product, operations and finances.

PART V

Appendices and Bibliography

Appendix A
TEXT COMMENTS

- Licensing Executives Society (U.S.A. and Canada), Inc. (LES) is a professional society comprising over 2,200 members who are actively engaged in the transfer of technology rights. Members have significant responsibilities in research, development, manufacture, use and marketing of technology. The society is a member of Licensing Executives Society International, with a membership of over 5,200 members in 22 national and regional societies representing 59 countries. LES (U.S.A. and Canada), and other LES chapters through various committees, provide considerable information to their members on a wide variety of subjects related to licensing, franchising and joint-ventures in the U.S. and Canada as well as Europe, Central and South America, and the Mid-East, Asian and Pacific Area countries. LES (U.S.A. and Canada) can be addressed at 71 East Avenue, Norwalk, Connecticut 06851-4903.

- Hoffman-LaRoche, Inc., Nutley, New Jersey, is a privately-held company and is a part of F. Hoffman-LaRoche & Company, Ltd., a worldwide Swiss firm with headquarters in Basel, Switzerland, operating in 50 countries and Research Centers in Switzerland, U.S.A., England and Japan. We are indebted to John S. Saxe, Vice President, Licensing and Corporate Development, for his assistance in explaining the Hoffman-LaRoche approach to licensing.

- American Intellectual Property Law Association (AIPLA) is a professional society of lawyers dealing with matters of patents, trademarks, copyrights. The AIPLA book, *How To Protect And Benefit From Your Ideas*, is available from: AIPLA, Inc., Suite 203, 2001 Jefferson Davis Highway, Arlington, Virginia 22202. This publication discusses the patenting and protecting of inventions.

Appendix B
SOME OF THE PROFESSIONAL ORGANIZATIONS INVOLVED IN LICENSING CONSIDERATIONS

- Licensing Executives Society (U.S.A. and Canada), Inc.
  (Abbreviated as LES.)
  71 East Ave., Suite S
  Norwalk, CT 06851-4903

  Phone:(203) 852-7168
  Telex:476 1226 ZAP UI
  Fax:(203) 838-5714

- American Intellectual Property Law Association, Inc. (Abbreviated as A.I.P.L.A.)
  Suite 203, 2001 Jefferson Davis Highway
  Arlington, VA 22202

  Phone:(703) 521-1680

Appendix C
SEMINARS AND CONSULTATION
GENERALLY AVAILABLE

- Licensing Executives Society (see page 271)

  Annual 3-Day Seminar Course usually held in May in New York City.

  Annual Beginners Licensing Course — A 2-hour course given in conjunction with the LES (U.S.A. and Canada) Annual Meeting normally held in the fall of the year.

  Small Business Consultation System (Write LES (U.S.A. and Canada) headquarters in Norwalk, CT to determine availability.)

  International Technology Directory (For LES members only.)

- American Intellectual Property Law Association, Inc. (see page 271)

  Consultant Reference System

- Franklin Pierce Law Center
  2 White Street
  Concord, NH 03301

  Course and Seminars on Patents and Licensing, held regularly in Concord, NH and Boston, MA.

- Patent Development and Biotechnology Transfer Programs

  Academic/Industry Interface, Annual Conference of University of Missouri, Office of Continuing Education and Extension
  in cooperation with Monsanto Corporation
  MA 215 Health Sciences Center, Colombia, MO 65212

- International Licensing, Technology Transfer and Distribution Annual Symposia November Date
The World Trade Institute
One World Trade Center
55W New York, NY 10048

- International Licensing and Negotiation for the Technology Manager
3-day Course by
The Center for Professional Advancement
P.O. Box 964
East Brunswick, NJ 08816-0964

BIBLIOGRAPHY

Reference marks and notes:

**** — Anyone who directs or has charge of a licensing activity should have this, also all those business, engineering, technical and legal persons who are involved with a licensing activity. In addition, good text and reference for all business schools.

*** — Excellent reference material, consider for your library. If your lawyer or consultant does not have it, find out why.

** — Very useful in its field.

* — A subscription might be a good idea if it covers your field.

No Stars — Should still be mentioned as pertinent background.

Notes: The Quarterly *les Nouvelles* is published each March, June, September and December by the Licensing Executives Society (U.S.A. and Canada), Inc. for the Licensing Executives Society International — Jack Stuart Ott, Editor-in-Chief.

Many articles which are listed for *les Nouvelles* have also been reprinted in Bibliography number 1. The articles are so indicated with the page number.

Copies of those *les Nouvelles* articles may also be obtained from the following:

Mr. Albert G. Tramposch
Director Center for Intellectual Property Law
John Marshall Law School
315 South Plymouth Court
Chicago, IL 60604

Mr. Karl F. Jorda
David Rines Professor of Intellectual Property Law
Franklin Pierce Law Center
2 White Street
Concord, NH 03301

Mr. Thomas H. Reynolds
Associate Law Librarian
University of California
Berkley, CA 94720-2499

****1. *The Law and Business of Licensing, Licensing in the 1980's.* Releases covering developments in 1980-89, ed. by Goldscheider, Arnold, Whipple, Poms, Blair and Jacobs, published by Clark Boardman Company, Ltd., New York, NY.

2. *Technology Licensing 1987.* Practicing Law Institute, New York, NY.

****3. *Technology Management: Laws/Tactics/Forms*, by Robert Goldscheider, published by Clark Boardman Company, Ltd., New York, NY.

4. *1982 Licensing Law Handbook*, published by Clark Boardman Company, Ltd., New York, NY.

5. *1983 Licensing Law Handbook*, published by Clark Boardman Company, Ltd., New York, NY.

6. *1984 Licensing Law Handbook*, published by Clark Boardman Company, Ltd., New York, NY.

7. *1985 Licensing Law Handbook*, published by Clark Boardman Company, Ltd., New York, NY.

8. *1986 Licensing Law Handbook*, published by Clark Boardman Company, Ltd., New York, NY.

9. *1987 Licensing Law Handbook*, published by Clark Boardman Company, Ltd., New York, NY — also *1988 Licensing Law Handbook* published by Clark Boardman.

10. *Domestic and International Licensing of Technology, 1980*, published by Practicing Law Institute, New York, NY

***11. *International Licensing*, Copyright December 1977. *International Licensing Management*, Copyright May 1988, published by Business International Corporation, New York, NY.

***12. *International Licensing and Trading (IL & T)*, published by Business International Corporation, New York, NY.

**13. *Competitive Alliances*, Copyright July 1987, published by Business International Corporation, New York, NY 10017.

***14. *Negotiating Compensation in International Licensing Agreements*, by F.R. Root and F.J. Contractor, published in *Sloan Management Review*, Winter, 1981. Sloan School of Business, Massachusetts Institute of Technology, Cambridge, MA.

15. "Ingredients for Success," a case history of successful technology transfer arrangements; hints for establishing beneficial relationship, by Andrew L. Ney, published in *les Nouvelles*, December 1979.

16. "Evaluating Licensee Candidates," by E.G. Tuttle, published in *les Nouvelles* of Licensing Executives Society, June 1982.

***17. *A Handbook for Inventors*, Copyright 1983, by Calvin D. MacCracken. How to protect, patent, finance, develop, manufacture and market your ideas, published by Charles Scribner's Sons, New York, NY, ISBN 0684179067.

**18. *How To Protect and Benefit from Your Ideas*, Copyright 1981, published by American Intellectual Property Law Association (A.I.P.L.A.), Suite 203, 2001 Jefferson Davis Highway, Arlington, VA 22202.

19. *Patent Law Fundamentals,* by Peter D. Rosenberg, published by Clark Boardman Company, Ltd., New York, NY.

20. "Get the Most Out of Your Trade Secrets," by Roger M. Milgrim, *Harvard Business Review,* Nov.-Dec. 1974.

21. "Trade Secret Licensing Definition, Duration and Disposition," by Kenneth E. Payne, *Licensing Law & Business Report,* June-July 1979, published by Clark Boardman Company, Ltd. New York, NY. Bibliography number 1, page 2A169.

22. *Trade Secrets Law,* by Melvin F. Jager, published 1985, Rev. 1986, by Clark Boardman Company, Ltd., New York, NY 10014.

23. *Protecting Trade Secrets 1986.* Practicing Law Institute, New York, NY.

24. "Patent Law for Programmed Computers and Programmed Life Forms," by James J. Myrick and James A. Sprowl, *American Bar Association Journal,* August 1982.

25. "Protection of Intellectual Property Rights in Computers and Computer Programs: Recent Developments," by Alan C. Rose, *Intellectual Property Rights, Pepperdine Law Review,* Vol. 9, 1982.

26. "Program Purloiners Doubly Deterred," by Roger M. Milgrim, *Datamation,* March 1983.

*27. *Computer Law Strategist,* published by Leader Publications, Division of The New York Law Publishing Company. A monthly newsletter on the legal developments involving computers.

**28. *Doing Business in (Country).* A series of publications covering virtually all of the commercially important countries of the world. Published by Price Waterhouse & Company.

**29. *Business Profile Series (Country).* A series of publications by the Hong Kong and Shanghai Banking Corporation, Marine

Midland Building, New York, NY. Series covers all east Asian countries and some mid-east countries.

30. "How to Use a Trademark Properly," by Sidney A. Diamond, from U.S. Trademark Association *Executive Newsletter No. 38*.

31. "A Trademark Is Not a Patent or a Copyright," by William M. Borchard, Cowan, Liebowitz & Latman, from U.S. Trademark Association *Executive Newsletter No. 39*.

***32. *Strategy in the Use of Intellectual Property*, by Derek Brian Momberg and Arthur Henry Ashton, published 1986 by Gerundive Press, The Business Centre, 1/F China Traders Centre, Regal Meriden Airport Hotel, Hong Kong.

33. "Trademark Licensing Abroad from U.S.," by James B. Gambrell and Wayne E. Webb, Jr., *les Nouvelles*, March 1983.

***34. *Attorney's Practice Guide To Negotiations*, by Phillip Sperber (1985), published by Callaghan and Company, Wilmette, IL 60091.

35. "Negotiators Abroad Don't Shoot From The Hip," *Harvard Business Review*, July-August, 1983, by John L. Graham and Roy A. Herberger, Jr.

**36. *Chinese Commercial Negotiating Style*, by Lucien Pyle, published by Oelgeschager, Gunn & Hain Publishers, Inc., Cambridge, MA, 1982.

**37. *Communist Country Negotiating Tactics*, U.S. Department of Commerce, January 1980.

38. *Negotiation*, by Roy J. Lewicki and Joseph A. Litterer, Copyright 1985, published by Richard D. Irwin, Inc., Homewood, IL.

39. "Business Through Joint Ventures," Ian S. Blackshaw, *les Nouvelles*, Licensing Executives Society Quarterly, March 1980. Bibliography number 1, page 2H-3.

40. *Licensing vs. Joint Ventures or Differences and Similarities*, J. Peter Killing and David J. French, Chapter 4 of 1982 Licensing Law Handbook, published by Clark Boardman Company, Ltd., New York, NY.

41. *Antitrust Guide Concerning Research Joint Ventures Nov. 1980*, by Antitrust Division of U.S. Department of Justice Chapter 17 of 1981 Licensing Law Handbook, published by Clark Boardman Company, Ltd., New York, NY.

**42. *201 Checklists*, published by Business International Corporation, New York, NY.

**43. *161 More Checklists*, published by Business International Corporation, New York, NY.

44. *Managing for Joint Venture Success*, by Kathryn Rudie Harrigan, Copyright 1986, DC Heath & Company, (published by Lexington Books), Lexington, MA, ISBN 0669116173.

45. *The Complete Information Bank for Entrepreneurs And Small Business Managers*, Copyright 1982, by Ron Christy and Billy M. Jones, published by The Center for Entrepreneurship and Small Business Management, Wichita State University, Wichita, KS, ISBN 0941958000.

46. *The Insider's Guide to Small Business Resources*, Copyright 1982, by David E. Gumpert and Jeffry A. Timmons, published by Doubleday & Company, Inc., Garden City, Long Island, New York, NY, ISBN 0385172621.

47. *The Small Business Survival Guide*, by Joseph R. Mancuso, Copyright 1980, published by Prentice Hall, Inc., Englewood Cliffs, NJ 07632, ISBN 0138142289.

48. *Franchising In The Economy 1985/87*, by U.S. Department of Commerce, International Trade Administration, Finance and Management Industries Division; $4.75 from Supt. of Doc., U.S. Government Printing Office, Washington, DC 20402.

49. *The Franchise Annual*, published by Franchise News, Inc., Lewiston, NY 14092. This publication is re-issued and updated on an annual basis.

**50. *Going International*, by Lennie Copeland and Lewis Griggs, Copyright 1985, published by Random House, New York, NY, ISBN 0394544501.

51. "Farming Out the Licensing Function," by Phillip Sperber, Vice President, REFAC International, Ltd., New York, NY, U.S.A., *les Nouvelles*, December 1980.

***52. "Mechanisms That Work," by Robert P. Whipple, President, Whipple International Development Company, *les Nouvelles*, December 1981. Bibliography number 1, page 2E243.

**53. "National Limits to Technology Transfer," by Deborah Hurley; Hinkley, Allen, Tobin and Silverstein, Providence, RI, *les Nouvelles*, June 1987. Bibliography number 1, page 2E681.

***54. "Evaluation, Selection of Technology," by Larry Evans, Director, Patent and License Division, The Standard Oil Company, Cleveland, OH, *les Nouvelles*, June 1981. Bibliography number 1, page 2E219.

**55. "Franchising Where It Fits In," by Howard Bellin, Managing Director, International Franchising, South Melbourne, Victoria, Australia, *les Nouvelles*, March 1981.

56. "Spin-Off Technology," by Tom Long, President, Tecktronix Development Company, Beaverton, OR, U.S.A., *les Nouvelles*, December 1985. Bibliography number 1, page 3E139.

57. "Basic Considerations in Licensing," by Tom Arnold; Partner, Arnold, White and Durkee, Houston, TX, U.S.A., *les Nouvelles*, September 1980. Bibliography number 1, page 2A73.

**58. *TIES Newsletter* Technical Information Exchange System, published by Development and Transfer of Technology Division, Department for Industrial Promotion, Consultation and Technology UNIDO P.O. Box 300 A1400, Vienna, Austria.

**59. "Finding New Sources of Technology," by William T. Nye, Vice President, CommTech International Management Corporation, Menlo Park, CA, U.S.A., *les Nouvelles*, December 1985. Bibliography number 1, page 3I109.

60. "The Art of Licensing Out," by Robert Goldscheider, Chairman, The International Licensing Network, Ltd., New York, NY, U.S.A., *les Nouvelles*, June 1984. Bibliography number 1, page 3I61, also Bibliography number 3, page 6.01.

**61. "Specifics of Finding Technology," by Richard L. DiCicco, President, Technology Catalysts, Inc., Falls Church, VA; and Willy Manfroy, Licensing Manager, The Dow Chemical Company, Midland, MI, U.S.A., *les Nouvelles*, June 1987. Bibliography number 1, page 3E175.

62. "Licensing in a Growth Company," by D.K. Layser, President, SAI Technology Company, San Diego, CA, U.S.A., *les Nouvelles*, September 1982. Bibliography number 1, page 3E67.

63. "Licensing of Know-How in U.S.," by Karl F. Jorda, Corporate Patent Counsel, Ciba-Geigy Corporation, New York, NY, *les Nouvelles*, June 1986. Bibliography number 1, page 2A783.

**64. "Hybrid Trade Secret Licensing," by Melvin F. Jager; Partner, Willian, Olds, Hoffer, Gilson and Lione, Ltd., Chicago, IL, U.S.A., *les Nouvelles*, December 1986. Bibliography number 1, page 2A889.

**65. "When Agreements Fail," by Crispin Marsh, F.B. Rice Company, Balmain, Australia, *les Nouvelles*, September 1983. Bibliography number 1, page 3D71.

66. "The Case Against Licensing," by William F. Silva, President, Catalysts and Process Systems Division, Union Carbide Corporation, Danbury, CT, U.S.A., *les Nouvelles*, March 1985. Bibliography number 1, page 3E129.

**67. "Transferring Biotechnology," by Waddell A. Biggart, Sughrne, Mion, Zinn, Macpeak and Seas, Washington, DC, *les Nouvelles*, March 1986. Bibliography number 1, page 3A281.

**68. "Capitalizing on Wealth in Biotechnology," by John H. Woodley, Sim and McBurney, Toronto, Ontario, Canada, *les Nouvelles*, June 1987. Bibliography number 1, page 3A401.

**69. "Fundamentals of Software Licensing," by Gerald E. Lester, Digital Equipment Company, Maynard, MA, U.S.A.

**70. "Protecting Semiconductor Chips in U.S.," by Charles N. Quinn, Miller and Quinn, Philadelphia, PA, U.S.A., *les Nouvelles*, September 1987.

71. "Profit and Technology Transfer," *les Nouvelles*, December 1987. Keynote address at LES (U.S.A. and Canada) Annual Meeting and International Conference, Toronto, Canada, September 1987, by Peter L. Waite, Director Davy Corporation, Chief Executive, Petroleum and Chemicals, Davy McKee International, Ltd., London, England. Bibliography number 1, page 3E191.

72. "Licensing Influence in Corporate Strategy," *les Nouvelles*, December 1986. Paper presented at LES (U.S.A. and Canada) Annual Meeting, Los Angeles, October 1986, by William S. Campell, Executive Vice President, Consumers Packaging, Inc., Toronto, Canada. Bibliography number 1, page 3F381.

73. "The Challenge of Licensing in a Research-Based Pharmaceutical Company," *les Nouvelles*, December 1987. Address to LES (U.S.A. and Canada) Annual Meeting and International Conference, Toronto, Canada, September 1987, by Edgar H. Philbrick, Jr., Vice President, Planning and Development, Merck and Company, Inc., Rahway, NJ.

**74. "Licensing In and Corporate Health," by Robert Goldscheider, Chairman, International Licensing Network Ltd., New York, NY, *les Nouvelles*, March 1988. Bibliography number 3, page 7.01.

*75. *Business America*, February 29, 1988 issue, published by U.S. Department of Commerce. Entire issue is devoted to the new Bureau of Export Administration and its operation.

**76. *Using Consultants*, A Consumer's Guide for Managers, by Thomas A. Easton and Ralph W. Conant, published by Probus Publishing Company, 118 North Clinton, Chicago, IL 60606.

***77. "Software Licensing Agreements   An Overview" from *Licensing Law and Business Report*, Vol. 10, No. 4, November-December 1987, by L.J. Kutten, published by Clark Boardman Company, Ltd.

**78. *Computer Software*, by L.J. Kutten, published by Clark Boardman Company, Ltd., Copyright 1987.

**79. *U.S. Computer Software Licensing Law   Quick Glance Reference*, Copyright 1988, by Licensing Executives Society available through LES (U.S.A. and Canada), Inc.

**80. *Venture Magazine* for entrepreneurial business owners and investors, October 1988 issue. Reference especially 5 articles:

> "The Practical Inventor"
> "It Pays To Patent"
> "Orphans No More"
> "Dream Weavers"
> "Franchising   Coming up with a great concept can be easier than protecting it"
> "Black Gold, Texas Tea"

****81. A New Era in Licensing by R.P. Whipple, *les Nouvelles*, September 1987. Bibliography number 1, page 2A895.

***82. *Valuation of Intellectual Property and Intangible Assets* by Gordon V. Smith and Russell L. Parr, Copyright 1988, published by John Wiley & Sons, New York, NY.

**83. *Copyrights, Patents and Trademarks: Protect Your Rights Worldwide* by Hoyt L. Barber; publ. by Tab Books, Inc., Blue Ridge Summit, PA, 17294-0850.

84. *Inventing: Creating and Selling Your Ideas* by Philip B. Knapp, PhD.; publ. by Tab Books, Inc., Blue Ridge Summit, PA, 17294-0850

*85. *Strategic Planning: Development and Implementation* by Dr. Bonita H. Melcher and Dr. Harold Kerzner, publ. by Tab Books, Inc., Blue Ridge Summit, PA, 17294-0850

**86. "Technology Acquisition Process" by Willy Manfroy, Wm. G. Paterson, Joachim W. Staackman. Dec. 1989 issue *les Nouvelles*.

**87. "Specifics of Finding Technology" by Richard L. DiCicco and Willy Manfroy, publ. in June, 1987, issue of *les Nouvelles*.

88. "International Franchising Problems" by Warren Pengilley publ. in March, 1987, issue of *les Nouvelles*.

**89. *Franchise Opportunities Handbook* — Stock No. S/N 003-009-00528-1, U.S. Supt. of Documents, U.S. Gov't Printing Office, Washington, DC.

**90. "Status of World Intellectual Property Protection" by Dr. Albrecht Kreiger — published in Sept., 1989, issue of *les Nouvelles*. Note: Dr. Kreiger is Director General in the Ministry of Justice of the Federal Republic of West Germany and Vice Chairman of the Administrative Counsel of the European Patent Organization.

**91. "U.S. Intellectual Property Law Sees Changes" by Alan Conrad Rose, publ. Sept. 1989, issue of *les Nouvelles*.

92. "High Technology as a Commercial Asset" by R. Adoutte, publ. in Dec. 1988, issue of *les Nouvelles*.

93. "Practical Considerations for Agreement" by Phillip M. Rice, publ. in Dec. 1989, issue of *les Nouvelles*.

**94. *International Computer Software Quick Reference Table* copyright 1988 and 1989 — published by Licensing Executives Society International. Copies may be purchased from LES (U.S.A. and Canada), Inc.

95. *The Basics of Licensing*, including the International License Negotiating Thesaurus — a publication written originally for inventors and entrepeneurs who want to have a very basic background in licensing. Published by and available from LES (U.S.A. and Canada), Inc.

**96. *Guide for Guarantee and Warranties* — published by United Nations Industrial Development Organization (UNIDO). May be purchased from UNIDO, P.O. Box 300, A-1400 Vienna, Austria.

97. The following publications were listed in the March, 1990, issue (p. 20) of *les Nouvelles* as having been compiled by LES U.S.A./Canada Biotechnology Licensing Committee for general background material for biotechnology licensings.

The following publications are available from the Industrial Biotechnology Association, 1625 K Street, N.W., Suite 1100, Washington, D.C. 20006; 202-857-0244.

1. Biotechnology at Work Series (order individually): Up to 10 copies of each pamphlet can be ordered at no cost. For bulk orders: 11-100 copies, 50 cents each; more than 100 copies, 40 cents each.

   a. *Glossary of Terms*
   b. *Agriculture and the New Biology*
   c. *Medicine and the New Biology*
   d. *Diagnostics*
   e. *Food for the Future*
   f. *Animals, People and Biotechnology*

2. *What is Biotechnology?* ($3 each)

3. The following are free for one copy; over that amount, 50 cents each:

   a. *The Role of Biotechnology in AIDS Research: A Progress Report*

   b. *U.S. Biotechnology: Meeting the Global Challenge*

c. *Answers to Commonly Asked Questions about Biotechnology Regulation*

d. *Careers in Biotechnology*

e. *Survey of State Government Legislation on Biotechnology*

The U.S. Office of Technology Reports

1. Office of Technology Assessment, U.S. Congress. *Mapping Our Genes — The Genome Projects: How Big, How Fast?* Washington, D.C. Government Printing Office, 1988, $10.

2. Office of Technology Assessment, U.S. Congress, *New Developments in Biotechnology, Ownership of Human Tissues and Cells*. 1987, $7.50.

3. Office of Technology Assessment, U.S. Congress, *New Developments in Biotechnology, Public Perception of Biotechnology*. Washington, D.C. Government Printing Office, 1987, $5.50.

4. Office of Technology Assessment, U.S. Congress, *New Developments in Biotechnology, Field-Testing Engineered Organisms: Genetic and Ecological Issues*. Washington, D.C. Government Printing Office, 1988, $7.50

5. Office of Technology Assessment, U.S. Congress, *New Developments in Biotechnology, U.S. Investment in Biotechnology*. Washington, D.C. Government Printing Office, 1988, $13.00

6. Office of Technology Assessment, U.S. Congress, *New Developments in Biotechnology, Patenting Life*. Washington, D.C. Government Printing Office, 1989, $8.50